The Global Politics of Jazz in the Twentieth Century

From the mid-1950s to the late 1970s, jazz was harnessed as America's "sonic weapon" to promote an image to the world of a free and democratic America. Dizzy Gillespie, Dave Brubeck, Duke Ellington and other well-known jazz musicians were sent around the world – including to an array of Communist countries – as "jazz ambassadors" in order to mitigate the negative image associated with domestic racial problems. While many non-Americans embraced the Americanism behind this jazz diplomacy without question, others criticized American domestic and foreign policies while also appreciating jazz – thus jazz, despite its popularity, also became a medium for expressing anti-Americanism. This book examines the development of jazz outside America, including across diverse historical periods and geographies – shedding light on the effects of jazz as an instrument of state power within a global political context.

Saito examines jazz across a wide range of regions, including America, Europe, Japan and Communist countries. His research also draws heavily upon a variety of sources, primary as well as secondary, which are accessible in these diverse countries: all had their unique and culturally specific domestic jazz scenes, but also interacted with each other in an interesting dimension of early globalization. This comparative analysis on the range of unique jazz scenes and cultures offers a detailed understanding as to how jazz has been interpreted in various ways, according to the changing contexts of politics and society around it, often providing a basis for criticizing America itself. Furthering our appreciation of the organic relationship between jazz and global politics, Saito reconsiders the uniqueness of jazz as an exclusively "American music."

This book will be of interest to students and scholars of international relations, the history of popular music, and global politics.

Yoshiomi Saito is Associate Professor in the Graduate School of Human and Environmental Studies at Kyoto University, Japan.

Routledge Advances in International Relations and Global Politics

137. Small States and Hegemonic Competition in Southeast Asia
Pursuing Autonomy, Security and Development amid Great Power Politics
Chih-Mao Tang

138. Empires of Knowledge in International Relations
Education and Science as Sources of Power for the State
Anna Wojciuk

139. Joining the Non-Proliferation Treaty
Deterrence, Non-Proliferation and the American Alliance
Edited by John Baylis and Yoko Iwama

140. New Geographies of Global Policy-Making
South-South Networks and Rural Development Strategies
Carolina Milhorance

141. Norm Dilemmas in Humanitarian Intervention
How Bosnia Changed NATO
Yuki Abe

142. American Hegemony in the 21st Century
A *Neo* Neo-Gramscian Perspective
Jonathan Pass

143. The Duty of Care in International Relations
Protecting Citizens Beyond the Border
Nina Graegar and Halvard Leira

144. The Global Politics of Jazz in the Twentieth Century
Cultural Diplomacy and "American Music"
Yoshiomi Saito

For information about the series: www.routledge.com/Routledge-Advances-in-International-Relations-and-Global-Politics/book-series/IRGP

The Global Politics of Jazz in the Twentieth Century
Cultural Diplomacy and "American Music"

Yoshiomi Saito

LONDON AND NEW YORK

First published 2020
by Routledge
2 Park Square, Milton Park, Abingdon, Oxon OX14 4RN

and by Routledge
52 Vanderbilt Avenue, New York, NY 10017

Routledge is an imprint of the Taylor & Francis Group, an informa business

© 2020 Yoshiomi Saito

The right of Yoshiomi Saito to be identified as author of this work has been asserted by him in accordance with sections 77 and 78 of the Copyright, Designs and Patents Act 1988.

All rights reserved. No part of this book may be reprinted or reproduced or utilised in any form or by any electronic, mechanical, or other means, now known or hereafter invented, including photocopying and recording, or in any information storage or retrieval system, without permission in writing from the publishers.

Trademark notice: Product or corporate names may be trademarks or registered trademarks, and are used only for identification and explanation without intent to infringe.

British Library Cataloguing in Publication Data
A catalogue record for this book is available from the British Library

Library of Congress Cataloging-in-Publication Data
Names: Saito Yoshiomi, 1976- author.
Title: The global politics of jazz in the twentieth century : cultural diplomacy and "American music" / Yoshiomi Saito.
Description: Abingdon, Oxon ; New York, NY : Routledge, 2020. | Series: Routledge advances in international relations and global politics ; 144 | Includes bibliographical references and index.
Identifiers: LCCN 2019018779 (print) | LCCN 2019019708 (ebook) |ISBN 9780429060595 (Ebook) |ISBN 9780429595363 (Adobe Reader) |ISBN 9780429594076 (Epub) |ISBN 9780429592782 (Mobipocket) |ISBN 9780367182984 (hardback)
Subjects: LCSH: Jazz–Political aspects–History–20th century. | Music and diplomacy–History–20th century. |United States–Foreign relations–20th century.
Classification: LCC ML3918.J39 (ebook) | LCC ML3918.J39 S2 2020 (print) | DDC 306.4/8425–dc23
LC record available at https://lccn.loc.gov/2019018779

ISBN: 978-0-367-18298-4 (hbk)
ISBN: 978-0-429-06059-5 (ebk)

Typeset in Times New Roman
by Taylor & Francis Books

Contents

Acknowledgements	vii
Abbreviations	ix
Introduction	1
1 The genealogy of "American music"	10
2 The scene changes in postwar jazz politics	29
3 Jazz ambassadors revisited	45
4 The politics behind the selection process	65
5 Anti-Americanism in the Western jazz discourse	84
6 Containing the Soviet jazz scene	106
7 Contesting discourses in East European jazz scenes	130
8 Making jazz great again	152
Conclusion	165
Bibliography	169
Index	184

Acknowledgements

Like all studies, this book would not have been possible without the support I received from many people and institutions. I would like to express my deepest appreciation to, first and foremost, James Llewelyn for his warm encouragement and vigorous support at various stages of this research. I also thank my colleagues at Kyoto University: Yuka Tsuchiya for reading a draft version of this book and providing her insightful expertise; Takeshi Sakade, Yu Sasaki and Toshiro Kamiya for providing me with much-needed arrangements for making this book a reality. I would like to also extend my appreciation to Mirza Redzic and Jasmina Gavrankapetanovic for their words of encouragement and inspiration. I am also obliged to the anonymous reviewers for their constructive criticism, which was invaluable in improving my manuscript. Any possible errors and shortcomings are, of course, solely my own.

Writing a book in the field of jazz will always be challenging, especially for non-American researchers. Fortunately, however, scholars have increasingly paid attention to the political dynamism of jazz outside America over the last decade, providing a diverse range of important sources to draw from. In addition, I received valuable support from a number of institutions. I am grateful to the following institutions: Japan Foundation, Tokyo, Japan; Library of Congress, Washington, DC, US; LSE Library, London, UK; National Archives and Records Administration, College Park, Maryland, US; The National Archives, Kew, London, UK; Radio Free Europe/Radio Liberty, Washington, DC, US; and University of Arkansas Library, Fayetteville, Arkansas, US. I also express my deep gratitude to Fatoumata Weston for her permission to use Randy Weston's personal reports for this book. Part of this research has been funded by a Grant-in-Aid for Scientific Research (C) from the Japan Society for the Promotion of Science (project number 25380193).

An earlier version of this book has been published in Japanese under the title of *Jazz Ambassadors: "America" no Ongaku Gaiko-shi*. While this book is a thoroughly revised and updated version, I nevertheless appreciate the publisher Kodansha, Japan, for allowing me to publish a revised version of this work. Special thanks are also due to Naotaka Kimizuka and Tateki Yokoyama for their previous support in the publication of the earlier Japanese version of this book. I also gratefully acknowledge the two editors at Routledge, Simon Bates and Tan ShengBin, who provided me with invaluable support and patience at various stages.

Finally, my family deserve special thanks. My wife Madoka and son Tokio have been patient throughout. They are a source of strength for me and make my life meaningful and rewarding. This book is dedicated to them.

Kyoto, March 2019

Abbreviations

AFHQ	Allied Forces Headquarters
AFN	American Forces Network
ANTA	American National Theatre and Academy
CCF	Congress for Cultural Freedom
CIA	Central Intelligence Agency
CND	Campaign for Nuclear Disarmament
Comintern	Communist International
CPUSA	Communist Party of the United States of America
CSCE	Conference on Security and Cooperation in Europe
CU	Bureau of Educational and Cultural Affairs
DTU	Deutsches Tanz- und Unterhaltungsorchester (German Dance and Entertainment Orchestra)
END	European Nuclear Disarmament
FBI	Federal Bureau of Investigation
FDJ	Freie Deutsche Jugend (Free German Youth)
GHQ/SCAP	General Headquarters, the Supreme Commander for the Allied Powers
HICCASP	Hollywood Independent Citizens Committee of the Sciences, Arts, and Professions
HUAC	House Un-American Activities Committee
JALC	Jazz at Lincoln Center
JATP	Jazz at the Philharmonic
KGB	Komitet Gosudarstvennoy Bezopasnosti (Committee for State Security)
Komsomol	Kommunisticheskiy Soyuz Molodyozhi (Communist Youth League)
MC	Master of Ceremonies
MFN	Most-Favored Nation
NAACP	National Association for the Advancement of Colored People
NATO	North Atlantic Treaty Organization
NHK	Nippon Hoso Kyokai (Japan Broadcasting Corporation)
NSC	National Security Council
ODJB	Original Dixieland Jazz Band

OWI	Office of War Information
POW	prisoner of war
RAA	Recreation and Amusement Association
RFE	Radio Free Europe
SALT	Strategic Arms Limitation Talks
SED	Sozialistische Einheitspartei Deutschlands (Socialist Unity Party of Germany)
SS	Schutzstaffel (Protective Echelon)
UN	United Nations
UNESCO	United Nations Educational, Scientific and Cultural Organization
USIA	United States Information Agency
USIS	United States Information Service
USO	United Service Organizations
VOA	Voice of America

Introduction

On the evening of 29 April 1969, an event at President Richard Nixon's White House saw many of America's most well-known jazz musicians freely mingling with senior US officials and politicians. This was one of those infrequent instances in the American capital when the usually unrelated worlds of Washington DC high politics and the royalty of American jazz collided – a musical occasion arguably more spectacular than anything ever held before in the White House. After dinner in the State Dining Room on the west side of the building, guests moved to the East Room, which was usually used for ceremonies and press conferences, to excitedly wait for the biggest event scheduled for the day, a birthday party for a respected jazz icon. There were many prominent figures from the American jazz scene in attendance, including trumpeters Clark Terry and Bill Berry, trombonists J. J. Johnson and Urbie Green, saxophonists Paul Desmond and Gerry Mulligan, pianists Dave Brubeck, Earl Hines, Hank Jones and Billy Taylor, bassist Milt Hinton, drummer Louie Bellson, guitarist Jim Hall, and vocalists Joe Williams and Mary Mayo. Willis Conover, who had been promoting jazz since the mid-1950s on his popular radio program *Music USA* – a segment on the US government's official radio station Voice of America (VOA) – served as the Master of Ceremonies (MC) at this distinctive event.

While the musically gifted guests essentially embodied the history of American jazz, they were simply there to celebrate the seventieth birthday of one of the most legendary figures of the American jazz scene: Edward Kennedy "Duke" Ellington. On this auspicious evening, Ellington and the other guests witnessed a unique performance by this line-up of jazz royalty, which opened with "Take the A Train," and was followed by a medley of other well-known pieces, including "Chelsea Bridge," "Satin Doll" and "Sophisticated Lady." Other popular numbers, including "In a Sentimental Mood," "It Don't Mean a Thing," "Caravan" and "Mood Indigo" also captivated the audience. Later in the evening, to everyone's delight, Ellington himself joined the performance by playing "Pat" on the piano, which he dedicated to President Nixon's wife.[1]

The formal highlight of the evening occurred when Nixon awarded Ellington the Presidential Medal of Freedom, the highest official award given to civilians. The President described decorating Ellington with this prestigious honor as "most appropriate" and went on to explain that:

> When we think of freedom, we think of many things. But Duke Ellington is one who has carried the message of freedom to all the nations of the world through music, through understanding, understanding that reaches over all national boundaries and over all boundaries of prejudice and over all boundaries of language.

Ellington, as praised by Nixon, enhanced the quality of "American music" and expanded the frontiers of jazz, while simultaneously retaining his individuality and freedom of expression – forming the very soul of this music. After graciously thanking the President, Ellington briefly spoke about the philosophy he lived by – passed on to him by his old friend and composer Billy Strayhorn – describing this life path as:

> Freedom from hate, unconditionally; freedom from self-pity; freedom from fear of possibly doing something that may help someone else more than it would him; and freedom from the kind of pride that could make a man feel that he is better than his brother.

Following this exchange, Nixon asked the audience to stand up and sing "Happy Birthday" to Ellington "in the key of G." Reflecting the festive nature of the event, and probably surprising many in attendance, Nixon himself played the piano for this final song.[2]

This snapshot of one evening at the White House could have been remembered superficially, as just another musical event at the White House, as musical performances were not uncommon. However, this event symbolizes the indivisible connection between jazz and freedom, best outlined by Strayhorn's way of life and the ideals behind the Presidential Medal of Freedom as awarded to Ellington. Moreover, in examining this event, we can see how jazz and global politics had become interwoven. For example, Conover transmitted jazz externally as a symbol of freedom and American democracy through the VOA. Many of the musicians invited to the White House that evening had also been involved in State Department-led cultural diplomacy, and had had direct experience at the forefront of the cultural Cold War pitting America against the Soviet Union. Therefore, this historic event – Ellington's birthday being celebrated at the White House – is symbolic of this book's major perspectives on the global politics of jazz.

Jazz and Americanism

Since its birth in the creole city of New Orleans, jazz has developed with improvisation as one of its fundamental features. From New Orleans jazz in the early twentieth century through the swing movement of the interwar period, and bebop after the Second World War to free jazz during the 1960s, jazz saw a variety of styles and evolutions emerge. Throughout this process, more or less, a freer mode of expression was pursued at each iterative stage, in contrast to classical music which tends to emphasize accuracy in music notation. Jazz has been, therefore, associated with the philosophy of freedom, as shown by its reliance on individual creativity. Herein lies the foundation as to why jazz relates to politics. Jazz has not only been understood as a genre, but also as a symbolic musical icon representing the notion of "America," embodying the ideals of the Founding Fathers.

The ideological conflict that defined global politics in the second half of the twentieth century set the context for a relationship between jazz and the public image of "America." As US-Soviet relations deteriorated in the postwar period, the two camps put forward competing political systems, thus initiating a battle for winning the hearts and minds at both domestic and international levels. In this context, cultural exchanges attracted much official attention as a means to influence and control global public opinion. While wearing an apolitical cloak, cultural programs were promoted as part of highly sophisticated Cold War strategies. The death of Joseph Stalin, General Secretary of the Soviet Communist Party, in 1953, triggered the Soviet cultural offensive, which emphasized traditional Russian high culture. For its part, the US government, long reluctant to encourage governmental involvement in international cultural exchanges – seeing them better catered for by the private sector – finally acknowledged their policy significance by the mid-1950s, at least as part of a counter-strategy against Soviet cultural influence.

Expectations for jazz to perform such a role were substantial. Under the Eisenhower administration, the State Department began dispatching notable jazz musicians around the world, including to an array of Communist countries. In addition to the musicians who played at Ellington's birthday party, many famed figures such as Louis Armstrong and Sarah Vaughan also conducted performances overseas in accordance with their own personal agendas. Ellington himself visited many Asian and African countries as a jazz ambassador, not to mention his successful Soviet tour in 1971. Jazz, as a symbol of freedom and democracy, was expected to dispel the negative image associated with America's domestic racial problems that were making global headlines at the time.

The cultural complexities of America vis-à-vis Europe also became another factor behind government interest in jazz, as a cultural and diplomatic strategy. Sometimes criticized as a "cultural desert" by some intellectuals, the US government undoubtedly felt compelled to improve America's global cultural image. While many believed classical music was a quintessentially European cultural asset, in similar fashion, jazz was seen as intrinsic to American culture. Just as Nixon had told Ellington, jazz had been identified as "American music." Or more precisely, jazz *had to* be "American music" in postwar America. In this sense, what jazz was expected to embody in America's postwar cultural diplomacy was American nationalism, or Americanism.

Functions of jazz

However, this book is not intended to provide another historical account of the relationship between jazz and Americanism. Rather, this book examines whether jazz functioned merely as a symbol of Americanism. Or more precisely, it offers new perspectives on a variety of discourses and interpretations of jazz outside America. The book therefore examines the extent to which jazz was understood as "American music" both inside and outside America. In this vein, considerable focus is placed on exploring the function of jazz as a means of criticizing America, thereby advocating the necessity to emancipate jazz from "American music." This relates closely to the fact that jazz historically served not only as a symbol of freedom, but also of resistance. Originally, jazz developed under the Jim Crow regime in America. For those seeking to put an end to the practice of segregation, jazz symbolized an act of protest. In this period, jazz's symbolic function as both expressing a thirst for freedom and a will to protest were two sides of the same coin. Therefore, listening to jazz in a society where basic freedoms were curtailed took on a critical tone against the existing order.

In America, that jazz could symbolize resistance was seen in the 1960s civil rights movement. Musicians in support of the movement were the manifestation of their objections to the existing reality of America, where they believed the ideals of the Founding Fathers had not been fulfilled. Notwithstanding this deep-seated philosophy of resistance, jazz was still able to maintain a distinct connection with Americanism. Whereas W. E. B. DuBois and several other notable civil rights activists abandoned their home country and moved to Africa, many stayed and dreamed of fulfilling their progressive ideals through pursuing domestic political and social reforms. To put it differently, those who stayed to reform the system from within embodied Americanism, in that they believed in the advent of an idealized future "America."

Rather ironically, despite the idea that jazz had distinctive American cultural roots – particularly the embedded notion of resistance – some European intellectuals used this core idea to criticize what they saw as insipid Americanism creeping into European life, a process derogatorily termed "Coca-Colonization."[3] The irony was clearly lost on many of France's postwar anti-American intellectuals who happened to be avid jazz fans, while also critical of parts of American culture. Existentialist thinkers such as Jean-Paul Sartre and Simone de Beauvoir ardently embraced jazz, believing it embodied their philosophy, while simultaneously publishing articles criticizing American racial as well as Cold War policies. At the same time, with France's international influence rapidly waning in the face of the new hegemon, French jazz journals lamented the reality of segregated America. In early postwar French society therefore, jazz provided these writers, and other leftist groups of the day, with a practical means through which to express anti-American feelings.

Additionally, jazz successfully encouraged transnational ties. In the State Department-led jazz diplomacy, jazz musicians soon engendered empathy with local musicians and fans outside America, well beyond what government officials had initially hoped. Through the medium of jazz, those in Communist bloc countries were also able to expand their transnational ties with people inside and outside the bloc. Looking at this historical evidence in light of global politics today, it is perhaps worth considering the potential jazz has clearly shown in helping build tolerance between cultures, overcoming political divides, and fostering inter-cultural dialogues.

Keeping these various contexts of jazz in mind, we should not limit jazz's historical role to Americanism and its associated ideas. Rather, there is a need to examine the development of jazz outside America, including across diverse historical periods and geographical places. Such an approach promises to shed important light on the effects of jazz within a global context.

Global political dynamism and jazz

In recent years, the study of jazz has been approached from various disciplines and perspectives, providing a rich repository of scholarly research for this book to draw upon. Taking a broad inter-disciplinary approach, this book reconsiders the unique functions jazz has played in the history of global politics, and discusses the global political dynamism that jazz generated. The definition of global politics in this book is relatively broad, as shown by not exclusively focusing on "inter-national" relations, but on transnational movements such as peace movements, the civil rights movement, decolonization and cross-cultural dialogues, among other related themes. In addition to government officials and musicians, a wide variety of non-state actors, such as producers, critics, intellectuals and dissidents, are set against a dynamic political context in various places around the world. More specifically, this book employs a rigorous, yet broad, historical inquiry approach covering many countries not previously examined in this context, including America, countries in Europe and Japan, as well as a number of Communist countries.

The existing literature on jazz diplomacy reveals at times problematic relations between artists and government officials. Penny M. Von Eschen's seminal work *Satchmo Blows Up the World: Jazz Ambassadors Play the Cold War* succeeds in illustrating the complex frictions jazz generated inside America – among policy elites, audiences and particular artists. Through her insightful research on US State Department-sponsored jazz tours, Von Eschen highlights the paradox of the US government's strategy of sending African American jazz musicians globally to represent America as a free and democratic country when its racial problems remained to be solved. Revealing interacting relationships of such factors as the Cold War, decolonization, race and cultural exchange, Von Eschen not only foregrounds the importance of jazz as a black culture to legitimize America's global strategy, but provides numerous stimulating examples of how musicians and the State Department pursued different agendas.[4] Investigating the same jazz program, Lisa Davenport's *Jazz Diplomacy: Promoting America in the Cold War Era* examines the role of jazz in transforming the US-Soviet relationship. Davenport uses similar but different sets of primary sources to Von Eschen's work, elaborating more on the specific contexts in which the jazz tours were carried out. Davenport also describes jazz diplomacy as affirming the existence of a cultural realm that was often unaffected by economic and strategic considerations.[5]

Incorporating multiple analytical perspectives other than the Cold War, Von Eschen defines the character of jazz as international and hybrid music. And this book concurs with her argument on this point. However, despite her best intentions to provide a perspective to examine the postwar dynamics of international politics, most of Von Eschen's source materials are limited to those archived or published in America, resulting in a body of work that falls within the confines of American history.[6] In so doing, Von Eschen neglects constructing a more balanced global history of jazz, which can only be achieved if the interpretations of the music both inside and outside America are examined. In order to broaden our understanding of jazz's characteristics and functions there is a need to incorporate more non-American jazz discourses. That is, jazz's encoded messages – or the political subtexts of jazz – were often negotiated in local contexts outside America, with the result being the emergence of multiple interpretations of the meaning and nature of the music. It is true that the US State Department and American jazz musicians pursued different agendas, but so did authoritarian regimes, intellectuals, leftist groups, critics, musicians and jazz aficionados outside America. To put it differently, this book is intended to introduce a more "globalized" view of jazz. Whereas Davenport's stated purpose of underscoring the power of jazz in diminishing the legitimacy of Communism only partly succeeds, due to the narrow historical parameters in which jazz's symbolic functions are examined.[7] Rather than giving the US-Soviet confrontation the highest analytical priority, what we need to do is de-bipolarize the historiography of jazz diplomacy, and incorporate a more diverse array of jazz discourses as seen inside and outside America.

Moreover, while both Von Eschen and Davenport set their research time frames somewhere between the mid-1950s to around the 1970s, this book contextualizes the US State Department's jazz diplomacy inside a broader framework, focusing on twentieth-century global political dynamics. This enables us to better trace the genealogy of the "American music" discourse. For this purpose, this book uses a variety of sources, primary as well as secondary, which were accessed in America, Europe and Japan. While there are emerging works reviewing the development of jazz outside America, they also tend to limit their perspectives to specific periods and places, failing to fully capture the power of jazz and its effects more globally. Among them, E. Taylor Atkins's edited book *Jazz Planet* shares the same objective as this book in examining jazz in a globalized context. Viewing jazz as a harbinger of globalization, Atkins and his other contributors successfully show how jazz was variously interpreted in different parts of the world.[8] While the essays in *Jazz Planet* all problematize nationalistic viewpoints found within previous jazz research, their perspectives are considerably diverse, including elements such as race, modernity and aesthetic values. Instead, this book provides a more in-depth analysis of the politics of jazz, effectively contextualizing this idea within jazz diplomacy. Through reevaluating the uniqueness of jazz – frequently seen as exclusively "American music" – this book ultimately allows us to deconstruct the exclusive relationship between jazz and its birthplace, America.

In the following chapters, while some sections cover similar case studies as the existing literature, and consult similar sources, they are being introduced in this book using new historical and comparative perspectives. Chapter 1 looks at the origins of the current jazz discourse, which equates jazz with "American music" both inside and outside America. The interwar period is examined to further explore the genealogy underpinning the "American music" discourse. During the New Deal era, some started to believe, supported by leftist groups, that jazz was quintessentially "American music" embodying the ideals of the Founding Fathers. Meanwhile, jazz outside America was gradually de-Americanized through various interpretations, which enabled Nazi Germany, Vichy France and Japan to propagate their own anti-American causes around jazz.

Chapter 2 considers the impact of postwar ideological confrontation against the context of domestic jazz scenes inside America and Communist bloc countries during the 1940s and 1950s. It argues that as American society problematized the infiltration of Communism, New Deal Liberalism of the 1930s was put in an awkward position. For example, Norman Granz, who is usually associated with Jazz at the Philharmonic (JATP) – the title of many recordings and numerous concerts – unequivocally advocated for racial integration. Because of this stance, however, he soon became a symbol of something un-American and was subsequently placed under the supervision of security authorities. Ironically, in the meantime, jazz followers in Communist bloc countries were persecuted precisely because jazz represented "American music."

Chapter 3 explores ideas around the universality and particularity of jazz by detailing five jazz musicians who were sent around the world during the 1950s: Dizzy Gillespie, Benny Goodman, Wilbur De Paris, Dave Brubeck and Jack Teagarden. The shift in global politics during the 1950s resulted in the US government recognizing the importance of government-sponsored cultural exchanges globally, while simultaneously promoting its own reinterpretation of jazz. Rapidly jazz, long denied any public status in representing America abroad, became "American music," reflecting the nation's founding principles. In this context, the US government's jazz ambassadors program commenced in the latter half of the 1950s. This chapter re-examines various local reactions found outside America to these musicians' performances, as well as the frictions that inevitably arose among State Department officials, American musicians and even local fans and musicians outside America, mainly due to a set of competing interpretations around the meaning of jazz.

Following the arguments presented in the previous chapter examining tensions in the jazz ambassadors program, Chapter 4 explores the discursive frictions of the 1960s over the external value of jazz, which arose among US officials, jazz musicians and music critics who were engaged in the jazz ambassador selection process. Race-conscious African tours by Louis Armstrong, Duke Ellington and Randy Weston were expected to strengthen cultural ties between America and Africa, but the represented "America" was socially problematic. Although Ornette Coleman's free-style jazz had been driving the Black Power movement in America – and he was highly regarded by critics selecting America's jazz ambassadors – State Department officials were nonetheless worried by the late 1960s about the unforeseen consequences of sending an ambassador abroad that might be too provocative. The gap in interpreting the strategic value of jazz among government officials, musicians and critics foregrounded the politics of who should represent America during the era of decolonization and the American civil rights movement.

Chapter 5 looks at the critical jazz discourse by examining the anti-American element of jazz in some Western countries in the period from the late 1940s to 1960s. In France, where jazz was understood as originating in black culture, the music rarely embodied Americanism but rather the weak and oppressed. The French Existentialists criticized America through *Les Temps modernes* while still loving jazz – a development perhaps not unrelated to the declining position of France in the postwar world. The situation was similar for another declining empire, Britain, where trad jazz revival reached its high point in the 1950s, reflecting certain imperial nostalgia. In West Germany, jazz served as a medium for overcoming a negative historical image, through which its own jazz ambassadors program commenced in the 1960s with the cooperation of the Goethe Institut. Whereas in Japan, jazz discourses in the 1960s turned "black" as they stressed the need for solidarity between the Japanese and "colored people." This chapter shows how jazz began to influence national identities in different and diverse corners of the world.

Chapter 6 discusses how the Soviet Union sought to contain the effects of jazz, while also providing the Communist regime with a reason for admitting American jazz ambassadors into the Soviet Union during the 1960s and the early 1970s. The Soviet authorities sought to improve relations with America, while minimizing the perceived risks to their people posed by American jazz and the idea of Americanism. Soviet tours by Benny Goodman, Earl Hines and Duke Ellington, as well as the unofficial jazz ambassador Gerry Mulligan, show the degree of official acceptance that occurred in parallel with the containment of their own jazz scenes and the Sovietization of the domestic jazz discourse. In this sense, the authorities' treatment of American jazz musicians provides a useful analytical lens through which to understand jazz's precarious position in the Soviet Union during this period.

Elaborating further on the jazz discourse in Communist countries, Chapter 7 looks at the local functions of jazz in Eastern Europe during the period from the mid-1950s to 1980s. As part of conciliatory measures toward its citizens, and to keep them away from rock music – a growing symbol of juvenile delinquency and decadence – jazz was gradually institutionalized and nationalized from the mid-1950s. This development paved the way for many American jazz ambassadors to visit Eastern Europe, much more frequently in the 1970s than in previous decades. Meanwhile, following détente in the early to mid-1970s, the politics of jazz again came to the fore in Czechoslovakia. When members of a small jazz fan group were arrested in 1986, this triggered a wave of transnational criticism by musicians, novelists and peace activists, soon generating a united front against the oppression of jazz in this country.

Chapter 8 explores the US government's jazz diplomacy after the 1980s, as well as how jazz might interconnect disparate groups of people in today's globalized world. Since the 1980s, the discourse equating jazz with "American music" saw a revival, in line with the US Congress repeatedly adopting resolutions celebrating the lofty idea of Americanism. However, controversy remains as to the ownership of jazz, and whether it is a symbol of racial integration in America or is solely symbolic of black culture. Further complicating the ownership questions, the United Nations Educational, Scientific and Cultural Organization (UNESCO) has determined that 30 April is International Jazz Day, disseminating values seen intrinsic to jazz such as cross-cultural dialogue, and respect for human rights and diversity. This chapter notes that although jazz has its roots in America, the music has become a shared cultural asset of the world, coming about via myriad historical routes.

The Conclusion summarizes the above arguments by reaffirming that jazz does not present, *a priori*, any specific or intentional message. Rather, it is through ourselves that jazz has been allocated a variety of messages. As time passed, places shifted and its styles changed, accordingly we found symbols of hope, fear, decadence and modernity in jazz through our own subjective interpretations. In that sense, jazz has long been a symbol of more than just music. Jazz was born in and remains a potent symbol of America. Still, jazz goes beyond Americanism. The various routes jazz followed in the process of expanding its popularity outside America obscure its roots, which has resulted in an enriched hybridity of jazz today.

Notes

1 Richard Nixon Presidential Library, Yorba Linda, California, US (Online), Box RC-2, WHCF: SMOF: Office of Presidential Papers and Archives, "President Richard Nixon's Daily Diary April 16, 1969–April 30, 1969," 29 April 1969. www.nixonlibrary.gov/sites/default/files/virtuallibrary/documents/PDD/1969/007%20April%2016-30%201969.pdf [assessed 27 February 2017].
2 Richard M. Nixon, *Public Papers of the Presidents of the United States: Richard M. Nixon, 1969* (Washington, DC: Government Printing Office, 1971), pp.338–39. For more on the event, see Edward Allan Faine, *Ellington at the White House 1969* (Takoma Park: IM Press, 2013).
3 Reinhold Wagnleitner, *Coca-Colonization and the Cold War: The Cultural Mission of the United States in Austria after the Second World War* (Chapel Hill: University of North Carolina Press, 1994).
4 Penny M. Von Eschen, *Satchmo Blows Up the World: Jazz Ambassadors Play the Cold War* (Cambridge: Harvard UP, 2006), p.4.
5 Lisa E. Davenport, *Jazz Diplomacy: Promoting America in the Cold War Era* (Jackson: UP of Mississippi, 2013), pp.4, 143.
6 Von Eschen, *Satchmo Blows Up the World*, p.24.
7 Davenport, *Jazz Diplomacy*, p.4.
8 E. Taylor Atkins (ed.), *Jazz Planet* (Jackson: UP of Mississippi, 2003), pp.xi–xxvii.

1   The genealogy of "American music"

Born in New Orleans, jazz emerged at the dawn of the twentieth century, musically influenced by ragtime and blues. Inexpensive musical instruments, procured by the southern states' military bands after the Civil War, turned out to be more than suitable for this music. When Storyville, a red line zone in New Orleans, closed following American participation in the First World War, many musicians moved north in search of work, allowing jazz culture to bloom in big cities like Chicago and New York. In the heady period after the war, the increase in material prosperity, innovations in science and technology, and a new dynamism in American society, led to the so-called Roaring Twenties. Urbanization and industrialization saw America's automobile industry grow rapidly through mass production, the movie and record industries expand exponentially, and a suite of new skyscrapers begin to reshape New York City's skyline – F. Scott Fitzgerald described America during the spectacular 1920s as the Jazz Age. In this period, "hot" jazz became one of the more popular styles, and was predominately played by African American musicians. Emphasizing a dynamic rhythm and improvisation, it was seen as posing a challenge to the Protestant norm of self-discipline, which was still held in esteem by America's middle class. In comparison, "symphonic" jazz, with its strong influence of classical music, was readily accepted by those who held these values. Paul Whiteman, a conductor who restricted improvisation and instead emphasized melodies, garnered broad support for this style and successfully grew his fame as the "King of Jazz." A typical example of the symphonic style was "Rhapsody in Blue," a piece composed by George Gershwin upon a request from Whiteman.

American society of the mid-1930s became familiar with swing as it recovered from the Great Depression. With the advent of this new style of jazz, orchestra composition grew in size, while improvisation became relatively restrained, resulting in arrangement coming to the fore instead. Swing's uplifting rhythm aligned with society's desire for bright and inspiring music in this era. The beginning of the swing era commenced when clarinetist Benny Goodman's national tour ended with great success in 1935. By January 1938, with the Goodman Orchestra having had resounding success in bringing its swing rhythm to Carnegie Hall – the Classical Music Hall of Fame – swing had become a social phenomenon.

Meanwhile, and despite the music's growing popularity, criticism of jazz remained. Jazz had once been called "jass" with distinctive sexual connotations, and was associated with images of deviation from social norms. Fans who danced with great energy to this music with a swinging rhythm were called jitterbugs. For them, swing overlapped with a desire for liberation from all kinds of private and social constraints that bound them as individuals. As detailed by jazz historians Lewis A. Erenberg and David W. Stowe, when fascism began emerging in Europe, jitterbugs and swing were accused of being "musical Hitlerism" symbolizing a decline of rationalism, while one Catholic archbishop even suggested that jitterbugs and their "cannibalistic rhythmic orgies" would lead the younger generations to "the primrose path to hell." For those who believed jazz and fascism were somehow intertwined, fans of Goodman were seen as fascists themselves. On one occasion, one University of Chicago professor recalled that jitterbugs cheered Goodman "with the abandon of a crowd of Storm Troopers demanding their Fuehrer or a Roman parade greeting its Duce." In response, however, acknowledging the music's political undertones, more cautious public voices arose to counter these criticisms. *The New York Times* advocated that swing should be understood not as a "doctrine set to music" but instead, as "a revolt against doctrine" – and in that sense "Dictators should be suspicious of swing."[1] Here, it would be enough to confirm that various jazz discourses existed in this period, ranging from those problematizing jazz and the doctrine of fascism, to those challenging the assumption of this association.

Keeping these various jazz discourses in mind, the following sections investigate the origins of the particular discourse of jazz that associates the music with Americanism, while also examining how its association was deconstructed outside America, notably in such countries as France, Germany and Japan – eventually engendering de-Americanized discourses of jazz. Reviewing the jazz scenes of these four countries in a comparative way provides us with a useful analytical lens through which to understand the dynamics that characterized the meaning of jazz both inside and outside America.

The emergence of "swing ideology"

It was during the New Deal era when some Americans started to advocate that jazz was "American music," thus embodying the ideals of the Founding Fathers. Stowe identifies this specific type of jazz discourse as "swing ideology." This ideology, demanding a freer and more democratic society, saw the formation of a loose anti-fascist cultural front that consisted of artists, labor unions and leftist intellectuals.[2] By clearly promoting the principle of racial integration when racial segregation remained in society from the hotel industry to public transportation, swing was able to connect people, therefore narrowing the gap between the ideal of freedom and democracy on the one hand, and the harsh reality of the times on the other. For example, it is well-known that Goodman hired pianist Teddy Wilson and vibraphonist Lionel Hampton, both African Americans. Ensuring his orchestra was racially integrated, he directly challenged the practice of racial segregation that still existed in the music industry. Also, Goodman financially supported African American bandleader Fletcher Henderson by asking him for musical arrangements.

Swing aimed to transcend race. While appealing to the black origins of the music – and by pushing a dynamic rhythm to the front – swing was usually played with a large ensemble with less collective improvisation. The music that put blues culture at its core was heard by a wide range of audiences from youth to the elite regardless of skin color. In this way, some believed that both white and black culture lived together in swing. Here a discourse that celebrated "American music" was born, aspiring to a racially integrated society. Goodman himself said: "difference of race, creed or color has never been of the slightest importance in the best bands." Viewing swing as democratic music, he also declared that "there's a sort of freedom about jazz." Swing, which was reaching explosive levels of popularity among the wider public, was here explicitly tied to the notion of Americanism. The discourse that associated jazz with "American music" developed through the New Deal in America, though it naturally posed the question as to how well it accurately reflected social reality. When a large segment of the public believed American society consisted of only white people, some people drawn to swing began to consider how music could be harnessed to overcome racial problems.[3]

Of the many organizations that made use of swing during the 1930s for their own causes, the case of the Communist Party of the United States of America (CPUSA) was the most striking. Expanding the influence to African American workers, particularly in the Harlem area of New York where the so-called Harlem Renaissance had been blooming since 1919, the CPUSA organized concerts and meetings advocating racial integration. While some members of the party showed a sense of disgust towards swing as bourgeois decadent music, the party's pragmatic policy of using the music for political purposes – deeply rooted in Harlem – prevailed after the high-profile Scottsboro case of 1931.[4] Eventually, the CPUSA modified its extreme left stance at the seventh World Congress of the Communist International (Comintern) in 1935 – the same year that saw the beginning of the swing era. With the adoption of anti-fascist popular front tactics, a wide range of leftist forces started to collaborate and associate themselves with the party. To garner further appeal, the CPUSA even started to explicitly link Communism and Americanism in its public statements. The party secretary Earl Browder's slogan, "Communism is 20th century Americanism," vividly demonstrated the left-leaning Americanism of the New Deal era.[5]

In the late 1930s, a wide range of anti-fascist circles declared support for Ethiopia following Italy's invasion of this country, also backing the Republican Army in the Spanish Civil War. At a fundraising event at Carnegie Hall for such causes, Cab Calloway, Fats Waller and Count Basie appeared. In addition, the party organ, the *Daily Worker*, regularly published essays on jazz. When Waller suddenly died, a memorial concert was organized by the party youth organization in cooperation with Basie, Duke Ellington and Billie Holiday. The *Daily Worker* was supportive in connecting the ideals of Americanism and swing by praising these musicians in its pages, stating the concert for Waller "was a testimonial to a 'good guy' who made music so that all people could live in a world where there aren't black people and white people any more than there are black keys and white keys on the piano."[6]

Among those fascinated with the idea of the popular front was Barney Josephson, known for opening Cafe Society in Greenwich Village, New York, in 1938. This jazz club broke the then normal practice of racial segregation and attracted such celebrities as Paul Robeson and Eleanor Roosevelt. Many fundraising concerts were held at this venue, including one for the Abraham Lincoln brigades that supported volunteer fighters in the Spanish Civil War. The cafe was also acknowledged as a place where John Hammond, a producer, critic and relative of Goodman through his youngest sister Alice's marriage, discovered Holiday, who later became known for her distinguished voice in the song "Strange Fruit." Interestingly, the composer of "Strange Fruit" was a Jewish high school teacher from New York, Abel Meeropol. Shocked by photographs of lynching incidents of African Americans, he accused the southern states of wanton violence with this song.[7] As an active CPUSA member, he later adopted the children of Julius and Ethel Rosenberg, who were arrested and sentenced to death for selling classified information on the atomic bomb to the Soviet Union in the early 1950s. Since Columbia records refused to produce the song due to its provocative lyrics, the record was eventually released under the independent Commodore Records label, which had been established in the same neighborhood as Cafe Society by producer Milt Gabler.[8] Inspired by the French jazz fan club, Hot Club de France, Gabler had formed United Hot Clubs of America with Hammond and other jazz fans in 1935.

Critic Marshall Stearns, a frequent contributor to *Down Beat*, believed that jazz was one of America's unique contributions to the art world. He insisted, in a similar way to Edgar Allan Poe, that jazz only became understood in America once it had been accepted overseas.[9] Stearns was in a sense right. Jazz was appreciated and better understood in Europe well before American society began dancing to swing's passionate rhythms. Since the 1920s, the relationship between jazz and America had been a major target of intense arguments in European intellectual circles.

Jazz à la mode

Local reactions outside America in encountering jazz varied. But there were some commonalities. In general, intellectuals, young people and musicians were considerably attracted to this music, due to its underlying modernism and cosmopolitanism as symbolic of the new era, while conservatives were often made to feel frustrated.

American participation in the First World War in 1917 brought jazz to Europe. In France, where 2 million American military personnel were stationed, particularly important was the 369th Infantry Regiment – dubbed the Harlem Hellfighters – band, led by Lieutenant James Reese Europe. Consisting only of African Americans, this regiment band conducted performances for Allied troops, bringing some joy to the battlefield. Due to their burgeoning popularity, John Pershing, Commander of the American Expeditionary Forces, ordered the regiment band to undertake a six-week French tour – the first tour of its kind – during which the band carried out jazz performances in 25 regional cities to wide acclaim.[10] While US President Woodrow Wilson had declared a democratic cause for entering the war, racial segregation in the American military forces caused many French people to resent this contradiction. However, it is not difficult to point out that France as a colonial state also had its own racial prejudices at this time. Unlike American soldiers who returned home once the war was over, immigrants from the distant colonies were designated as "others" from inside the empire – despite forming only 3.5 percent of all immigrants – and were treated as potential threats to society. Nonetheless, it is noteworthy that the positive reception the jazz-playing African Americans received from French locals strengthened their view of France as a freer country than America.[11]

Through the Jazz Age of the 1920s, this "American music" spread widely throughout the French cultural scene. Already in the late 1910s, the Original Dixieland Jazz Band (ODJB), generally believed to have recorded jazz for the first time, had established a great reputation after playing before King George V in London. Similar to the all-white ODJB, the Southern Syncopated Orchestra, made up of only African Americans, also established a solid reputation with its performances in Paris. Sidney Bechet, who accompanied the orchestra, stayed in London until 1923, and later participated in the legendary performance, *La Revue Nègre*, with singer Josephine Baker in 1925.[12] Their performances at the Champs Elysées Theater brought a great whirlwind of enthusiasm because of her naked costumes and dynamic Charleston dance. The enthusiasm was not limited to the masses. Well-known cultural figures such as composers Maurice Ravel and Darius Milhaud, and poet Jean Cocteau, also listened to jazz in their search for an innovation to the extant French culture of the day – that is, looking to learn something new from the exoticism of black culture. Behind this *négrophilie* cultural trend was the fear that the First World War would destroy European civilization. Accordingly, African Americans became a symbol of purity and strength, not polluted by destructive European civilization. Thus French society saw jazz and Charleston from the perspective of the noble savage. In other words, through indulging in this joyful pleasure – interweaving a melancholic blue note with their own precarious circumstances – these apprehensive Europeans found a certain catharsis in jazz.[13] In this way, jazz culture blossomed in Paris. When the other side of the Atlantic saw the Harlem Renaissance in New York, many artists visited "Harlem in Montmartre" in Paris, which became a base for their creative activities.[14] In an era when Jim Crow laws and a culture of segregation continued in America, the air of Paris connected jazz to the idea of freedom.

The situations in Germany and Japan were somewhat different, however. In Germany, where no *négrophilie* attitudes of the same extent existed, even if fans welcomed Baker and other jazz players, racial prejudice was stronger than France.[15] In Japan, where jazz entered society during the Taisho period (1912–26), opportunities to encounter African Americans were limited. With Japan unscathed by the destruction wrought upon Europe by the First World War, in contrast to French society, there was little desire to find a catharsis in the roots of black culture to overcome the destructive forces of a decaying Western civilization.[16]

At the same time, jazz was also seen as a symbol of modernity. America's mass consumerism and production systems were the icons of the dynamic machine age. America was defined by a variety of images, such as materialism, rationalism, efficiency and standardization, as well as trust in technology and pragmatic philosophy. In one allegorical example, the syncopated rhythm of jazz overlapped with the image of a steam engine and the movements of its pistons. Although some complained of jazz as a symbol of mass-produced frivolous culture, the influx of jazz meant the spread of modernism, which showed that jazz connoted something American even before swing ideology began to raise expectations for social change in America.[17]

The conservative backlash against jazz was a common phenomenon in many countries. In France, the reasons behind this criticism were diverse, such as it being anti-French and eroding "truly French music" – it was seen as incompatible with French culture in social circles that respected order and self-discipline. Two kinds of reactions emerged from these criticisms. The first was an effort to make jazz less improvisatory and instead to emphasize melody and harmony, which enabled fans, critics and musicians to point out jazz's closeness to traditional French music. Here, rather than blackness as the origin of jazz being stressed, its "civilized" nature was highlighted. In reality, despite *négrophilie* already being widespread, symphonic European-style jazz, à la Paul Whiteman, was popular in French music halls. For example, "Gregor and His Gregorians" and "Ray Ventura and His Collegians," who both played jazz à la Whiteman with reduced improvisation, soon became very popular, with the latter performing in New York in 1929.[18] Another result of this criticism was the emergence of a new jazz movement that, despising symphonic jazz as overly commercialized, proclaimed that the dynamic improvisation of hot jazz was "authentic" jazz. Here, too, the similarity of hot jazz to traditional French music was emphasized. Critics Hugues Panassié and Charles Delaunay formed the core of this movement. Panassié was a member of the right-wing Action Française, but ironically loved the music that was now left-leaning in America. When visiting Harlem, he observed good old French traditions in African American society, starkly different to the overly commercialized society around him, allowing him to feel a "purified" spirit in swing. Panassié established the Hot Club de France, and launched the magazine *Jazz Hot*, while also establishing the new record label Swing. When he promoted the Quintette du Hot Club de France with Django Reinhardt and Stéphane Grappelli in the hope of establishing "French jazz," Panassié felt something primordial in these musicians.[19]

Already from the early 1930s, starting from Duke Ellington (1933), well-known American jazz names were visiting France. Despite this, the anti-jazz discourse strengthened in France, alongside the rise of Nazism in Germany. However, due to the efforts of Panassié and Delaunay, jazz gradually took root in French society beyond what could be considered as Americanization or

Africanization of France. Fused with chanson and musette, jazz was now believed to represent a genuine aspect of French culture, despite the enduring controversy as to whether or not to admit blackness as a part of this music. In any event, Paris become the epicenter of the interwar global jazz scene, with the Hot Club de France even leading to the creation of its American counterpart, the aforementioned United Hot Clubs of America.[20]

The localization of jazz in French society, therefore, occurred in parallel with another process, in which the meaning of jazz was negotiated and reinterpreted. This process of reinterpreting jazz continued during the Second World War, constructing a distinct style of national jazz while depriving it of its distinctive American-ness. After the northern part of France was occupied by Germany and the Vichy regime was established in the south in 1940, French jazz found itself surrounded by Nazi Germany's theories on race. Although the authorities did not completely ban this popular music, partly because it functioned as an outlet for people's complaints, jazz was subject to state control as a regressive or amoral music. After America entered the war against Germany, the French jazz scene became more restrictive. Against this background, jazz's Frenchification was further encouraged. On behalf of Panassié, who left Paris for his hometown, Delaunay, now the chairman of the Hot Club, set the localization of jazz as its primary survival strategy. In addition to holding a jazz festival focusing on French jazz at the Salle Pleyel in Paris, Delaunay proclaimed in *Jazz Hot* that the goal of the Hot Club was "the development of 'Jazz Français'," while at the same time accusing American jazz of being degenerating, due to its commercialism.[21] In an article in *Down Beat* in 1940, Delaunay declared: "jazz is not white, nor black, nor Jewish, nor Aryan, nor Chinese, nor American! ... Jazz is much more than an American music – it is the first universal music." His aim was to separate jazz from all things American.[22]

The Frenchification of jazz was sometimes implemented strategically. For example, "St. Louis Blues," a masterpiece frequently played around the world, was renamed "La tristesse de St. Louis" following the German occupation. Its motif was taken from the discriminatory situation Louis Armstrong found in America. Further modifications to suit the political climate of the day included: "Take the A Train" was changed to "L'attaque de train," "Honeysuckle Rose" to "La rose de chevrefeuille," and "Sweet Sue" to "Ma chère Suzanne." "Sweet Georgia Brown" was renamed "Douce Georgette" by simply translating the English title into French. "Tiger Rag" was now "La Rage du Tigre," a song based on the French traditional dance Quadrille. Furthermore, the change from "I Got Rhythm" to "Agatha Rhythm" was an example of changes made based on the similarity of pronunciation.[23]

As shown above, Django Reinhardt was a key figure who contributed to the rise of French jazz, but he had multiple handicaps that could have made his life difficult in occupied France. Firstly, he was a Roma. The Vichy regime persecuted the Roma people in line with German racial ideology, sending countless of them to forced labor camps. Secondly, jazz was seen as "degenerate art" in Germany, as detailed below. And lastly, he had a physical deformity in two of his fingers. Despite these disadvantages, in occupied France his fame increased. In contrast to Grappelli who remained in London from the beginning of the war, Reinhardt returned to Paris and vigorously continued his music activities. The German authorities utilized the cultural capital of Paris to the fullest extent, as they needed to appease local citizens and also provide entertainment for the German army. Theaters and clubs reopened their businesses immediately after the collapse of Paris. Notably, among the clientele was the German Air Force Lieutenant, Dietrich Schulz-Köhn, also called "Dr. Jazz," who was an enthusiastic fan of swing and one of the first German members of the Hot Club de France. A unique surviving photograph from this period shows "Dr. Jazz" in full military uniform alongside Django, one Jew, and four black musicians in front of the French jazz club La Cigar.[24]

Jazz as a form of resistance in Germany and Japan

In Weimar Germany, the image of America brought disgust and fear to conservatives, for whom jazz lacked spirituality and was a threat to German *Kultur*. Still, jazz enjoyed some support from contemporary musicians, including composers Paul Hindemith and Kurt Weill, who were known for reinvigorating classical music. In particular, Weill composed one of jazz's better-known masterpieces "Mack the Knife" in *The Threepenny Opera*, which was written in 1928 by Bertolt Brecht who was himself a committed Communist. Showing that jazz's standing among some leftist intellectuals was uneven at best, however, some intellectuals loudly denounced the music as bourgeois, seeing it as sapping the resistance of the workers. Whereas it is well known that Theodor Adorno, one of the Frankfurt School's most prominent cultural critics and intellectuals, denied the significance of improvisation, syncopation and jazz's musical significance on the whole.[25]

Furthermore, as described earlier, the recognition that jazz was black music made the German jazz scene more restricted than in France. In the 1920s, the Chocolate Kiddies led by Sam Wooding, as well as Josephine Baker and Sidney Bechet, visited the country and gained popularity, but black musicians were rarely employed in domestic bands. Also, its commercial image tied jazz to anti-Semitism. The Jews were accused of waging "Negro-Jewish war," and poisoning German culture by exploiting the culture of black origins for profit.[26] After Adolf Hitler's rise to power, jazz was harshly suppressed under the banner of "degenerate" culture, and seen as polluting Germany's ethnic purity. A poster at the "Entartete Musik" (degenerate music) exhibition in 1938 showed a black musician – depicted as a monkey – playing a saxophone with the Jewish star of David pinned to the right side of his chest, portraying the appalling manner in which jazz was viewed in official German circles in the Third Reich. Still, jazz did not completely disappear from German society. The definition of jazz was ambiguous, and authorities lacked a sufficient understanding to distinguish this music from other genres. Fans, on their part, frequently attempted to smuggle in jazz records when returning from Scandinavian countries. Musicians from countries such as Sweden, the Netherlands, and Belgium, who were only loosely controlled by local authorities compared with local German musicians, were able to play swing frequently. To avoid sanction, German jazz musicians changed the titles of their songs. "How High the Moon" was renamed "Serenade an den Mond," while "Tiger Rag" became "Schwarzer Panther," and "St. Louis Blues" was played as "Lied des blauen Ludwig."[27]

Moreover, the propaganda director Joseph Goebbels, rather than seeking the total demise of jazz in Germany, sought to employ it as a form of entertainment, somewhat preferable to foreign broadcasts that were promoting jazz across Europe. The popular demand for dance music had necessitated a music that eliminated intense hot rhythms and improvisation. The answer was to create a new "German Jazz" composed of sweet melodies of violin instead of saxophone or trumpet. Now jazz was being nationalized in Nazi Germany. Notwithstanding these attempts, this music was officially recognized as light music and was never regarded as jazz.[28]

During the Second World War, the value of jazz increased, as a musical genre to provide comfort to the German army. An official radio program, which originally targeted the Allied forces, began to play Glenn Miller numbers, soon also attracting German troops to its listening audience.[29] Even the leading German fighter ace, Werner Mölders, was one of those attracted to jazz. Dissatisfied with the dearth of swing on German radio stations, he complained directly to Goebbels, creating a potential new opportunity for the German jazz scene. Goebbels had already become concerned that the Luftwaffe pilots were becoming vulnerable to the influence of swing, due partly to their high education levels and English ability. In 1942, the Deutsches Tanz- und Unterhaltungsorchester (DTU; German Dance and Entertainment Orchestra) was established in this context. The orchestra aimed to satisfy people's appetite for an entertainment style of music. Symbolizing its significance, the DTU was seen as on par with the Berlin Philharmonic. However, since the orchestra played a melodious music that did not swing enough, it was ultimately unable to attract many jazz fans. The worsening of the war situation forced its headquarters to move to Prague in 1943, while its musicians also started to be drafted to the front. Eventually, the DTU ceased activities in early 1945.[30] So, among many contemporaries who feared that American culture would result in degenerating German *Kultur*, Goebbels occasionally exploited the potential of jazz, while suppressing hardline voices calling for its thorough repression. There were periods, therefore, when German authorities sought to restrict jazz, while at other times use it for their own specific purposes. Cultural historian Michael H. Kater underscores this paradoxical position of jazz in the Third Reich as stemming from the improvisational character of the totalitarian regime.[31]

Looking to the everyday politics of jazz reveals that jazz served as a tool for expressing objections to conformist culture. It is widely known that the Hitlerjugend (the Hitler Youth) was established within the Nazi party for physical training and brainwashing German youth. There were also groupings of young people who opposed the Nazi regime, who formed the Weiße Rose (the White Rose), and the Edelweißpiraten (the Edelweiss Pirates). Alongside these groups, jazz fans formed the Swingjugend (the Swing Youth), mainly composed of middle-class youth in large cities. They were known as jazz freaks who danced to a hot swing beat. Dressed in a unique fashion, the Swingjugend often collided with the Hitlerjugend. For the young people of the Swingjugend, a feeling of relative deprivation gave swing a special meaning, and America represented hope and promise, while they were also empathic toward African Americans who faced discrimination. The Hitlerjugend in contrast viewed swing with deep suspicion.[32] As detailed by historian Detlev Peukert, a Hitlerjugend internal report clearly expressed a high degree of distrust and enmity towards a February 1940 Hamburg swing festival, in the following way: "At the entrance to the hall stood a notice on which the words 'Swing prohibited' had been altered to 'Swing requested'."[33] Not that the Swingjugend engaged in political resistance to the same degree the Edelweißpiraten did. Still, by greeting one another with "Swing Heil" instead of "Sieg Heil," setting up an illegal jazz club and secretly holding dance parties, they clearly opposed the conformism of authority. The very existence of the Swingjugend clearly challenged the heart of the Nazi ideology, and therefore Heinrich Himmler, the director of the Schutzstaffel (SS; Protective Echelon), ordered: "All the ringleaders, and I mean ringleaders both male and female, and all teachers with enemy views who are encouraging the swing youth, are to be assigned to a concentration camp." Peukert confines the influence of the Swingjugend to social and cultural fields compared to the Edelweißpiraten that had a degree of political power as well. However, it should be noted that the act of listening to jazz in search of a more open society had significant political implications.[34]

A similar phenomenon was seen in wartime France, where a youth group called the zazou challenged conformist culture. Wearing long hair and zoot suits, a fashion popularized by the jazz singer Cab Callaway – an icon of American counter-culture since the 1930s – members of the zazou listened to jazz as a symbolic act of resistance to their parents' values. Like the Swingjugend, the zazou had little political will to rebel against the ruling government. They did not participate in the resistance movement, nor did they join Charles de Gaulle's Forces françaises libres. One of the few examples in which they took up a political cause was when they wore a yellow star-shaped badge with "Swing" marked on their chests in June 1942, in response to the Jews who had been ordered to put a yellow star that read "Juif" on their clothes. Nonetheless, the zazou were condemned as being anti-French, and conservative newspapers negatively portrayed the zazou as cooperating with Allied leaders. For the authorities, they were easier to condemn as morally corrupt enemies to social order, and therefore anti-French, than the invisible resistance movement groups.[35]

The existence of the Swingjugend and the zazou reveals how jazz functioned as a protest against conformism, regardless of whether the target of the resistance was a repressive regime or their parents. Jazz was here interpreted as a cultural icon of resistance, supporting people's hope for freedom. Musician and music critic Mike Zwerin observes that "Rarely, if ever, has any art affected the lives of 'normal' human beings as directly as jazz in Nazi-occupied Europe."[36] When repression produced resistance, the Vichy regime finally relaxed measures against the zazou. Instead of seeing jazz and the zazou as anti-French, authorities attempted to depoliticize both of them, manifesting in the discourse of critics like André Cœuroy, who advocated jazz's French origins. The wholesale reinterpretation of jazz, therefore, made it compatible to both love jazz and also be patriotic.[37]

Meanwhile, Japanese musicians were resisting conformist culture in their own ways. As mentioned above, the origins of Japanese jazz can be traced back to the Taisho period (1912–26), when five graduates of the Tokyo Music School, led by Fukutaro Hatano, formed a band while working on the ship Toyo Maru – whilst employed by the Japanese steamship company Toyo Kisen. The band encountered foxtrot and ragtime rhythms while ashore on the west coast of America, where the band members also bought musical instruments and cultivated their musical skills. Demand for jazz for dancing gradually increased in Tokyo and Yokohama, but Japanese jazz culture first blossomed in Osaka in western Japan, after the Great Kanto Earthquake destroyed large parts of Tokyo in 1923. The first Japanese jazz band, Laughing Stars, was formed in Kobe by violinist Ichiro Ida.[38] Later he left Kobe and Osaka, the city of jazz, for Tokyo because local dance halls had closed out of respect for the passing of Emperor Taisho. Like trumpeter Fumio Nanri and composer Ryoichi Hattori, who also shifted their jazz activities from Osaka to Tokyo and eventually to Shanghai, Japanese jazz musicians were fascinated by this "American music." When the *mobo* (modern boy) and *moga* (modern girl) came to embody the look of this new era, jazz's association with cosmopolitanism was one of the reasons behind its wide acceptance among Japan's youth.

And yet, there were not a few social strata in Japan that saw jazz and its associated modernism as uncivilized. The Immigration Act of 1924 limiting Japanese immigration to America had caused anti-American feeling to foment in Japan. Tadataka Ikezaki, a literary critic who later served as a member of the House of Representatives, harshly criticized jazz in his book *Americanism That Threatens the World*, published in 1930. Ikezaki argued that war between the US and Japan was "destined" to occur, while specifically criticizing Americanism as the "machine of evangelism and imperialism." He also warned that jazz represented a "culture of barbarism" that threatened Japan's unique culture. This grave sense of concern over Americanism – a notion allegedly embodying "the hedonistic life" and "the desire of the savage for short-lived gratification" – was an extension of his overall disgust with modernism.[39]

As the war with America drew closer, the local jazz scene became more strained. Although there were no counterparts to the Swingjugend or the zazou in Japan, musicians made strenuous efforts to maintain their freedom to play jazz. Through keenly reading the trends of the time and skillfully resisting pressure from the authorities, they continued to pursue their interests in jazz. As jazz historian E. Taylor Atkins elaborates, in a society where the Japanese aesthetic sense and spirituality were believed to be outstanding, musicians sought to adapt Japanese jazz to the times. Hattori was a central figure, arranging folk songs and nursery rhymes like "The Mountain Temple Priest" and "Oedo Nihombashi" to follow the swing style. By around 1940, well-known Japanese music, such as "The Moon over the Ruined Castle," "Kiso-Bushi," "Yagi-Bushi," "Yasugi-Bushi," "Sho-Jo-Ji

(The Hungry Raccoon)" and "Kutsu-ga-Naru" were being played in Dixieland, symphonic, swing and boogie-woogie styles to avoid unwanted attention from authorities. Reflecting the atmosphere in Japan around the second Sino–Japanese war, the lyrics of "Canton Blues" or "China Tango" showed a distinct pan-Asianism influence. Just before the outbreak of the Pacific War, "Over the Kunlun Shan" espousing the unity of Asia was played "à la Fletcher Henderson" by Japan's well-known Columbia Orchestra, seen as epitomizing the official military ideology of the Great East Asia Co-Prosperity Sphere.[40]

In similar fashion to Germany and occupied France, jazz and patriotism were also compatible in wartime Japan, although it came under stifling state control. When the National Mobilization Act came into force in 1938, the Ministry of the Interior took legal control over surveilling the Japanese jazz scene. A translation of an internal Cabinet Intelligence Bureau memo titled "An Opinion Regarding the Control of Jazz Music" shows a sophisticated understanding of the social influence of jazz in Japan and a realization by the authorities that it could be harnessed in support of Japan's national goals.[41] This memo officially acknowledged that jazz had a "bad influence" on other musical genres, as the music was viewed as "obscene" and "decadent." Officials nonetheless understood it was "necessary to admit some jazz as a compromise stance" in support of their domestic political agenda. Accordingly, the memo advocated that simply "arguing against modern music while ignoring the existence of jazz is to ignore aspects where it could prove beneficial." In response, authorities recognized that an official music policy could not afford to reject jazz outright, but instead "remove as much unhealthy elements as possible." In this context, similar to Germany during the same period, Japanese authorities pursued a policy that sought to encourage music that was light, cheerful and wholesome. Thus, Japan's wartime government prescribed jazz to be: "melodic and emphasizing the different ethnicities of different countries; cheerful and enlightening; humorous and light; lyrical; and containing notions of heroism." Interestingly, Japan's government also made clear what type of jazz was to be officially "excluded." Raising the ire of Japanese officials at the time would have been jazz numbers which had "riotous rhythms lacking melody; any music that generated overly embarrassing or amorous feelings; and decadent or ruinous music that makes people indolent."[42]

With the outbreak of the Pacific War, and Japan turning sharply away from the West, many foreign words that had been simply reproduced as they sounded, were renamed in hard Japanese characters. Jazz instruments were no exception. The saxophone was renamed "kinzoku seihin magari shakuhachi (bent metallic flute)" and the trombone became "nukisashi magari kin cho rappa (sliding bent long gold trumpet)." Eventually the use of the mute, a device used for softening and altering the tone of an instrument, even became restricted. However, it soon became clear that authorities lacked an in-depth knowledge of jazz. The difference between Duke Ellington and Mozart was lost on them, thereby permitting musicians to cleverly play "Unter dem Doppeladler" and "O Sole Mio" openly with jazz-like arrangements, while military songs were also played with a jazz rhythm. Finding loopholes in the web of official restrictions was a routine tactic for Japanese jazz musicians. Hattori, who embodied Japanese jazz of the time, later recollected how he could even manage to play standard New Orleans numbers when recording the *Light Music Hour* program for Japan's national radio broadcaster, Nippon Hoso Kyokai (NHK; Japan Broadcasting Corporation). To a nosy junior official who had listened to "Tiger Rug" and asked him whether it was American jazz, Hattori answered: "No, this is a song of a brave Malayan tiger hunt. You can hear lots of sounds like the roar of tiger. I think this sums up my current situation perfectly."[43]

This relative latitude given to jazz, however, was not to last. As the war dragged on, Japan's jazz scene became more restrictive. In January 1943, the Cabinet Intelligence Bureau directed "the expulsion of Anglo-American music" from Japan on grounds that "The Great East Asia War is not only an armed war but also a war of culture, thought and the like, and in particular, the destruction of Anglo-American thought is the root of everything."[44] Articles condemning jazz continued to appear in *Ongaku Bunka Shimbun* (Music Culture Press), a journal published by Japan's Music Culture Association – a body established and supported by the Ministry of the Interior and the Imperial Rule Assistance Association. Likely referring to jazz in an article printed in July 1943, the magazine firmly requested its readers to "discard musical scores of an inappropriate kind." The propagandistic piece also expressed the hope that Anglo-American music records would be "wiped out" in Japan. Undoubtedly taking its cue from the mood of the day, the author observed that Japan's record industry "is now ready for battle." Another article published in *Ongaku Chishiki* (Musical Knowledge) the following year asserted that Anglo-Americans were the musical "have-nots." According to the author, "Rhapsody in Blue" was "a flood of sound and was just noisy" and failed to enrich one's soul, suggesting it would be pointless to even discuss recordings by Paul Whiteman and Benny Goodman. The article goes on to add that compared with German music, admired as "food for thought for our people," jazz had "no creativity nor artfulness," yet would seek to corrupt the culture of the world.[45]

Propagating swing during the Second World War

In the 1941 State of the Union address, President Franklin D. Roosevelt put forward the Four Freedoms as a means of rallying the American people to fight fascism. Once joining the war, America provided jazz with a wartime role in representing the nation itself. Roosevelt himself recognized that music would play a role in winning the war, advocating music could help to maintain national morale.[46]

Glenn Miller became a central figure in this campaign. Disbanding his orchestra at the height of its popularity, he enlisted at the age of 38, and formed the Army Air Force Band to support US forces by conducting live performances for soldiers on the front line, while also making recordings for the V Discs provided to the military forces. While sweet numbers like "In the Mood" and "Moonlight Serenade" helped maintain morale, Miller's music was also expected to serve as a propaganda tool against Germany by enhancing the image of America as a bridgehead of freedom. The Office of War Information (OWI) broadcast the radio program *German Wehrmacht Hour* during which they played his music, propagating Roosevelt's Four Freedoms in the German language in between sets. As jazz historian Lewis A. Erenberg points out, the fact that Miller never returned home following his flight across the English Channel in 1944 was enough to transform him into a symbol of sacrifice for freedom and democracy.[47]

Meanwhile, enlisted African American musicians directly experienced the gap between swing's lofty ideals and the reality. Not all these musicians had enlisted like Miller, and some like Louis Armstrong and Duke Ellington, who were all already over the age of 40, were not recruited at all but were instead required to be involved in performances for the United Service Organizations (USO). Many younger musicians were directly recruited to become combat troops and soon found themselves deployed to areas which saw heavy fighting. Not all cases fitted this pattern, however. Lester Young of the Count Basie Orchestra was recruited in 1944 at the age of 30, but following a military trial for drug use was dishonorably discharged in 1945. Even though Miller put together Jewish and Italian musicians from all over America in order to promote a unified patriotic front, African American musicians were kept out of sight. Nonetheless, the fact that swing ideology came to represent a part of a national cause raised expectations that racial integration was possible. Critics such as John Hammond and Leonard Feather maintained critical stances against the Musician's Union and radio stations that continued to practice racial segregation. To Hammond, racial segregation was an explicit threat, albeit a domestic one, when he exclaimed that "We are fighting Hitler and Hitlerism, and yet we are practicing Hitler's own racial theories." Frank Sinatra, who had experienced anti-Italian sentiment in his own childhood, also repeated calls for racial integration. Meanwhile, black newspapers and the National Association for the Advancement of Colored People (NAACP) had initiated the "Double V" campaign for winning the war and eliminating domestic segregation at the same time. When an Illinois hotel refused entry to Ellington, the *Pittsburgh Courier* loudly decried this blatant discrimination, pointing out that an event like this did not occur even in Berlin or Tokyo. Against this backdrop, as the war drew to an end, some African American musicians started to feel disillusioned with the possibility of social reform, which would eventually lead them to develop a new style of jazz, bebop.[48]

What should be stressed in this context is that jazz was not the exclusive property of American wartime propaganda. During the Second World War, German radio stations strategically broadcast special programs utilizing swing music. The formation of Charlie and His Orchestra shows that the Nazi regime was comfortable employing jazz as a medium for propaganda. Led by saxophonist Lutz Templin, with Karl Schwedler as "Charlie" singing in fluent English, the orchestra ridiculed the American and British leaders. After singing a popular song with the original lyrics, Charlie then changed the lyrics to reflect recent German victories or military accomplishments against the Allies. For example, during the London air raids, when he sang "St. Louis Blues," he depicted the voices of London's citizenry worrying about the evening arrival of the German Luftwaffe. He also exploited the idea of Winston Churchill's weak leadership in performing "The Sheik of Araby." Moreover, following the outbreak of Soviet–German conflict in June 1941, whereupon Churchill was reluctant to fulfill Stalin's request for opening up a western front, the orchestra performed "Blue Moon" to show discord among the Allies. Similarly, lyrics directly criticizing the Americans appeared following Japan joining the Axis powers. When Singapore fell, "Continental" praised the Japanese, while employing lyrics to describe Roosevelt as mourning the loss of one of Britain's important strategic bases. Even when the tide of the war began to shift against Germany after the battle of Stalingrad, it was the predicament of the Allies that was sung in "Daisy."[49] In the meantime, from the end of 1940, members of the orchestra began to be conscripted to join the fighting at the front. New musicians were sourced from occupied territories such as Belgium and the Netherlands, and Axis powers like Italy, which soon made the orchestra quite multinational in character. When the war further deteriorated for Germany in 1943, the headquarters moved to Stuttgart, but later, following the main radio station being destroyed by Allied air raids in 1945, all the orchestra activities ceased.[50]

The case of a jazz band being established in a German-controlled concentration camp perhaps provides the ultimate example of jazz being grotesquely manipulated in support of a national purpose. In 1944, an investigation team led by the International Red Cross Committee entered the Theresienstadt camp on the outskirts of Prague to verify whether reports of forced labor and the killing of Jews in gas chambers had substance. In an attempt to counter the rumors, the camp was cleaned, and some prisoners were sent to Auschwitz to reduce overall numbers. To show that prisoners experienced a cultural side during their imprisonment, musical instruments were brought in, and the jazz band the Ghetto Swingers was formed. When the Red Cross team arrived at the camp, they were welcomed with a jazz performance. Later, the Ghetto Swingers appeared in the propaganda film *Adolf Hitler Gives the Jews a City*, produced to create the distorted image of a colorful and rich life in the camps. Ironically, some of the camp's band members had been interned for singing "Tiger Rug" in a public place with an Armstrong-like scat, and were later forced to play the same jazz for official propaganda purposes. Ultimately very few of these members survived, including Martin Roman (who had once played with Django Reinhardt, Coleman Hawkins and Lionel Hampton when living in Amsterdam), Coco Schumann and Eric Vogel, with many seeing out their final days in Auschwitz.[51]

Like in America and Germany, jazz found a place in the national war strategy of Japan. In 1942, when the Military Relief Department of the Army dispatched a band of musicians led by *Shochiku*, a leading film company, to Southeast Asia, some of these musicians included well-known jazz names such as Fumio Nanri. Another troupe, organized by the *Mainichi Shimbun*, one of Japan's major newspapers, was sent to the same region with a host of musicians, including well-known composer Takio Niki, saxophonist Shin Matsumoto and trumpeter Hisashi Moriyama to entertain Imperial Japanese Army personnel at this distant battle front.[52]

Moreover, Japan launched new propaganda broadcasting programs in anticipation of increased feelings of desperation among Allied forces, incorporating news they could not listen to on the air otherwise. The NHK's radio program *Zero Hour*, as one example, originated from a proposal by Lieutenant Shigetsugu Tsuneishi within the propaganda section of the Second Division of the Army General Staff. The program started as a daily edition running for 70 minutes from six in the evening, sending captives' messages to their family and covering American domestic news, while also playing jazz. Australian Major Charles Cousens – a former radio commentator who became a prisoner of war (POW) of Japan – and Filipino jazz fan Lieutenant Norman Reyes, were recruited for this project, as well as various female MCs collectively known as Tokyo Rose (notably Iva Toguri D'Aquino).[53] According to *Newsweek*, following the launch of the program, American soldiers preferred to listen to this jazz program rather than American radio programs. However, even if American listeners were in search of good jazz, this did not mean that Tokyo Rose propaganda messages were effective.[54]

Putting the propaganda impact of the radio programs aside, for Japanese musicians, radio stations provided a sanctuary for jazz. In the recording studios for the propaganda program *Sunday Promenade Concert*, musicians in an orchestra mostly composed of the Columbia Jazz Band could play swing without fear of retribution from authorities. The members of the orchestra included: bassist Ryo Watanabe, saxophonist Shin Matsumoto, two American-born *Nisei* musicians, trumpeter Hisashi Moriyama and vocalist Tib Kamayatsu, and two Filipino émigrés, pianist Francisco "Kiko" Reyes and clarinetist Raymond Conde. Despite all heralding from different backgrounds and origins, they enjoyed to the fullest extent the limited swing space allowed in wartime Japan. While in America swing represented the cause for joining the war against Japan, jazz was played in Tokyo with an anti-American tone. The theme song of the aforementioned propaganda program was "Moonlight Serenade" composed by Glenn Miller, the symbol of wartime Americanism, but no one in Japan saw this glaring contradiction. Jazz had a legitimate place also in wartime Japan by seeking out the possibility of going beyond Americanism. Also ironically, clarinetist Artie Shaw, who had joined the US Navy and formed a military band, reportedly heard "Begin the Beguine" on Japanese broadcast radio – a song he had arranged – while deployed at Guadalcanal. Moreover, when the Occupation Forces needed jazz for amusement and recreation after the war, it was these same musicians who were preferentially hired by the American military clubs across Japan. The advent of the jazz boom in postwar Japan arguably cannot be understood without considering the role jazz played during the turbulent early and mid-1940s.[55]

Being American and non-American simultaneously, jazz outside America had already started to take on a certain hybridity in the interwar period. With the rise in the popularity of swing, jazz was interpreted in various ways. In that process, jazz's American-ness was gradually diluted, creating room for the Axis powers to strategically exploit the music as an anti-American propaganda medium. As the postwar ideological conflict deepened, the relationship between jazz and America evolved into yet a new phase. The next chapter explores the standing of

"American music" in the early postwar period in America and Communist bloc countries, through investigating the interaction between the changing global political environment and domestic jazz scenes in these countries.

Notes

1 Lewis A. Erenberg, *Swingin' the Dream: Big Band Jazz and the Rebirth of American Culture* (Chicago: University of Chicago Press, 1998), pp.37–40; David W. Stowe, *Swing Changes: Big-band Jazz in New Deal America* (Cambridge: Harvard UP, 1998), pp.23–24, 52–54.
2 Stowe, *Swing Changes*, pp.73–74; Michael Denning, *The Cultural Front: The Laboring of American Culture in the Twentieth Century* (Brooklyn: Verso, 2011), p.xix.
3 Erenberg, *Swingin' the Dream*, pp.xi–xvi, 69–83, 90–91; Stowe, *Swing Changes*, pp.13–14.
4 For jazz's social standing in Harlem, and more on the Scottsboro case as well as well-known jazz musicians' involvement with this case, see Jonathon Bakan, "Jazz and the 'Popular Front': 'Swing' Musicians and the Left Wing Movement of the 1930s–1940s," *Jazz Perspectives*, vol.3 no.1, 2009, pp.36–42.
5 Walter LaFeber, Richard Polenberg and Nancy Woloch, *The American Century: A History of the United States Since the 1890s*, 7th Edition (London: Routledge, 2013), pp.148–49.
6 Erenberg, *Swingin' the Dream*, pp.133–35; Stowe, *Swing Changes*, pp.64–66.
7 Erenberg, *Swingin' the Dream*, pp.144–47. For the background of "Strange Fruit," see David Margolick, *Strange Fruit: Billie Holiday, Cafe Society, and an Early Cry for Civil Rights* (Philadelphia: Running Press, 2004).
8 Barney Josephson and Terry Trilling-Josephson, *Cafe Society: The Wrong Place for the Right People* (Urbana: University of Illinois Press, 2009), p.50.
9 Erenberg, *Swingin' the Dream*, pp.137–39.
10 Matthew F. Jordan, *Le Jazz: Jazz and French Cultural Identity* (Urbana: University of Illinois Press, 2010), pp.43–45.
11 Ch. Didier Gondola, "'But I Ain't African, I'm American!': Black American Exiles and the Construction of Racial Identities in Twentieth-Century France," in Heike Raphael-Hernandez (ed.), *Blackening Europe: The African American Presence* (London: Routledge, 2003), pp.202–10; Jeffry Jackson, *Making Jazz French: Music and Modern Life in Interwar Paris* (Durham: Duke UP, 2003), pp.16–17. For more on exoticism and racial discrimination in France, see Brett A. Berliner, *Ambivalent Desire: The Exotic Black Other in Jazz Age France* (Amherst: University of Massachusetts Press, 2002).
12 Cary D. Wintz and Paul Finkelman (eds.), *Encyclopedia of the Harlem Renaissance: A-J* (London: Routledge, 2004), p.384. For the reaction the ODJB received in Britain, see Catherine Parsonage, *The Evolution of Jazz in Britain, 1880–1935* (London: Routledge, 2005), pp.124–43.
13 Ludovic Tournes, *New Orleans sur Seine: Histoire du jazz en France* (Paris: Fayard, 1999), pp.17–24; Karen C.C. Dalton and Henry Louis Gates, Jr., "Josephine Baker and Paul Colin: African American Dance Seen through Parisian Eyes," *Critical Inquiry*, vol.24 no.4, 1998, p.907; E. Taylor Atkins, *Blue Nippon: Authenticating Jazz in Japan* (Durham: Duke UP, 2001), pp.122–23; Jordan, *Le Jazz*, pp.49–53, 72.
14 William A. Shack, *Harlem in Montmartre: A Paris Jazz Story between the Great Wars* (Berkeley: University of California Press, 2001).
15 Michael H. Kater, *Different Drummers: Jazz in the Culture of Nazi Germany* (Oxford: Oxford UP, 2003), p.18.

16 Atkins, *Blue Nippon*, pp.99, 122–23.
17 Frank Costigliola, *Awkward Dominion: American Political, Economic, and Cultural Relations with Europe, 1919–1933* (Ithaca: Cornell UP, 1988), pp.20–22, 167; Jackson, *Making Jazz French*, pp.72–79; David Ellwood, *The Shock of America: Europe and the Challenge of the Century* (Oxford: Oxford UP, 2012), p.74.
18 Tournes, *New Orleans sur Seine*, pp.27–29; Jackson, *Making Jazz French*, pp.108–16, 128–35; Jordan, *Le Jazz*, pp.111–17.
19 Tournes, *New Orleans sur Seine*, pp.40–58; Jackson, *Making Jazz French*, pp.159–86; Jordan, *Le Jazz*, pp.142–43, 161–69; Tom Perchard, *After Django: Making Jazz in Postwar France* (Ann Arbor: University of Michigan Press, 2015), pp.23–33.
20 Jackson, *Making Jazz French*, pp.123–24, 167–68, 187–90; Jordan, *Le Jazz*, pp.173–76.
21 Mike Zwerin, *Swing under Nazis: Jazz as a Metaphor for Freedom* (New York: Cooper Square Press, 2000), pp.149–51; Jordan, *Le Jazz*, p.191.
22 Rashida K. Braggs, *Jazz Diasporas: Race, Music, and Migration in Post-World War II Paris* (Oakland: University of California Press, 2016), p.68.
23 Shack, *Harlem in Montmartre*, p.117; Michael Dregni, *Django: The Life and Music of a Gypsy Legend* (Oxford: Oxford UP, 2006), p.164.
24 Dregni, *Django*, pp.157–69.
25 Mary Nolan, "America in the German Imagination," in Heide Fehrenbach and Uta G. Poiger (eds.), *Transactions, Transgressions, Transformations: American Culture in Western Europe and Japan* (New York: Berghahn Books, 2000), pp.5–7; Uta Poiger, *Jazz, Rock, and Rebels: Cold War Politics and American Culture in a Divided Germany* (Oakland: University of California Press, 2000), pp.20–21.
26 Michael H. Kater, *Different Drummers*, pp.18–20; Berndt Ostendorf, "Subversive Reeducation?: Jazz as a Liberating Force in Germany and Europe," *Revue Française d'Etudes Américaines*, vol.5, 2001, pp.60–61.
27 Michael H. Kater, *Different Drummers*, pp.32, 51, 64; Ralph Willett, "Hot Swing and the Dissolute Life: Youth, Style and Popular Music in Europe 1939–49," *Popular Music*, vol.8 issue 2, May 1989, pp.157–58; Hans-Joerg Koch, *Das Wunschkonzert im NS-Rundfunk* (Köln: Böhlau, 2003), p.60. Song titles and musicians' names were changed also in Italy. "St. Louis Blues" became "Le tristezze di San Luigi," and "In the Mood" to "Tristezze," while "Stompin' at the Savoy" was played as "Savoiardi." Louis Armstrong was renamed Luigi Bracciaforte, Benny Goodman was now Beniamino Buonomo, Duke Ellington became Del Duca, and Coleman Hawkins was known as Correa. See Franco Minganti, "Jukebox Boys: Postwar Italian Music and the Culture of Covering," in Fehrenbach and Poiger (eds.), *Transactions, Transgressions and Transformation*, pp.151–52.
28 Kater, *Different Drummers*, pp.47, 52.
29 Ibid., pp.118–9; Christina L. Baade, *Victory Through Harmony: The BBC and Popular Music in World War II* (Oxford: Oxford UP, 2011), pp.189–93.
30 Zwerin, *Swing under Nazis*, p.31; Kater, *Different Drummers*, pp.126–29, 170.
31 Kater, *Different Drummers*, p.202.
32 Willett, "Hot Swing and the Dissolute Life," p.160; Frank McDonough, *Opposition and Resistance in Nazi Germany* (Cambridge: Cambridge UP, 2001), pp.17–18.
33 Detlev J. K. Peukert (trans. Richard Deveson), *Inside Nazi Germany: Conformity, Opposition, and Racism in Everyday Life* (New Haven: Yale UP, 1987), pp.166–67.
34 Ibid., pp.199–200. See also Michael H. Kater, *Hitler Youth* (Cambridge: Harvard UP, 2004), pp.140–66.
35 Tournes, *New Orleans sur Seine*, pp.87–90; Julie Kathleen Schweitzer, *Irresponsibly Engage: Boris Vian and Uses of American Culture in France, 1940–1959* (MA Thesis, University of Maryland, 2005), pp.21–23; Jordan, *Le Jazz*, pp.201–22.
36 Zwerin, *Swing under Nazis*, p.44.
37 Tournes, *New Orleans sur Seine*, pp.85–6; Jordan, *Le Jazz*, pp.222–32.

38 Koichi Uchida, *Nihon no Jazz-shi* (Tokyo: Swing Journal, 1976), pp.5–44.
39 Chuko Ikezaki, *Sekai wo Kyoi Suru Americanism* (Tokyo: Tenjinsha, 1930), pp.33–49.
40 Atkins, *Blue Nippon*, pp.132–36; Masahisa Segawa, *Jazz de Odotte* (Tokyo: Seiryu Shuppan, 2005), pp.367–68; Masahisa Segawa and Yoshio Otani, *Nihon Jazz no Tanjo* (Tokyo: Seidosha, 2008), pp.109–12, 133–49; Toshihiko Kishi, *Higashi Asia Ryukoka Hour* (Tokyo: Iwanami Shoten, 2013), pp.151–55.
41 "Jazz Ongaku Torishimarijo no Kenkai (Showa 16 nen 7 gatsu)," reprinted in Yoshimi Uchikawa (ed.), *Gendaishi Shiryo: Mass Media Tosei*, 2nd edition (Tokyo: Misuzu Shobo, 1973), pp.347–54. This memo has been discussed in detail in Atkins, *Blue Nippon*, pp.139–46.
42 "Jazz Ongaku Torishimarijo no Kenkai (Showa 16 nen 7 gatsu)," pp.347–54.
43 Atkins, *Blue Nippon*, pp.130–63; Ryoichi Hattori, *Boku no Ongaku Jinsei* (Tokyo: Nihon Bungeisha, 1993), pp.199–200, quoted in ibid., p.157. See also Masato Mori, *Nippon Swing Time* (Tokyo: Kodansha, 2010), pp.240–41, 257–58.
44 "Eibei Ongaku no Tsuiho," reprinted in Jun Kobayashi, "Jazz Gohatto no Jidai ga Atta," in Mainichi Shimbunsha, *Nihon no Jazz* (Tokyo: Mainichi Shimbunsha, 1982), pp.77–80. See also Atkins, *Blue Nippon*, pp.147–49.
45 "Tekikoku no Gakuhu Haiki," *Ongaku Bunka Shimbun*, vol.53, 1943, and Araebisu, "Teki Beiei no Onban," *Ongaku Chishiki*, vol.2 no.11, 1944, both reprinted in Tatsuhide Akiyama, *Nihon no Yogaku Hyakunen-shi* (Tokyo: Daiichi Hoki Shuppan, 1966), pp.559, 566–67.
46 Erenberg, *Swingin' the Dream*, p.184.
47 Ibid., pp.181–209.
48 Ibid., pp.188–89, 202–8; Stowe, *Swing Changes*, pp.156–67.
49 Horst J. P. Bergmeier and Rainer E. Lotz, *Hitler's Airwaves: The Inside Story of Nazi Radio Broadcasting and Propaganda Swing* (New Haven: Yale UP, 1997), pp.153–74, 306–14.
50 Kater, *Different Drummers*, pp.131, 167, 170.
51 Zwerin, *Swing under Nazis*, pp.25–27; Fabrice D'Almeida, *High Society in the Third Reich* (Cambridge: Politi, 2008), p.212; Larry Ross, "Jazz Musicians in Europe: 1919 to 1945," in James L. Conyers Jr. (ed.), *Engines of the Black Power Movement: Essays on the Influence of Civil Rights Actions, Arts, And Islam* (Jefferson: Mcfarland, 2006), pp.37–38. Vogel later detailed the situation of the time in *Down Beat*. See Eric Vogel, "Jazz in a Nazi Concentration Camp (Part 1, 2, 3)," *Down Beat*, vol.28 no.15, 16 and vol.29 no.1, 7 December, 21 December 1961 and 4 January 1962.
52 Uchida, *Nihon no Jazz-shi*, pp.139–48; Kishi, *Higashi Asia Ryukoka Hour*, pp.153–54.
53 Atkins, *Blue Nippon*, p.157; Masayo Duus, *Tokyo Rose* (Tokyo: Bungeishunju, 1990), pp.74–83.
54 Takashi Watanabe, *Propaganda Radio* (Tokyo: Chikuma Shobo, 2014), pp.136–64.
55 Atkins, *Blue Nippon*, pp.157–59; Stowe, *Swing Changes*, p.152; Segawa, *Jazz de Odotte*, p.372; Mori, *Nippon Swing Time*, pp.281–85; Kishi, *Higashi Asia Ryukoka Hour*, pp.151–55.

2 The scene changes in postwar jazz politics

The end of the Second World War coincided with the demise of the swing era. Emerging from this period was a new style of jazz, which pursued more expressive freedom through emphasizing improvisation with a small combo, named bebop. Symbolizing the complaints voiced by many African American musicians that social expectations for racial integration once embodied in swing had failed to materialize, this new style of jazz emphasized blackness. Bebop was different from swing in this respect, but its relationship with politics was nevertheless as close as swing. Big name musicians such as Charlie Parker and Dizzy Gillespie were interested in social issues including the civil rights movement, and both were influenced by activists such as Paul Robeson. It was Gillespie who refused the role of entertaining white audiences, while he advanced the notion of bebop as a "manifestation of revolt." He therefore, thought little of Louis Armstrong who Gillespie believed was foregoing a needed political role.[1]

The dawn of modern jazz also witnessed the rivalry of two superpowers that both held universal – yet incompatible – value systems. In America many argued for standing firm against Communism through a policy of containment, as articulated by the State Department's well-known Sovietologist George F. Kennan, manifesting in his so-called "X" article and the Truman Doctrine. In such an environment, the concept of New Deal Liberalism of the interwar period, during which swing embodied the idea of freedom and democracy, suddenly found itself in an awkward position. People who had advocated racial integration were increasingly seen as representing un-American values, even leading to some being placed under the supervision of security agencies. Whereas in Communist countries, ironically, jazz became a target of oppression by party functionaries just because the music stood out as "American music." In the following sections, the early postwar jazz scenes – from both inside and outside America – will examine the contested discourse of jazz in the early postwar period.

Racial integration and bebop's resistance

The trajectory of record producer and social entrepreneur Norman Granz exemplified these changes in the postwar jazz scene, as well as the philosophy of resistance symbolized by bebop. Granz, who had played an active part in promoting the idea of racial integration through "American music" during the war, believed that jazz had a part to play in postwar America. The son of Jewish Russian immigrants and coming from a modest childhood, Granz played with friends of various ethnic origins around Central Avenue, Los Angeles. Granz was influenced by the socialist ideas of Harold Laski as a college student, during the latter's tenure as a visiting lecturer at the University of California.[2] In postwar America, Granz became a suspected Communist and eventually came under formal investigation by the Federal Bureau of Investigation (FBI).

Granz is usually associated with the JATP label, the title of numerous recordings and concerts organized both inside and outside America until 1957. The JATP was launched at the Philharmonic Auditorium in Los Angeles on 2 July 1944 as a means of protesting against the Sleepy Lagoon case, an incident involving the arrest and prosecution of hundreds of Mexican youths, despite flimsy evidence, for a murder near an eastern Los Angeles reservoir in 1942. Granz was involved in a fundraising concert for the defendants. Coincidentally, the launch of the JATP at the Auditorium took place exactly 20 years before the enactment of the Civil Rights Act on 2 July 1964. How the JATP represented Americanism is evident in a well-known declaration publicly issued in its literature at the time:

> Jazz is America's own. It is the music which grew out of a young and vigorous melting-pot nation. It is a product of all America, deriving much of its inspiration and creation from the Negro people. Jazz holds up no superficial bars. It is played and listened to by all peoples – in harmony, together. Pigmentation differences have no place in jazz. As in genuine democracy, only performance counts. Jazz is truly the music of democratic America. It is an ideal medium for bringing about a better understanding among all peoples.[3]

The uniqueness of Granz lies in the fact that he was a social entrepreneur working to resist a segregated society. Through JATP concert tours, he not only produced high-quality jazz, which served to enhance its social status, but also tried to eliminate racial segregation by making jazz a viable commercial enterprise. Taking advantage of the logic of the market differentiated him from other like-minded critics who were also engaged in tackling racial problems through jazz periodicals. For Granz jazz was not a genre of music for dancing – it should be a music for musicians themselves. Bored with swing that had come to be seen as overly commercialized and restrictive with little room for self-expression, beboppers had advanced the technique of improvisation in an experimental space in jam sessions after work during the war. Their participation in the JATP tours in turn grew their popularity, leading to significant business successes for the organizer, as well as the musicians themselves.[4] Certain business practices upheld in the course of planning and carrying out the JATP concerts illustrated bebop's deep-seated philosophy of resistance. As detailed by Granz's biographer Tad Hershorn, from the ticket sales to the audience's seat allocation, Granz banned racial discrimination by inserting clauses into contracts, imposing a stiff financial penalty on anyone who dared violate them. In an interview with the black paper the *Pittsburgh Courier*, Granz proclaimed that through his management of these tours "enlightenment is gradually spreading all over the nation." However, the tours with racial clauses written into their contracts were not always profitable, as shown by an annual loss of US$100,000 Granz incurred in 1947. Still, Granz adhered to his philosophy, employing various practical methods to express it. For instance, after booking a room at a first-class hotel, Granz arrived at this same venue with a racially mixed band, threatening the hotel with litigation if it canceled his accommodation. Granz also sought solidarity with other band leaders, requesting them to explicitly insert similar racial clauses into their contracts when planning public performances. Granz's creed can be summarized in his own words: "Prejudice is an economic matter. Make it unprofitable."[5]

However, bebop's aspiration for social reform and its deep criticism of the social order of the day were vulnerable in postwar America. John Edgar Hoover had already started investigating John Hammond and his leftist connections in swing ideology. Duke Ellington, on his part, also had many reasons to become a target of the FBI. He had appeared in the Fats Waller memorial concert organized by the CPUSA, while also playing in a concert supporting CPUSA candidate Benjamin J. Davis from Harlem.[6] Another figure, Artie Shaw, had worked alongside Ellington in the leftist organization, the Hollywood Independent Citizens Committee of the Sciences, Arts, and Professions (HICCASP), during a critical period when Communism was thought to be influencing Hollywood. As a result, Shaw was later summoned to testify in front of the House Un-American Activities Committee (HUAC), which had been established in 1938, later becoming a ruthless tool aimed at rooting out postwar Communism.[7] Notably, Frank Sinatra also worked for HICCASP, serving as the vice-chair from 1946. In 1945 Sinatra won an Oscar for the short film *The House I Live In* – a movie tackling the problem of discrimination against Jews – for which Abel Meeropol composed the movie's theme song. Eventually, however, the relationship between Sinatra and the popular front would be noticed by the HUAC.[8]

New York's Cafe Society, a well-recognized meeting place for leftist intellectuals, was one such venue affected by the changing environment of postwar global politics. Leon Josephson, one of the owner's older brothers, a lawyer and open Communist, was suspected of collaborating with Soviet agents. When he was summoned to the HUAC in 1947, the chairman Richard Nixon heard Josephson's motion contesting "the right, the legality of this committee, to examine me."[9] Making his doubts public about the legality of the HUAC and refusing to testify, Josephson was later imprisoned, which suddenly affected the profitability of Cafe Society, resulting in its closure.[10]

Prior to its closure, the cafe had had its own orchestra, with trumpeter Frankie Newton as its leader. The Marxist historian Eric Hobsbawm was fascinated with this open Communist who had once recorded "Strange Fruit" with several other notable musicians, and he used "Francis Newton" as his *nom de plume* when publishing books on jazz. Just as jazz musicians were placed under the supervision of the FBI in America, the British intelligence agency, MI5, monitored Hobsbawm, because he was recognized as a member of the Communist Party of Great Britain.[11] Importantly, Hobsbawm (Newton) called jazz a "music of protest and rebellion." According to his views, when jazz and politics mixed in the West, "they have been pretty invariably with the left." Just like Granz and Cafe Society sought to promote a more racially integrated society around them, Hobsbawm asserted that any jazz lover should protest racial discrimination, which could only be legitimized by the right.[12]

As the Americanism of the 1950s continued to search for flag bearers to publicly call for racial integration, suspicions of Granz as un-American eventually led to his arrest and formal questioning by the FBI. In October 1955, Granz was arrested by the Houston city police during a JATP tour in America's southern states. When musicians including Dizzy Gillespie and Illinois Jacquet were playing a low-key dice game between performances, they were all arrested by plain-clothes law enforcement officials who burst into their room unannounced. Although they were released after paying a $50 fine, Granz spent $2,000 on an expensive lawyer to fight the case, which he later won.[13] This represented the way he tackled racial problems – through paying scant attention to the financial costs involved. The following year, when 35 people in the music industry were summoned to the HUAC, Granz was originally included on the list. But he could escape these difficulties by staying abroad and keeping an eye on the activities of the HUAC from afar. In any event, Granz was formally accused of being a member of the CPUSA at a hearing in his absence. Following this, the State Department tasked its overseas missions to locate Granz and seek an affidavit from him denying his relationship with the party. In 1957, when he appeared at the US consular office in Zurich to renew his passport, it was refused because, contrary to the State Department's expectations, he indicated he still held membership in the CPUSA. Consular officials only issued him with a temporary passport to enable him to return to America. But again, Granz hired a prominent lawyer, won the lawsuit against his government, leading to his passport being officially renewed. Meanwhile, not wanting to bring his and the JATP's social standing into disrepute, Granz himself arranged to meet with the FBI to answer all their questions. After explaining the principal reason for accepting membership in the CPUSA stemmed from his interest in racial problems, as well as his relations with the film director Edward Dmytryk – one of the Hollywood Ten found guilty for refusing to testify at the HUAC – the FBI assessed that Granz presented no threat.[14] Nevertheless, in the fall of 1957, at the end of the annual national tour, Granz put an end to JATP activities. Only sporadic tours would be held in America, Europe and Japan in later years, as he would spend most of his life in Switzerland.

The success of the JATP shows the continued popularity of jazz in America during the early postwar period, but Granz's life experiences reveal a marked difference in social conditions surrounding the heyday of swing and the rise of bebop. Although the number of CPUSA members peaked at 80,000 during the war, around when the civil rights and social security reformer Henry Wallace lost the presidential election to Harry Truman in 1948, the number had dropped to 60,000 and continued to decline. Voicing concerns over racial problems was almost akin to declaring oneself a Communist, which in turn ran counter to the notion of Americanism.

Against the context of these shifts in the American cultural and societal landscape was the Cold War. Ironically, however, followers of jazz in many Communist countries were persecuted precisely because this music stood out as "American music." As such, we need to examine how various jazz scenes in the Eastern bloc were affected by the emerging Cold War structure in global politics.

Swings in Soviet jazz policy

Russian society first encountered jazz in 1922, after poet Valentin Parnakh returned from six years in Paris, whereupon he formed "the First Eccentric Orchestra of the Russian Federated Socialist Republic – Valentin Parnakh's Jazz Band." During the 1920s, the Chocolate Kiddies led by Sam Wooding conducted a tour of Russia featuring symphonic jazz, while Benny Peyton's Jazz Kings with Sidney Bechet played hot jazz, both receiving favorable reviews at the time. Under the New Economic Policy period, the middle class and government officials were fascinated with the music's distinctively new rhythm. Jazz was also an art form for the workers, prompting Anatoly Lunacharsky, the People's Commissariat for Education, to dispatch a composer to America to carry out jazz research.[15] During the same decade, American-style production systems began penetrating the Soviet Union, as shown by General Electric signing a contract with the Soviet government in 1928 for $25 million. Ford Motor Company also signed large commercial contracts with Soviet partners. Indicating Henry Ford's popularity, his autobiography was a hit with Soviet readers. In addition, showing an upswing in economic – and cultural relations – by the early 1930s, America had become the Soviet Union's second largest trading partner after Germany.[16]

Even so, criticism directed at jazz arose, with some critics seeing it as anti-revolutionary and causing moral corruption. For writer Maxim Gorky, jazz was the "music of grossness," a symbol of homosexuality and lust. Jazz did not disappear, however, as it had already penetrated deep into society as a dance music. The interpretation of the music as art for America's discriminated workers – such as African Americans and Jews (this analogy was close to the way jazz was represented by the Nazi regime) – allowed the jazz scene to survive in Soviet society. Furthermore, the categorizing of jazz into "authentic/good" and "bad" facilitated the promotion of a certain type of jazz, even during Stalin's rule. As detailed by jazz historian S. Frederick Starr, herein arrived the "red jazz age" perfectly in tune with Communist ideology's call for solidarity among oppressed peoples. These developments eventually led to the establishment of the State Jazz Orchestra in 1938 with the aim of legitimizing the existence of the music in a Communist state.[17]

When the German/Soviet Nonaggression Pact was violated by the invasion of German forces into Soviet territory in June 1941, the Soviet jazz scene was further legitimized by the image that jazz was being suppressed in Germany. Soviet musicians began performances on the front line, maintaining the morale of soldiers with patriotic lyrics. Jazz was a symbol of powerfulness, youthfulness and vivacity, which, as in France after the fall of Paris, provided them with a temporary reprieve from the hardships of war. At this time, the Soviet Union's State Jazz Orchestra visited various places in response to requests from frontline commanders. Among many numbers, "Katyusha" was one of the most popular at the time, which described a young lady's longing for her beloved soldier who was bravely defending his homeland. Known as a Russian folk song but actually written in 1938, "Katyusha" was played as part of a repertoire of the orchestra, stimulating patriotism during difficult times. Likewise, a number of small jazz-playing divisions were organized within the Red Army. At Leningrad, the Baltic Fleet Jazz Orchestra continued to stoically perform even when coming under attack by German forces, greatly lifting the morale of the local people. In this way, the status of jazz gradually improved during the war. In 1944, the film *Sun Valley Serenade*, which featured the Glenn Miller Orchestra and its hit numbers "In the Mood," "Chattanooga Chu Chu" and "Moonlight Serenade," was released in the Soviet Union, enhancing the popularity of jazz even further.[18]

The early life of Eddie Rosner – a beloved musician nicknamed the "Tsar" – found significant support from the Communist Party, testimony to the rising popularity of jazz in Soviet society. Born in 1910 to Jewish parents in Berlin, Rosner was later active in Germany as a member of the Weintraub Syncopators. After the rise of the Nazi party forced him to move to Poland, Rosner again immigrated to the Belorussian Soviet Socialist Republic following the German invasion of Poland. Under the protection of the Communist jazz fan Panteleimon Ponomarenko, the first secretary of the Communist Party of Belorussia, Rosner assumed leadership of the Belarus State Jazz Orchestra. According to Starr, even the far-right nationalists were more likely to accept jazz in the war period than at any other time, despite the music's association with the idea of Americanism.[19] In this favorable environment, Rosner could play jazz with dignity and record popular numbers like "St. Louis Blues" and "Caravan." Compatibility between being an ardent jazz fan and being a good Communist was graphically demonstrated when Rosner performed an unusual concert at Sochi in 1941. Surrounded by secret police, he conducted a two-hour program at a theater with seemingly no audience in attendance. The next day his manager received a phone call from the Kremlin reporting that Stalin had enjoyed Rosner's performance. The Sochi performance had turned out to be a "royal performance" in front of another Tsar, Josef Stalin himself.[20]

Despite this, the beginning of the Cold War cast a shadow over the Soviet jazz scene. In 1946, a rigid ideological campaign commenced, seeing a strengthening of cultural controls by Andrei Zhdanov, who loudly criticized all abstract art as formalism. As the campaign extended to the music world, composers such as Dmitri Shostakovich and Aram Khachaturian were accused of being bourgeois, decadent and modernist. In the background of this Zhdanov doctrine there was Stalin's aim to purify his society by shutting out foreign culture, and thereby reinforce social control and restore legitimacy to the Communist Party's rule. Based on a wealth of primary sources, historians of Soviet diplomacy Vladislav Zubok and Constantine Pleshakov stress the domestic drivers underpinning this new campaign rather than external influences.[21] Still, we should not ignore the role that the image of America played in the implementation of this new cultural policy. By 1947, the emergence of an enduring East–West confrontation manifested through a series of historically significant events. The Truman Doctrine, for instance, depicted the world through a dualistic lens that contrasted two ways of life – one characterized by "free institutions" and "representative government" and the other based on "terror" and "oppression." Whereas Zhdanov provided another, somewhat dichotomous world view, which described the Western world as plagued with "imperialism." In this context, once represented as a progressive democratic power, America had become a decadent, uncultured and racist country associated with exploitation, unemployment and the lynching of minorities – in the minds of Soviet officials at least and reflected in their propaganda. Americans caricatured in domestic journals in this period were depicted as rough-looking gangs with cigarettes or as grotesque animals. Accordingly, jazz was soon expelled from official culture, becoming a symbol of barbarism, bourgeois decadence and sexual deviation. Saxophones were forbidden, and techniques used to play jazz were severely curtailed by the authorities – vibrato in the brass section and the use of a blue note were explicitly prohibited as techniques associated with jazz. Aimed at vilifying jazz in Soviet society, new idiomatic expressions even entered the discourse, such as "today he plays jazz and tomorrow he sells his whole country" and "from saxophone to knife – one step," clearly showing how the discursive tide had shifted against jazz.[22]

In the same vein, as jazz's closeness with America became indisputable, Rosner's celebrated life and career began to implode, graphically showing how the postwar Soviet jazz scene was rapidly shifting and becoming increasingly politically charged. He was personally targeted by a new ideological campaign and shortly thereafter arrested trying to leave the country illegally in November 1946. Later he was interned in a gulag at Kolyma in northeastern Siberia. Following imprisonment, however, he was ordered to organize an ensemble for the same music that had made his fame and fortune. As one who once reigned in the Soviet jazz scene as the "Tsar," Rosner received an enthusiastic welcome from his fellow prisoners. Although he was later released following Stalin's death, the authorities continued to refuse to issue him a visa to leave to Berlin until 1972, when Richard Nixon visited Moscow for the first time as the US President to hold summit talks with Leonid Brezhnev.[23]

Although jazz was suppressed in postwar Soviet society, these draconian efforts did not lead to its extinction as a musical genre, nor did jazz fans fade away into obscurity. Since popular music for dancing was not issued by the state, Red Army officers stationed in the German Democratic Republic (East Germany) brought back jazz records from Berlin. Moreover, and somewhat paradoxically, Duke Ellington's popular numbers featured in anti-American dramas and films. In "Brother Can You Spare a Dime," Leonid Utesov – a singer and comic actor, known for his theatrical "Thea-Jazz" – sang about poor job conditions in interwar America with a hint of jazz. Born in Odessa, a city with a cultural diversity like New Orleans, Utesov often joked that jazz originated in Odessa.[24]

A more explicit phenomenon of resisting the official policy towards jazz was shown by the emergence of the stilyagi, a counterculture youth group. The way they cared about fashion and dancing – wearing zoot suits with long hair and nicknaming Moscow's main Gorky street "Broadway" – was reminiscent of the Swingjugend and the zazou in Germany and France during the war, when jazz represented freedom and resistance. The stilyagi's "delinquency," such as disdain for work or frequent visits to foreign restaurants, were signs of protest against their parents and conformism. Although the Kommunisticheskiy Soyuz Molodyozhi (Komsomol; Communist Youth League) were highly critical of them, members of the stilyagi were not necessarily politically minded. Rather, jazz provided them with a means to escape from the unpleasantness of official culture, thus offering a momentary catharsis in the gray life of Soviet society. The style of jazz the stilyagi usually followed was either swing or boogie-woogie. But in a certain sense, the spirit they embodied resonated with the philosophy of resistance found in bebop. We can note that bebop underpinned and drove complicated improvisation, which was clearly antithetical to conformism. Witnessing the rise of the stilyagi, the US ambassador in Moscow, Charles Bohlen, noticed the value of jazz and proposed the launch of a new radio program, which later materialized as *Music USA* from 1955.[25]

It was Stalin's death that brought about a major change in the standing of jazz in postwar Soviet society. As Ilya Ehrenburg depicted in his novel *The Thaw*, Soviet leaders began to take a more relaxed stance on cultural matters, resulting in the easing of restrictions regarding playing and listening to jazz. The cultural "thaw" at international level manifested in a series of cultural agreements the Soviet Union concluded with Western countries, which enabled Soviet citizens to access Western culture easier than before. Approximately 70,000 Soviets traveled abroad in 1957, while 2,700 Americans visited the Soviet Union in the same year.[26] Even though state regulations still prevented a totally free press and information was still controlled, earlier prejudices towards the West began to wane, which, according to historian Robert D. English, allowed a foundation to form around more reformist foreign as well as domestic policies of later decades.[27]

Following Nikita Khrushchev's secret speech denouncing Stalin at the Twentieth Congress of the Communist Party of the Soviet Union on 25 February 1956, jazz became more accepted by the authorities. The military intervention to quell the Hungarian Uprising in October the same year forced the Soviet government to show its "openness" to the world as a means of preventing further deterioration of its international image. As a result, the sixth World Festival of Youth and Students in 1957 became an important part of Soviet public diplomacy, seeing 34,000 people from all over the world, including 160 people from America, gather in Moscow.[28] At this festival, jazz featured frequently, with local Muscovites fascinated by Michel Legrand from France, as well as Krzysztof Komeda from Poland who played a series of Miles Davis numbers.[29] According to Alexey Kozlov, a Soviet saxophonist and himself a stilyagi, the festival irreversibly spurred the collapse of Stalinist society, and eventually the whole Soviet system.[30] While this is a debatable point, it could be argued that the festival certainly symbolized the scene changes in post-Stalin Soviet society.

De-Americanizing jazz discourse in Eastern Europe

While geographically close to the West, jazz had a special meaning in postwar Eastern Europe. Although the music entered the region in the interwar period and was popular, the relatively tolerant cultural policy in the early postwar period ended as the Cold War progressed and the relationship with the West became increasingly tenuous. Furthermore, the arrival of the Zhdanov doctrine led to the imposition of the ideology of socialist realism, defining the value and landscape of the entire art scene.

In Poland, jazz had experienced high popularity since during the interwar period. Despite its temporary disappearance from society following the German invasion, the local jazz scene saw a healthy revival after the war. Jazz was again widely enjoyed in Polish restaurants, bars and the like, with the YMCA serving as a contact point organizing jazz concerts and holding jazz-related books and records. However, in keeping pace with the Zhdanov doctrine, the Union of Polish Composers sought to banish this music, criticizing it as rooted in American ideology. Under this barrage of criticism, the YMCA was forced to close, and jazz began to be treated with deep-seated enmity, becoming a symbol of formalism, commercialism and bourgeois decadence. Still, this "forbidden fruit" survived as a symbol of resistance. Jazz went underground to escape monitoring by authorities, which marked the beginning of the somewhat romantic "catacombs" period in the Polish jazz scene.[31] Notably, surveillance by Moscow across the region was carried out by sending monitoring missions made up of known Soviet artists to supervise the implementation of these official directives. For instance, in Czechoslovakia, composer Aram Khachaturian, after attending a jazz concert, harshly criticized a trumpeter's performance as "despicable, whining, like a jungle cry!," reflective of a new wave of suppression emanating from Moscow. Under this "guidance" from Moscow, jazz was identified as "American music," which resulted in the local jazz scene disappearing from official culture. Nevertheless, elements of resistance remained, shown by Karel Vlach's swing orchestra continuing to perform even after Khachaturian's vocal criticisms. When the authorities critically pointed out the jazz numbers from Stan Kenton's repertoire, Vlach replied that he would stop playing swing if the Soviet Union could replace these numbers with better music.[32]

The greater the risks involved with playing and appreciating jazz, the more it became a music of freedom and resistance. Although musicians generally did not go out of their way to become politically active, they did oppose ever-increasing restrictions from their government, and often renamed their song titles to reflect this.[33] Like the Swingjugend, the zazou and the stilyagi, young jazz fans in Eastern Europe dressed in a unique fashion, read Western novels and listened to jazz. Naturally, they were always associated with juvenile delinquency by party officials, and derogatorily called "bikiniarze" in Poland, "jampecek" in Hungary and "pasek" in Czechoslovakia. Taking "pasek" as an example, they wore a conspicuous tie and striped socks, hanging out in central Prague's Wenceslas Square, where they stared at people walking by while chewing gum.[34]

In the American Cold War strategy, the Soviet satellite countries became targets to be "liberated." However, while rhetorically useful, implementing a liberation strategy was impractical as it required significant resources for intensive political warfare initiatives and para-military operations. When the East Berlin workers' uprising broke out in 1953, which must have been what the US government had been hoping for, the Americans had no concrete strategy or means by which to grasp this opportunity and intervene in support of the disgruntled workers.[35] In a report subsequently issued by the Central Intelligence Agency (CIA) Secretary Allen Dulles, it was assessed that covert operations against regimes in the East were unlikely to succeed, with official caution against this course of action. Similarly, the National Security Council (NSC) report adopted in 1956 (NSC 5602/1) proposed more moderate policies to change the status quo, such as cultural and educational exchanges.[36]

Meanwhile, Radio Free Europe (RFE), funded by the CIA and supported by political exiles from Eastern Europe, was broadcasting polemic programs back to exiles' home countries. By this time RFE had also acknowledged the possibility of jazz as an agent for political transformation in the region. From interviews with escapees from the East, RFE took note of the existence of non-conformist "juvenile delinquents" who listened to jazz, raising some expectations that political conditions in the East could be potentially influenced through a cultural approach. In the early 1950s, RFE internally reported that a Bulgarian orchestra had played forbidden jazz rhythms, and that some young people were arrested after dancing Jitterbug – they were reportedly punished ruthlessly by the authorities.[37] RFE was also aware of social conditions inside Czechoslovakia, conscious that many young people were interested in modern jazz, and vastly preferred lively American fashion partly due to the drab Communist society around them. Reports also reached RFE that a group of young Czechs – in defiance of the authorities – regularly hosted private bebop parties at weekends. Providing a picture of the political and social context of the day, it was noted these youths were desirous of greater freedoms, despite efforts by the authorities to drive them towards Communism.[38]

It should be stressed here that the region's jazz scene also became a focus of US diplomatic missions. When the State Department's jazz diplomacy was on the verge of commencing operations, the US legation in Hungary sent detailed reports on the local music scene back to the State Department in Washington DC. As such, it is worth a detailed analysis here for better understanding what jazz represented in the eyes of American officials.

In July 1955, ignoring warnings from authorities not to play jazz, a Czechoslovakian swing orchestra led by Karel Vlach visited Hungary and entertained 5,000 fans with six hours of swing. Stimulated by the orchestra, some of the musically inclined fans in attendance put on a free jazz performance for their excited peers some months later, deceiving local police by promising they would only play folk music.[39] Earnest A. Nagy, America's vice consul who witnessed Vlach's performance, noted that based on the orchestra's composition – saxophone, trumpet, trombone, piano, bass, drum and guitar – as well as the way the members of the orchestra dressed, "the American influence was unmistakable." Tellingly, Nagy observed that Vlach's style was "one hundred percent American," reminiscent of the strong influence of Les Brown, Woody Herman and Glenn Miller. Recalling the orchestra's theme was Miller's "Moonlight Serenade," which was played in an "unmistakable Miller manner," he went on to praise the orchestra's skill in performing standard numbers such as "Rhapsody in Blue," "Blue Skies," "Charmaine," "Song of the Moulin Rouge," "Jealousy" and "Stardust." Also, Nagy praised the orchestra as "the best European swing band" he was aware of, believing it had obviously "spent many hours listening to Western radio broadcasts." Moreover, he noted that improvisations by trumpeters, saxophonists and a trombonist were "in the best jazz tradition." In addition, according to this reporting, the audience riotously welcomed a medley consisting of "Adios," "Chattanooga Chu Chu," "Sunrise Serenade," "I Know Why" and "In the Mood," which were all dedicated "to the memory of the great Glenn Miller." When "In the Mood" was played again, the audience reportedly erupted in excitement, disrupting the concert moderator. According to Nagy, the audience's mood positively changed in response to increases in tempo, improvisation and as "jazziness" increased.[40]

Although this particular diplomatic reporting from the US legation in Hungary was no more than a series of reflections and observations of a single musical event in Budapest, there are nonetheless two important points to note. First, the acceptance of jazz in Hungary was understood here as the acceptance of "America." In this respect, Nagy was hardly surprised. Instead, there was a feeling of pride in the "terrific influence that jazz of the best and most modern kind exerts with young people all over the world." The most encouraging point for the American diplomat in Hungary, however, was that many young Eastern Europeans showed a great interest in jazz, regardless of the negative official labels describing it as "reactionary" and "decadent." Second, because of his pride in this American product, there was frustration – arguably widely shared among American officials in the region – that their leaders could not understand jazz's potential. As Nagy deplored:

> I feel that this American product, one of America's outstanding contributions to the art forms of the world and perhaps our most popular export, remains singularly unexploited. I fear that most of our leading people do not like or understand jazz for various reasons and are, in fact, ashamed of jazz music.

Although it is uncertain whether the legation recognized the positive effects of the VOA's radio program *Music USA*, which had commenced broadcasting half a year earlier, Nagy's expectations for jazz were nonetheless increasing, as shown by the comment:

> I am sure that a performance in Budapest by Norman Granz's Jazz at the Philharmonic troupe or by either the Les Brown, Woody Herman or especially the Stan Kenton orchestras would be worth more from a propaganda and public relations standpoint than six weeks of VOA broadcasting or high level conferences.[41]

The vital question here is whether the popularity of jazz in Eastern Europe signified the wholesale acceptance of "American music" per se.[42] It seems certain that jazz culture was at least blossoming there in the 1950s. However, we should not hastily conclude this was only the result of the ubiquitous pressure of postwar Americanization. Instead, local authorities had their own self-serving reasons for approving jazz. Thus, the politics of reinterpreting "American music" needs to be considered once again.

Jazz in East Germany is a case in point. After its establishment in 1949, jazz in this country faded into the shadows as authorities placed more importance on traditional German cultural figures such as Goethe, Schiller and Beethoven. As a self-imposed anti-fascist nation, it was logically possible to appreciate jazz, as it had been suppressed by the Nazi regime. But its image remained largely as it had been in the 1930s – a music representing sexual deviation, corruption and decadence. As detailed by European historian Uta G. Poiger, at the time of the East Berlin uprising in June 1953, local newspapers criticized the incident by associating the "provocateurs" with cowboys and striped socks, so as to impress upon readers that American culture was morally depraved.[43]

Notably, however, RFE had already identified an element of change two years before this uprising. What had been treated as "reactionary," "tasteless," "Jungle tam-tam" and a "capitalist-imperialist pest," jazz was being gradually accepted and associated with "Negro folk music," rooted in an empathy with American "Negro slaves." The emphasis on jazz's blackness, therefore, became harmonized with the logic of anti-Americanism. In concerts held in East Berlin and Dresden, which were hosted by the Cultural Association of the Democratic Reconstruction of Germany, concert posters propagated "The Call for Freedom" and "Negro Lyric – Negro jazz." To represent jazz as originating in the culture of those persecuted, Dixieland jazz thus became a natural choice for the authorities.[44]

This was a similar categorization of jazz as once seen in the Soviet Union. By distinguishing a tolerable "authentic" jazz from a commercialized version, the local jazz scene partly recovered. Through influential people such as Reginald Rudorf, a lecturer at the University of Leipzig and a member of the ruling party, the Sozialistische Einheitspartei Deutschlands (SED; Socialist Unity Party of Germany), the importance of New Orleans and Dixieland jazz was propagated. These "authentic" styles of jazz were highly appreciated as stimulating German *Kultur*. Whereas swing and modern jazz were criticized as commercialized, decadent and formalistic music symbolizing imperialistic culture, at a time when American society was witnessing the heyday of bebop. For Rudorf, Charlie Parker and Dizzy Gillespie were seen as pursuing a goal of soulless technical superiority in the music industry, separating themselves from the black liberation struggle.[45]

During the mid-1950s, the Communist youth organization, the Freie Deutsche Jugend (FDJ; Free German Youth), started to warm to jazz. Newly opened unofficial jazz clubs enjoyed the approval of the FDJ, legitimizing their activities as propagating a struggle against cultural Americanization, which was in line with the political missions of the SED and FDJ. In addition, memory of the Nazi past was found useful in stressing that "true" jazz was anti-fascist, resulting in the FDJ admitting officially in 1956 that jazz was "an old folk music of oppressed Negroes." In order to protect jazz fans from "false" jazz developed by American "imperialists," the FDJ had finally found an interest in utilizing a particular type of jazz.[46] These changes were not unrelated to Khrushchev's secret speech denouncing Stalin. According to RFE, official approval of jazz was the SED's strategy of maintaining social order by means of advancing a cultural "thaw" domestically. At the same time, RFE had been observing changes in the East German jazz scene, noting the FDJ's inability to attract young people to Communism. RFE reporting indicates that SED Central Committee directives urged jazz concerts to be organized following two-hour official forums to discuss domestic political questions and Communist dogma, indicating that jazz was used as a youth recruiting tool for authorities.[47]

In this context, it should be noted that jazz was seen as a markedly lesser evil than rock music, which was increasingly associated with violent and juvenile delinquency. In this sense, party leaders retained a sense of caution and remained wary about jazz. What proved fatal in this regard was that Rudorf openly demanded political reform through jazz at Karl-Marx University in the chaotic aftermath of the Hungarian Uprising. He had been on officials' radar for some time, in fact, as he had previously organized a concert in collaboration with a church, thus incensing authorities. As a onetime collaborator of the Stasi himself, Rudorf had by now come under surveillance by this same organization. Exceeding the tolerance threshold of authorities, he was finally arrested in March 1957 on a charge of using jazz to covertly commit political crimes, serving two years' imprisonment for this offence.[48]

Curiously, when a new set of jazz discourses emerged in some Communist bloc countries that were compatible with Communist ideology, the Eisenhower administration was becoming aware of the popularity of jazz outside America, even inside the Communist bloc. This culminated in a review of the strategic value of jazz, shortly thereafter resulting in the US State Department sending star jazz musicians around the world. Although this new project was accompanied by a philosophy of racial integration – unlike swing ideology – the driving rationale behind the project was no longer based on New Deal Liberalism. Instead, the project now took on a distinctly anti-Communist flavor. The next chapter revisits the nature of this jazz diplomacy with fresh eyes.

Notes

1 Erenberg, *Swingin' the Dream*, pp.225–30.
2 Tad Hershorn, *Norman Granz: The Man Who Used Jazz for Justice* (Berkeley: University of California Press, 2011), pp.18–20.
3 Stowe, *Swing Changes*, p.237; Ingrid Monson, *Freedom Sounds: Civil Rights Call Out to Jazz and Africa* (Oxford: Oxford UP, 2007), p.79; Yusuke Torii, *Swing Ideology and Its Cold War Discontents in United States-Japan Relations, 1944–1968* (PhD Thesis, George Washington University, 2007), p.49.
4 Hershorn, *Norman Granz*, pp.4–5; Torii, *Swing Ideology*, pp.31–64.
5 Hershorn, *Norman Granz*, pp.76, 96, 104–12.
6 Erenberg, *Swingin' the Dream*, pp.242–45; Stowe, *Swing Changes*, pp.50, 67–71. In addition to Ellington, the FBI created files for Cab Calloway, Louis Armstrong, Nat King Cole, Charles Mingus, among others. Andrew W. Lehren, "Jazz and the FBI: Guilty until Proven Innocent," *Jazz Times*, April 2009.
7 Dening, *The Cultural Front*, p.334.
8 Erenberg, *Swingin' the Dream*, p.243; Bakan, "Jazz and the 'Popular Front'," pp.49–50. See also Gerald Meyer, "Frank Sinatra: The Popular Front and an American Icon," *Science & Society*, vol.66 no.3, 2002.
9 Committee on Un-American Activities, *Investigation of Un-American Propaganda Activities in the U.S. (Regarding Leon Josephson and Samuel Liptzen): Hearings before the United States House Committee on Un-American Activities, Eightieth Congress, First Session, on Mar. 5, 21, 1947* (Washington, DC: Government Printing Office, 1947), pp.24–25.
10 Josephson and Trilling-Josephson, *Cafe Society*, pp.236–37.
11 Bakan, "Jazz and the 'Popular Front'," pp.51–52. An MI5 document created in 1959 shows there was an argument with informants as to whether a jazz book written under the name of Francis Newton was actually written by Hobsbawm. The National Archives, Kew, London, UK, KV 2/3985, "Extract from LASCAR Material," 29 May 1959.
12 Francis Newton, *The Jazz Scene* (New York: Da Capo, 1975), p.261.
13 Hershorn, *Norman Granz*, pp.244–46.
14 Ibid., pp.248–51.
15 S. Frederick Starr, *Red and Hot: The Fate of Jazz in the Soviet Union 1917–1991* (New York: Limelight Editions, 2004), pp.54–55, 62, 66–68; Martin Lücke, "The Postwar Campaign against Jazz in the USSR (1945–1953)," in Gertrud Pickhan and Rüdiger Ritter (eds.), *Jazz behind the Iron Curtain* (Bern: Peter Lang, 2010), pp.83–84.
16 Costigliola, *Awkward Dominion*, pp.157–64; Irina Suponitskaya, "The Americanization of Soviet Russia in the 1920s and 1930s," *Social Science*, vol.45 no.2, 2014, pp.33–40.
17 Starr, *Red and Hot*, pp.90–91, 96–101, 107–13, 177–78; Lücke, "The Postwar Campaign against Jazz in the USSR (1945–1953)," pp.85–90.

18 Starr, *Red and Hot*, pp.182–93; Richard Stites, "The Ways of Russian Popular Music to 1953," in Neil Edmunds (ed.), *Soviet Music and Society under Lenin and Stalin* (London: Routledge, 2004), p.28.
19 Starr, *Red and Hot*, p.203.
20 Ibid., pp.196–203.
21 Vladislav Zubok and Constantine Pleshakov, *Inside the Kremlin's Cold War: From Stalin to Khrushchev* (Cambridge: Harvard UP, 1996), pp.114–23.
22 Starr, *Red and Hot*, pp.208–11; Lücke, "The Postwar Campaign," p.92; Timothy Johnston, *Being Soviet: Identity, Rumor, and Everyday Life under Stalin, 1939–53* (Oxford: Oxford UP, 2011), pp.169–79.
23 Elisabeth Kolleritsch, "Jazz in Totalitarian Systems (Nazi Germany and Former USSR): The Life of the Trumpet Player Eddie Rosner," *European Scientific Journal*, vol.2, May 2015, pp.261–62.
24 Starr, *Red and Hot*, pp.144–47, 223–25; Lücke, "The Postwar Campaign," pp.95–96.
25 Starr, *Red and Hot*, pp.236–43; Lücke, "The Postwar Campaign," pp.96–97; Timothy W. Ryback, *Rock around the Bloc: A History of Rock Music in Eastern Europe and the Soviet Union* (Oxford: Oxford UP, 1990), pp.9–10.
26 Vladislav Zubok, *A Failed Empire: The Soviet Union in the Cold War from Stalin to Gorbachev* (Chapel Hill: University of North Carolina Press, 2009), p.172.
27 Robert E. English, *Russia and the Idea of the West: Gorbachev, Intellectuals and the End of the Cold War* (New York: Columbia UP, 2000), pp.51–80. See also Zubok, *A Failed Empire*, pp.164–65.
28 Yale Richmond, *Cultural Exchange and the Cold War: Raising the Iron Curtain* (University Park: Pennsylvania State UP, 2003), p.11.
29 Starr, *Red and Hot*, pp.248–50.
30 Zubok, *A Failed Empire*, pp.174–75.
31 Keith Hatschek, "The Impact of American Jazz Diplomacy in Poland During the Cold War Era," *Jazz Perspectives*, vol.4 no.3, 2010, pp.254–60; Igor Pietraszewski, *Jazz in Poland: Improvised Freedom* (Bern: Peter Lang, 2014), pp.48–55; Marta Domurat-Linde, "From 'Jazz in Poland' to 'Polish Jazz'," in Gertrud Pickhan and Rüdiger Ritter (eds.), *Meanings of Jazz in State Socialism* (Bern: Peter Lang, 2015), pp.81–82; François Fejtö, *Stalin Jidai no Touo* (trans. Toru Kumada) (Tokyo: Iwanami Shoten, 1979), pp.334–37.
32 Ryback, *Rock around the Bloc*, pp.11–13.
33 Pietraszewski, *Jazz in Poland*, pp.54–57.
34 Djurdja Bartlett, "Socialist Dandies International: East Europe, 1946–1959," *Fashion Theory: The Journal of Dress, Body and Culture*, vol.17 no.3, 2013, pp.254–81; Karl Brown, "Dance Hall Days: Jazz and Hooliganism in Communist Hungary, 1948–1956," in Pickhan and Ritter (eds.), *Jazz behind the Iron Curtain*, pp.271–75; Ryback, *Rock around the Bloc*, pp.9–10.
35 Bennett Kovrig, *Of Walls and Bridges: The United States and Eastern Europe* (New York: NYU Press, 1991), p.72; Sarah-Jane Corke, *US Covert Operations and Cold War Strategy: Truman, Secret Warfare and the CIA, 1945–53* (London: Routledge, 2007), pp.159–61.
36 US Department of State (ed.), *Foreign Relations of the United States* (hereafter FRUS), *1955–1957, Volume XIX, National Security Policy* (Washington, DC: Government Printing Office, 1990), pp.242–68, "NSC 5602/1, National Security Council Report, Basic National Security Policy," 15 March 1956.
37 Open Society Archives at Central European University, Budapest, Hungary, Records of Radio Free Europe/Radio Liberty Research Institute (hereafter Open Society Archives), HU OSA 300-1-2-29762, "Night Life in Sofia: Youth Loves Jazz," 13 January 1953.
38 Open Society Archives, HU OSA 300-1-2-33929, "Young Czechs Defy Communist Disapproval of Jazz," 28 April 1953.

39 Don Gold, "Behind the Iron Curtain," *Down Beat*, vol.24 no.1, 9 January 1957.
40 National Archives and Records Administration, College Park, Maryland, US (hereafter NARA), Record Group (hereafter RG) 59, Central Decimal File (hereafter CDF) 1955–59, Box 82, 032, "Czech Orchestra Plays American Jazz in Hungary," 29 July 1955.
41 Ibid.
42 Davenport endorses what Nagy analyzed in the latter's report on jazz in Hungary. See Davenport, *Jazz Diplomacy*, pp.44–45.
43 Poiger, *Jazz, Rock, and Rebels*, pp.37, 59–63. See also Ryback, *Rock around the Bloc*, p.12.
44 Open Society Archives, HU OSA 300-1-2-5868, "Authorities Allow Jazz as 'Negro Folk Music' and Use It to Present Themselves as the Champions of the Oppressed," 3 September 1951.
45 Poiger, *Jazz, Rock, and Rebels*, pp.150–53.
46 Ibid., pp.154–60.
47 Open Society Archives, HU OSA 300-1-2-76774, "Pankow Recognizes Jazz," 27 March 1956; HU OSA 300-1-2-69371, "Fighters for Jazz," 27 November 1956.
48 Poiger, *Jazz, Rock, and Rebels*, pp.161–62; Christian Schmidt-Rost, "1956: A Turning Point for the Jazz Scenes in the GDR and Poland," in Pickhan and Ritter (eds.), *Meanings of Jazz in State Socialism*, pp.44–62.

3 Jazz ambassadors revisited

Charlie Parker, legendary trumpeter who led the bebop revolution, died in March 1955. It had been two years since the death of Stalin, and the Soviet leaders had commenced a vigorous set of cultural exchange programs, as seen by sending icons of traditional Russian culture – such as the Bolshoi Ballet and the Leningrad Philharmonic Orchestra – to a diverse range of countries, even including those that fell into the Western camp. We can imagine the Soviets held a deep-seated sense of superiority behind this cultural offensive vis-à-vis the Americans in the field of high culture.[1] Shortly afterwards, the Eisenhower administration started to modify its long-held reluctance to engage in government-funded cultural exchanges. The search for a new policy course was in line with the administration's emphasis on maintaining fiscal equilibrium at home, thereby shifting its focus toward a non-military containment policy against the expansion of Communist influences.[2] As the Soviets propagated the idea of America being a cultural desert, and materialistic and racist in nature, the need was increasingly felt in American policy circles to show the world not only that American culture was contributing to the world of arts, but that racial relations were also improving. In the State Department, cultural exchanges came to be recognized as practical tools for refuting the discourse underlying virulent state-directed anti-American propaganda. In this sense, cultural exchange programs quickly became "instruments of the cold war." In providing an "answer to questions of image," the State Department explicitly proposed they should work to alleviate these negative charges against America.[3]

The year 1955 was an especially symbolic year in connecting international politics and culture, manifesting in two important international meetings held this year. One was the Geneva Summit. The leaders of the so-called Big Four (America, Britain, France and the Soviet Union) met to discuss issues on culture, disarmament and German reunification. The Western leaders emphasized the necessity of freer exchange of people and information and called for the cessation of jamming radio broadcasts, as well as calling for the establishment of information centers. Although these proposals were not accepted by the Soviet side, attempts to promote domestic changes in the East from below – using cultural infiltration methods – continued to be part of a suite of Cold War strategies discussed by major Western countries. The other significant meeting was the

Asian-African Conference, known as the Bandung Conference. As the postwar wave of decolonization swept the world, the demand for solidarity and unity among the newly independent states of the Third World was growing. The conference declared a set of ten-point principles governing international relations, and as a result, the presence of countries in Asia and Africa increased more than ever before. These developments heightened the need for the US government to mitigate the image of America as racist – as promoted by the Soviet propaganda.

As the existing literature has argued, the changing international environment led to the discovery of jazz by the Eisenhower administration, which saw that winning the hearts and minds of people in other countries was now an integral part of national security policy.[4] Jazz, long denied any public status in representing "America" abroad, was suddenly reinterpreted to become "American music," thus symbolizing the country's liberalist founding principles. The following sections revisit some of the external tours by American jazz ambassadors through focusing on local reactions, contesting discourses of jazz, and the universality of the music.

Ironies in the discovery of jazz

That jazz came to represent America was ironical in some ways. Firstly, while countries outside America had already encountered and then reinterpreted "American music" during the interwar period, it took decades before the US government officially acknowledged the external value of this music. Even in the postwar period – as Parker's cause of death indicated – bebop's association with drugs and alcohol in many people's minds did not enhance the social standing of jazz, and was often portrayed as anti-social. However, in November 1955, eight months after the death of Parker, when Louis Armstrong was performing a series of highly successful concerts across Europe, the *New York Times* wrote on the huge popularity of "Ambassador Satch" in Europe. The article explicitly noted the usefulness of jazz in diplomacy, describing it as America's "secret sonic weapon."[5] Although it is difficult to gauge to what extent this article influenced official planning for the American jazz ambassadors program, the article suggests there was a significant gap in the social standing of jazz between inside and outside America. In this sense, the irony lies not so much in the fact that the State Department-nominated jazz ambassadors were rarely sent to Western Europe – because the music was already established and popular there – but rather in the fact that the value and status of jazz had to be reimported from outside America, where the music had long been considered serious.[6]

The second irony relates to the principal agents behind the reinterpretation of jazz. While swing ideology, first propagated by the popular front during the New Deal era (specifically the CPUSA), promoted the idea of racial integration, jazz had now become a tool by which to win the cultural Cold War against the Soviet Union. The music took on an explicit anti-Communist role, resulting in jazz becoming an integral part of the practical propaganda strategy against Communism led by the highest levels of the US government. As the result of this reinterpretation of jazz, America's unique jazz discourse previously engendered by leftist groups, resurfaced with different agendas in the context of the Cold War confrontation. One typical example can be found in the philosophy of *Music USA*, a music program operationalized by the VOA. Willis Conover, who would later organize Duke Ellington's birthday party at the White House, served as the MC on this program. In a well-cited interview conducted by the *New York Times Magazine* in 1959, he described what jazz meant for him as follows: "The musicians agree on tempo, key, and chord structure but beyond this everyone is free to express himself. This is jazz. And this is America. That's what gives this music validity. It's a musical reflection of the way things happen in America."[7] One unmissable point here is his essentialist view of jazz. For Conover, the notion of freedom of expression – the embodiment of improvisation – was inseparable from the history of America, and should apply regardless of race. *Ipso facto*, according to Conover's line of reasoning, jazz could exist only in America. The interrelationship between jazz and Americanism was similar to swing ideology, but the "American music" discourse had now found official sponsorship and support in the State Department and its associated organizations. In fact, Conover was a thorough individualist in the selection of jazz to be broadcast on his program. Having a solid philosophy of treating any music fairly if they were "good" in quality, he decided what was to be played only after carefully paying attention to multiple musical factors from length, tempo and mood, to the flow of solo segments.[8] His attitude to set standards only around the level of musical quality – regardless of the style or the performer – resonated with the idea of color-blind Americanism. Still, the image of "Mr. Cool" – he liked to create poetry and lyrics introspectively – contrasted with the open and dynamic character of "America" that listeners imagined through his voice.[9]

When Soviet propaganda condemned America as a racist country, the real America had to catch up with the ideal of color-blind Americanism. In this regard, Conover was optimistic, as shown by his comments reported by the *New York Times Magazine*: "Jazz corrects the fiction that America is racist." And showing a deep understanding of the relationship between jazz and America he added: "Minorities have a tough time everywhere but the acceptance and success of so many Negro musicians and singers in jazz in the United States makes it obvious that someone like Louis Armstrong, for instance, is not an exception." Even though Conover was not ignorant of racial issues, nor tried to ignore them, this could nonetheless be seen as somewhat overly optimistic in light of the domestic social situation, and the general state of race relations in America in the late 1950s.[10]

Another tangible result of the reinterpretation of jazz by officialdom was seen in the launch of the jazz ambassadors program in 1956, which ran until 1978. As a part of the Cultural Presentations Program initiated under the Eisenhower administration, jazz musicians were tasked with propagating the American ideal of racial integration. Under the program, prominent American jazz figures were sent to areas where commercial tours were thought difficult to organize. Exchanges with local people or sessions with local musicians were another important task for them, thus the performer's personality was an important factor – in addition to high artistic standards – during the selection process for becoming an official American jazz ambassador.[11] The initial proposal was made in November 1955, not long after the publishing of the "secret sonic weapon" article in the *New York Times*. As has been detailed in existing work, the idea was robustly supported by Adam Clayton Powell Jr., a member of Congress from Harlem, who appealed to journalists that America should send what he believed as its rare export product to the world. Dizzy Gillespie, a close friend of Powell, was staying in Washington DC for his performance when Powell pronounced "I'm going to propose to President Eisenhower that he send this man, who's a great contributor to our music, on a State Department sponsored cultural mission to Africa, the Near East, Middle East, and Asia."[12] For Powell, it was not creative to fight the Bolshoi Ballet with sending American ballet companies or symphony orchestras. He instead saw it as imperative to have the world experience "real Americana," by dispatching a form of art born in America that no one could compete with. Perhaps Powell felt the need to project himself as a Cold War warrior. His wife, jazz pianist Hazel Scott, had once been a target of the HUAC for alleged Communist activities. Also, at the Bandung Conference, Powell strenuously rebutted accusations of racial problems in his home country.[13]

Since the State Department was not familiar with the quality of artists to be sent under the Cultural Presentations Program, the Music Advisory Panel was established within the American National Theatre and Academy (ANTA) for the selection of musicians. Critic Marshall Stearns, who had been making a considerable effort to improve the status of jazz in America, was one of the experts on the panel. Under a strategy named "Operation Jazz," he taught jazz at New York University while establishing the Institute of Jazz Studies in 1952 to institutionalize jazz research. Stearns, as a racial integrationist, was well aware that jazz symbolized resistance during the war, and knew the value of this music as a weapon against totalitarian states.[14]

Asked who to nominate as the first jazz ambassador, Stearns recommended Louis Armstrong, Duke Ellington, Count Basie, Stan Kenton and Dizzy Gillespie. Of these, the first four were eliminated due to cost, aviophobia (fear of flying), or scheduling difficulties, leaving only Gillespie as a suitable candidate. Stearns thought highly of Gillespie, describing him as an "intelligent comedian, cultivated, with novelty acts, and his musical material is interesting." Importantly, a band that Gillespie would lead was expected to be racially mixed, thus acting as a symbol of racial integration. More importantly, there was an insightful comment made during this selection process that many scholars have overlooked. Foreshadowing future contention over the program, William Schuman – a talented composer and president of the Juilliard School of Music – noted "there has been a lot of controversy about the inclusion of jazz in our Program; some people feel that we are selling out on the more serious work." To this, another member of the Panel, general manager of ANTA Robert C. Schnitzer, replied: "there is a division of opinion as to whether jazz represents a boon or a handicap to our nation."[15] Here, therefore, is another irony – even though jazz had secured official sponsorship from none other than the American government, the "American music" discourse would be constantly contested by alternative discourses during the course of the program.

Gillespie and competing jazz discourses

In March 1956, a group of 18 musicians led by Gillespie set off on a tour around South Asia, the Middle East and Southern European countries. Describing the composition of the band that included trumpeter Quincy Jones, saxophonist Phil Woods and female trombonist Melba Liston, Gillespie wrote in his autobiography that it was "a complete 'American assortment' of blacks, whites, males, females, Jews, and Gentiles in the band."[16] Stearns accompanied the tour as a lecturer and subject matter expert on jazz.

Importantly, the American assortment label for the tour manifested itself also in the basic set list for these performances. It was divided in two parts. The first half, starting with "St. Louis Blues," was named the "History of Jazz" part. This was followed by, for instance, an African drum rhythm performance, "Sometimes I Feel like A Motherless Child" and "Joshua Fit the Battle of Jericho" (both spiritual), "When the Saints Go Marching In" and "I'm Confessin'" (New Orleans/Dixieland jazz), "Mood Indigo," "For Dancers Only," "King Porter Stomp," "Rockin' Chair" and "One O'Clock Jump" (all swing), while Gillespie's "Groovin High" was performed as one of the last numbers for each performance. The second half consisted mainly of bebop, including "Cool Breeze," "A Night in Tunisia," "Ooh-Shoo-Be-Doo-Bee" and "The Champ." Overall, the contributions of various musicians to the history of jazz were presented, regardless of race, making jazz feel like "American music."[17]

The tour was originally planned to go westward from India, but the Indian government canceled the invitation for Gillespie's band at the last moment. As a result, the tour started from the Iranian city of Abadan, with the band traveling to Pakistan (Dacca and Karachi), then on to Lebanon (Beirut), Syria (Damascus and Aleppo), Turkey (Ankara and Istanbul), Yugoslavia (Zagreb and Belgrade), and finally to Greece (Athens).[18] Right after the start of the tour, King Faisal II of Iraq asked the US embassy in Bagdad to also bring Gillespie's concert to Iraq. Although this unusual request from one of the region's better-known jazz fans was seriously considered by the State Department, Secretary of State John Foster Dulles politely declined his request on grounds that it was "too late."[19]

All the US diplomatic missions in these countries reported excited local reactions. According to the US consul general in Dacca, William L. S. Williams, the Gillespie band's "final performance ran nearly an hour overtime," which was characterized by "Tremendous applause, whistling, clapping, and all the other earmarks of a dedicated jazz audience." Blaring trumpets could "reach right into the very back row of the theater and shake a customer by the scruff of the neck." The consul's reporting emphasized there was "no doubt that Dacca acquired an ear and a taste for American jazz … [and] Dizzy Gillespie pioneered promising new territory." In Turkey, fans waiting for Gillespie at the airport held a banner saying "Welcome Dizzy Gillespie," moving him to comment to one embassy staff member that "he had not had so warm a welcome anywhere else on his trip." The performance was reportedly "unprecedentedly successful," and the jam session with local musicians was also seen as a huge success.[20]

The favorable reaction to the tour can be gauged from a review in the press. According to a critical review in the music magazine *Metronome*, the band members had a style that was so precise and enthusiastic, and they noted the audience's rapturous applause after every performance. *Metronome* went on to note that trumpeters had "sharp-edged" bright sounds and trombonists were "sober and smooth," while the reed instruments kept a "tonal fullness." The performances of Liston in "Stella by Starlight," the trumpet solo of Joe Gordon in "A Night in Tunisia," and the powerful performance of tenor saxophonist Billy Mitchell were all highly acclaimed. Alto saxophonist Woods's performance was described as blending "the influences of Bird [Charlie Parker], [Lee] Konitz and [Paul] Desmond in a way to avoid the accusation of derivativeness." Whereas Gillespie's solo performance was "softer, his phraseology more refined." *Metronome* confidently concluded – with some foresight – in declaring that the Gillespie band would be looked back on by jazz aficionados ten years later as an "all-star band."[21]

Scholars have argued the importance of the band's performance in Athens. It was carried out in the midst of rising local anti-American sentiment, partly influenced by domestic leftist groups. Since the concert hall had to be shared with a Russian folk ballet group, matinee and evening performances were alternately held, which in practice positioned the jazz ambassadors at the forefront of the cultural Cold War. Initially, the US embassy in Athens was concerned about the reaction of the audience, but it turned out that the students, who had previously been throwing stones at US government facilities, enthusiastically welcomed the band, shouting "Dizzy! Dizzy!"[22] Compared with the performances in Greece, Gillespie's tour to Yugoslavia showed another important dimension of the global tour. According to reporting from the US embassy, "jazz lovers, diplomats and gentle white-haired ladies alike jostled elbows and squeezed sardine-like" into the local concert hall. It was also reported that the Gillespie band "gave Belgrade its longest musical ear-beating in history." Significantly, this local reaction was interpreted as "a triumph for the West, and particularly for self-expression as a phase of the American way of life."[23] American officials ostensibly strengthened their convictions of color-blind Americanism when a local critic in Belgrade published an article in the local weekly magazine *Republika*, which reported: "the structure of the Gillespie orchestra is democratic and anti-segregational. We could find there Negroes and Whites playing together. Even a young Negress played a trombone."[24]

However, musicians and officials were not monolithically united in their aim to maintain the hearts and minds of local people, as has been suggested by many observers. First of all, there was a difference of opinion regarding for whom "American music" should be played. In Ankara, seeing many local young fans denied entry to a reception held at the US embassy, Gillespie refused to perform, protesting to the US ambassador: "I won't have any segregation here. I won't play until the people outside the fence are let in."[25] In Damascus, where the performance was scheduled in the month of Ramadan, the band respected local customs and voluntarily abstained from eating any food until sunset.[26] These two stories are sufficient to show how Gillespie and his band members frequently had a different agenda from that of the State Department, for whom the main purpose of the tour was to disseminate the American idea of color-blind democracy.[27] Second, jazz ambassadors also disputed the legitimacy of the program. Prior to the tour, the State Department tried to contact Gillespie, who was on the JATP tour in Western Europe, in order to brief him on domestic racial problems. This infuriated him. "I sort've liked the idea of representing America, but I wasn't going over to apologize for the racist policies of America," Gillespie later recollected in his autobiography. When progress toward improving racial conditions in America somewhat stalled, jazz ambassadors were asked to rationalize their government's racial policies at home. Notwithstanding these pressures and contradictions, Gillespie also found profound meaning in representing America in a racially mixed band. Gillespie described the state of racial problems in his own way by stating: "We have our problems but we're still working on it. I'm the leader of this band, and those white guys are working for me. That's a helluva thing."[28]

What needs to be stressed in this context is that Gillespie's tour revealed a significant gap in the interpretation of jazz within America. Strong objections lingered domestically about embracing the discourse of jazz and equating it with "American music," let alone providing the music with government funding. Senator Barry Goldwater angrily criticized the Assistant Secretary of State for "the recent tour of a Negro band leader, Dizzy Gillespie, which apparently involved an expenditure by the Federal Government of the outrageous sum of $100,839." In fact, the Gillespie band's relatively princely salary of $2,150 per week exceeded that of even President Eisenhower.[29] No doubt irritating his critics further, his overseas tour incurred expenditure exceeding $84,000.[30] For Senator Allen J. Ellender, Gillespie's music was "pure noise." He showed his concern at the Senate that by sending a jazz band, people would believe "we are barbarians."[31] The jazz ambassadors program was initiated as a calculated response to mitigate the effect of anti-American propaganda, which described America as racist, yet the same program in fact revealed a strand of racial prejudice inside Congress. The State Department asked for understanding that jazz, as "a musical form uniquely American in origin," was evoking a special reaction worldwide, and "to the young people in almost every country jazz represents freedom, vitality and a new kind of expression." The Under Secretary of State Christian Herter replied that these first-class cultural figures were sent overseas in order to represent "as many phases of American cultural life as possible."[32] Faced with this significant gap in the interpretation of jazz, Gillespie bemoaned: "Jazz is too good for Americans."[33] In this sense, Gillespie's tour allowed him to experience for himself what African American musicians like Josephine Baker and Louis Armstrong had also experienced outside America.

The gap in the interpretation of jazz also surfaced rather unpleasantly when trombonist Wilbur De Paris toured a number of African countries for two months from March 1957. His tour was unique in that he led an all-African American troupe, anticipating the future transformation of the foundational idea of a color-blindness concept to one more akin to color-consciousness. De Paris's tour to Africa takes on a particular importance against the background that the band visited areas where decolonization was occurring, or had recently taken place. Ghana, the first country of their visit, had enormous political significance, as the country had just attained independence from Britain on 6 March 1957. De Paris was tasked with the role of goodwill ambassador – he participated in the Independence Ceremony and met with Prime Minister Kwame Nkrumah.[34] In Ethiopia, Haile Selassie I awarded a gold medal to each of the band members, and the Imperial Body Guard also presented them with a plaque and insignia as a memento of their visit and in honor of De Paris's musical achievements. Curiously, in diplomatic reporting from Addis Ababa, the chargé d'affaires ad interim, Paul B. Taylor, was delighted that the band's reception by the local people had been "excellent" from a public diplomacy viewpoint. According to Taylor, one Ethiopian bodyguard was astonished to hear that one American band member had purchased a new home and owned his own automobile. This bodyguard told American embassy staff that discussions with the jazz ambassadors had changed his perception of the state of domestic affairs in America.[35] In Kenya, De Paris explained to the audience not only that personal capabilities and experience were the keys to success in America, rather than racial factors, but that race also did not prescribe social status.[36] According to the US ambassador to Tunisia, G. Lewis Jones, the American jazz musicians "did more to obviate current misconceptions prevalent here regarding this question than any number of Embassy and USIS [United States Information Service, the overseas branch of the US government's information policies] efforts has ever been able to accomplish."[37]

However, these musicians faced significant criticism at home. When De Paris was about to leave Africa, a member of Congress protested to Secretary of State Dulles, questioning the significance of the tour on the ground that an entertainment like jazz was not accepted by most Americans. These accusations mirrored in similar ways the same ones levelled over Gillespie's tour, particularly the accusations of misusing public funds, as the Congressman complained that the Founding Fathers had never allowed such waste of tax money. The State Department sought to legitimize the jazz ambassadors program by stating that a true representation of today's American music scene had to also include jazz. American officials believed that their superiority and leadership in the field of jazz were widely known all over the world, and this "American music" attracted a wide public interest as well as important intellectuals.[38] What the American musicians experienced in this early period of the jazz ambassadors program would be replicated over the coming decade, as the result of the continued existence of various interpretations of jazz, both inside and outside America.

Goodman at the front line in the cultural Cold War

The bold American proposal to send jazz musicians to various parts of the world was made against the background of an unprecedented increase in the presence of Asian and African countries in the global arena following the Bandung conference. This became an important strategic variable in Washington's Cold War thinking, as it sought to prevent Communism from infiltrating these developing countries. Indicating this policy orientation, of the six jazz ambassadors who toured various parts of the world during the late 1950s after Gillespie, four visited these countries.[39]

The first musician nominated as a jazz ambassador after Gillespie was Benny Goodman, who performed in several Asian countries from the end of 1956 to January the following year. The creed of racial integration that he had espoused since he was called the "King of Swing" during the 1930s, was completely in tune with the State Department's notion of color-blind Americanism. Accordingly, the racially integrated Goodman band consisted of 16 musicians, including tenor saxophonist Budd Johnson, pianist Hank Jones and bassist Israel Crosby. To some extent, therefore, one could be well justified in arguing that Goodman's Asia tour had significant connotations of politics of race underpinning it. However, an alternative aspect emerges when reading closely how jazz critics discussed Goodman and his music during the last stages of the tour.

Southeast Asia was the place where Goodman's tour first hit the world spotlight. And, as the existing literature demonstrates, this was the region where the "King of Swing" received several royal welcomes. Thailand's King Bhumibol was known for his unrivaled love for jazz. The jam session organized for the king continued in the royal palace until four o'clock in the morning, following which Goodman reportedly said: "He's not bad at all."[40] Cambodian Prince Norodom Sihanouk was also known as a jazz fan, raising official expectations with the State Department that the tour "has great political possibilities if appropriately prepared." While "Goodman is no counterweight to Chou En-Lai," it was reported from the US embassy in Phnom Penh, "all here are convinced his visit has political potentialities greater than the airforce band." Although Sihanouk declined participating in a jam session alongside Goodman, preferring to "sulk in his tent in Siem Reap," 1,500 people came to the concert held in front of the royal palace. Goodman voluntarily refrained from using his title "King of Swing" as a way to show his respect to the local king, which further boosted his popularity. Notably, at the formal reception provided to Goodman, King Norodom Suramarit awarded him the Royal Order of Monisaraphon.[41]

Whereas, in Rangoon, Burma, the Goodman band targeted two groups: elites and student groups. At the public premiere of the band at Aung San Stadium on New Year's Eve, attended by ministers and diplomats, the former Prime Minister U Nu appeared backstage to greet Goodman. Furthermore, U Thant (would-be third Secretary-General of the United Nations) also cordially greeted Goodman backstage, handing him a bouquet of red roses. Afterwards, the band played in a jam session at a local nightclub with local musicians, which continued until early the next morning, bringing in New Year's Day. In the first performance of the New Year, the Burmese national anthem saw an improvised iteration by the Goodman band, inviting an enthusiastic response from the audience. At a later date, a tape recorder was brought to the concert hall under the direction of the Chief of Staff of the Burmese Forces Ne Win (later Prime Minister and President), and the improvised version of the national anthem was recorded for posterity presumably. However, the biggest success in Burma was arguably a jam session at Rangoon University, where 1,000 students gathered, despite the fact that the performance was only announced in local newspapers that same day. According to the local paper, the *Nation*, excited students jumped for joy over Mel Davis's powerful trumpet performance in "Bugle Call Rag" and "And the Angels Sing," while the brilliant tone of Budd Johnson's tenor saxophone in "One O'Clock Jump" and "Sing Sing Sing" were also reported as being huge hits with the local Burmese audience.[42]

The last stop of the tour, Japan, was an important front of the cultural Cold War. The country was known for having many ardent jazz fans. Here, interestingly, an element of the US–Soviet artistic competition foregrounded more than jazz diplomacy's racial element per se. *Swing Journal* had featured articles two months before Goodman's arrival, in which the political nature of the tour was broadly discussed by Japanese jazz critics. In an interesting dialogue between well-known jazz critics Shoichi Yui and Jiro Kubota, Yui observed that Goodman's tour appeared to be "an American counter measure against the cultural offensive by the Soviet Union, which had recently sent Lev Oborin abroad to showcase Russian culture." Kubota noted that the 1956 Gillespie tour and the Goodman tour were targeting those countries with the strongest Communist influences, with the latter finally coming to Japan. Along the same line of thought, Teruo Isono, a Japanese staff member of the USIS, also explicitly noted the political undertones of Goodman's tour and an almost tit-for-tat pattern of superpower cultural diplomacy taking place in Japan:

> During the last year, violinist David Oistrakh's successful visit to Japan was soon followed by the visit of Symphony of the Air. At this time [the Goodman tour] occurred shortly after the Russian pianist Oborin's highly acclaimed performances across Japan. Ultimately, Japan-Soviet high-level negotiations [for a peace treaty] seem to have affected the tour. Against such a backdrop, it was also widely reported at this time that Dizzy Gillespie's band had had an unequivocally successful visit to the volatile Middle East.[43]

It was against this context that Goodman arrived in Japan in January 1957 to play at Tokyo's Sankei Hall, receiving an enthusiastic welcome by Japanese jazz fans upon arrival. However, the critics' reactions were mixed. On the one hand, Japanese musicians including Fumio Nanri, George Kawaguchi and Shoji Suzuki, who represented the postwar Japanese jazz scene, warmly welcomed Goodman at the formal reception for him at Sanno Hall – an event hosted by the American embassy in Tokyo. He also received a rousing welcome for the jam session in Ginza Esuya Hall planned by the American Center. At this event, when clarinetist Suzuki played "Memories of You," Goodman performed the same number with Suzuki's clarinet, greatly exciting the local audience.[44] However, on the other hand, at a roundtable discussion by several prominent Japanese critics and musicians, Goodman's old-style jazz became a target of their criticism. One local critic observed that Goodman seemed somewhat "satisfied just playing the hits of yesteryear," while another critic lamented that Goodman had "lost a sense of youth" in his live performances. The overall sense of disappointment by this eminent group of Japanese jazz critics can be best summarized by the remark that Goodman's clarinet performances "had not really developed since he first played the big jazz hits of twenty years ago." Interestingly, they also pointed out that there had been a noticeable divergence in styles within the Goodman band itself. It was noted that while Goodman stuck to his favorite swing style, his "young players are all modern, but play in the style of Benny Goodman."[45] Somewhat presciently, this foreshadowed a problem that would arise during jazz tours to the Soviet Union in the early 1960s.

Brubeck, Teagarden and the universality of jazz

While the underlying principle of the jazz ambassadors program was selling jazz as "American music," it also sometimes deeply interacted with local music in various countries the tours visited. Ostensibly then, the distinctly "American" nature of jazz was put on hold, and musical commonalities – or joint synergies – instead came to the fore. This universality in jazz encouraged an interchange of musical ideas between jazz ambassadors and local people. With this theme in mind, the following two cases focus on how American jazz and local musical scenes interacted.

The first case involved white pianist Dave Brubeck, representative of the cool West Coast jazz musicians. His quartet, consisting of Brubeck, alto saxophonist Paul Desmond, bassist Eugene Wright and drummer Joe Morello, set out to tour the Middle East and South Asia for eight weeks from March 1958. Although the initial plan was to perform in Poland for two weeks, the schedule was extended to cover other areas in response to strong requests from many US embassies in the region. Brubeck had been treated like a star in the State Department, which saw him as "unusually well qualified" to be a jazz ambassador. Educated under Darius Milhaud and Arnold Schoenberg, Brubeck was recognized as a "serious jazz artist with some classical training and background," and someone who could importantly help dispel existing prejudices about jazz. The State Department expected that by vanquishing "certain overseas misconceptions on American jazz," and showing that this music was not for dancing but for appreciation, local people in far-off countries would deepen their interest in sophisticated American culture.[46]

The most significant moment of the Brubeck tour, which started from Turkey, arguably came during a series of concerts in India. While the quartet went through various parts of India, receiving resoundingly positive reactions, the final performance in Bombay was reportedly nothing short of a "smash hit." Attended by an element of the local wealthy class, as well as Indian classical musicians and young fans, the quartet's brilliant performance greatly impressed the audience, persuading them of the value of jazz as "a musical form that deserves serious consideration." American embassy officials were particularly encouraged by the reaction from students who had been invited to the event "Jazz Concert under the Stars" supported by the Delhi University Music Society. They sat on dhurries and became intoxicated by the quartet's musical sophistication. In contrast, Madras was thought to be a more culturally conservative city, and American officials were concerned about how the local audience might react. They need not have worried. The audience "succumbed to the artistry of the four tall young men from America, before half a dozen bars of 'Take the A Train' were played." According to reporting from the US embassy in New Delhi, "a sizable proportion of the audience [was] composed of people who came out of curiosity but went away converted." Aside from official diplomatic reporting, the upbeat local response was also reported in the *Times of India*. According to the paper, while the pianist was outstanding, the "alto saxophonist has all the sax appeal (pardon me!) that he needs." The audience was described as having been impressed with the beauty of Brubeck's musical interpretation, as well as his extraordinary mastery of musical techniques and rhythm making.[47]

Two critical points underscored the success of this jazz tour to India. The first was the friendly nature of the quartet members and their close interactions with the Indian people. The quartet cheerfully accepted pre-arranged exchanges with local people, while happily performing unscheduled regional performances upon request. The members also interacted with the local media professionally. Although people seeking their autographs constantly visited their hotel, often infringing upon their privacy, Brubeck and his band members never exhibited any intemperate behavior. Arguably, they contributed to a sharp increase in the popularity of jazz locally at this time. At least part of this new-found interest could possibly be attributed to a large public seminar sponsored by the Bombay Music Society, during which they provided a detailed history of jazz and the origins of the quartet's formation – they also gave practical demonstrations of their instruments and showed their audience a number of improvisational techniques. Since the quartet's diplomatic and friendly character made it easy to interact with the local Indian people, American officials proclaimed them to be "the most congenial group of artists ever to be handled" and "cooperative to the point of heroism." In Madras, the quartet co-starred with Palani Subramania Pillai, a prominent figure in *mridangam* (a South Indian percussion instrument) at a jam session hosted by a local radio station. The American drummer Morello was so fascinated with Pillai's musical techniques that he visited Pillai's home the next day to practice with the Indian instrument, further deepening their friendship. Pillai, on his part, was also interested in Morello's musical skills, and therefore, the exchange resulted in a truly reciprocal cultural dialogue. The quartet also had a chance to perform in a jam session at the home of well-known Indian *veena* player Sundaram Balachander (a master of the ancient Indian stringed instrument).[48]

The second factor behind the success of Brubeck's Indian tour, and somewhat related to the first point, is the commonality between Indian classical music and jazz – both are characterized by their distinctive improvisatory rhythms. The State Department expected from the start that jazz's "emphasis on improvisation relates it to the Indian approach in music, and its rhythmical character is readily appreciated in a land that gives such attention to the drum." The US embassy in New Delhi reported that Brubeck's concert performance in Bombay engendered a sense of closeness among the audience, as it naturally fell somewhere between classical Indian music and jazz. Similar diplomatic reporting noted this was also why the performance in Madras was successful. Although many Indians "expected vulgarity" before attending each concert, they were pleasantly surprised this was not the case. American diplomats observed that "On the contrary there was unexpected melody, intricate rhythm, disciplined improvisation and the spontaneous joy of creating alternately lacy and Gothic patterns of sound from the bare bones of musical materials." Once the quartet's jazz was recognized as resembling classical Indian music, the local audience's reaction became increasingly positive. Seemingly pleasantly surprised soon after the performance started, the local audience soon began to tap their feet and cheer just like American jazz aficionados. It seems undeniable that this musical commonality encouraged many positive and genuine interactions between the American quartet and the local Indian people.[49]

Selling jazz as a serious genre of music and emphasizing its proximity to Indian classical music had another advantage of clearly delineating jazz from rock music. According to US embassy reporting at this time, many Indians still tended to equate jazz with "wild and undisciplined" rock music, thus the performance by Brubeck, who had a classical music background, was able to show jazz's sophistication and intelligence behind this particular genre of music.[50]

The musical commonality worked even after the quartet left India. In Dacca, despite the State Department's initial concern over a possible negative reaction from locals due to their general unfamiliarity with Western music, the audience warmly welcomed the quartet's performances. The US consul Williams opined that the "Blues note or fourth" in jazz shared common elements with the structure of Bengali music, while its rhythm was similar to Bengali classical music.[51]

When trombonist Jack Teagarden, known for his Dixieland style, started his Asian tour in September 1958, he was fortunate in that he was able to capitalize on the positive atmosphere left by his predecessor, the Brubeck quartet. Especially in India, Brubeck's visit in the spring of the same year had maintained local intellectuals' interest in jazz. The US embassy and consulates were conscious of this synergistic effect. Teagarden's "Dixieland beat," according to official reporting, prompted even higher audience turnouts than Brubeck had received. The audience reacted excitedly to Teagarden playing the *tablas* (an Indian percussion instrument) with local musicians, as well as to his sextet's powerful sound when they performed "When the Saints Go Marching In." A review in the *Times of India*, posted by an Indian classical music authority, praised the precise rhythms of the piano, bass and drums, as well as the melodic weavings of the clarinet, trumpet and trombone, which combined to produce "a great experience" for the audience. The sextet members' personality and active musical exchanges with local people both inside and outside the concert halls also created a resounding impact during the tour. The local *Indian Express* voiced an appreciation for the glimpses of humor that were interspersed throughout the live performances. Their commitment was also impressive. In Madras, some members including Teagarden became ill, but they continued to exhibit professionalism without complaint. American officials seemed to be convinced that "a distinctively favorable impression of American jazz can be created even in conservative outposts like Madras."[52]

Teagarden's popularity continued after his sextet left India. According to US embassy reporting, the performance in Kuala Lumpur in the Federation of Malaya received an "enthusiastic audience response," causing "thunderous applause" each time a solo part was played during the concert. In the ancient city of Malacca, an "overwhelming" audience reaction saw five encores, while in Ipoh the performance starting with "Original Dixieland One Step" thrilled fans.[53]

Favorable audience reactions were more difficult to achieve in the early stages of the tour, however. In Kabul, the first scheduled stop of their tour, the sextet failed to excite the audience. Still, it did fascinate Russian embassy officials, with even one official suggesting that jazz was a "universal form of music." The main idea conveyed here was that jazz should not be regarded exclusively as "American music." This idea should be kept in mind, especially in light of the Soviet jazz scene beginning to open up at this time.[54]

In some places they performed, there was only a limited understanding of Teagarden's jazz at best. In Burma, where the Goodman tour had been welcomed excitedly by university students two years before, listening to jazz of any kind was still a rare experience for many citizens, and the US embassy in Rangoon reported that some "seemed puzzled by it, uncertain how to react to it," while others "found it too strong for their musical tastes." For one 13-year-old youth, "it was very noisy and I didn't like it very much." Still, responses from Burmese government officials were very favorable. Among the range of highly positive comments frequently made to American diplomats, a government clerk commented that "I always liked jazz but now I have madly fallen in love with it." According to a state agricultural marketing board official, he had never listened to the music nor liked it but "now that I have seen Teagarden play and heard the music at the same time you can say that there is one more jazz fan in the world." Nonetheless, reactions like "I should learn how to Rock 'N Roll even to keep up with the times" suggested that the difference between jazz and rock music was still unclear to some locals. As a result, US embassy reporting noted that the sextet had left a positive impression "On the whole," somewhat indicating a nuanced reception across the board in Burma.[55]

During the final stage of the tour, the sextet experienced further health problems. In Hong Kong, Teagarden arrived with laryngitis, but he "carried out his responsibilities in the best tradition of 'the show must go on'."[56] However, just before arriving in Korea, one member suffered appendicitis and traveled to

Okinawa for emergency surgery. Making matters worse, Teagarden's prostate condition deteriorated during the tour, while he also suffered a hernia. In addition to the accumulated fatigue at the end of this long international tour, official concerns increased over the general health of the band members. Accordingly, it was suggested to Secretary of State Dulles that Teagarden return home to undergo surgery and rest. But it was Teagarden himself who wished to complete the tour no matter what condition his health was in. In Busan, South Korea, he seemed "close to collapse," and all local musical exchange events were canceled, except at the very final stage of the Korean tour. Notably, the performance in Seoul coincided with a large political demonstration organized by the local opposition party against the Syngman Rhee administration. The central city was blockaded by barricades set up by the government, driving down attendance markedly at this concert.[57]

The atmosphere changed when the sextet arrived in Japan, where, in addition to eight performances in Tokyo, Osaka, Nagoya and Hiroshima, a video recording for Radio Tokyo also took place. Tickets had sold out quickly and concert halls were subsequently packed with devoted fans. It was reported that even scalpers had difficulty sourcing tickets, although the ones they could acquire were sold at triple the original price. Although the band members were still recovering from various medical issues and illnesses, numerous musical exchange events with local musicians were organized. Once word got out, hundreds of musicians brought their instruments to participate in impromptu jam sessions with the visiting Americans. Citing a Dixieland revival at jazz cafes throughout Japan, much of which was stimulated by Teagarden, the US embassy in Tokyo reported that the tour was "undoubtedly a success."[58]

But the importance of Teagarden's visit to Japan was best shown by him unintentionally raising the notion of the universality of jazz. During an interview with a Japanese jazz critic at Tokyo's Imperial Hotel, Teagarden insisted: "jazz could have been born not only in America but anywhere in the world." He went on to emphasize the universality of "lamentation," "the ability to appeal from the heart" and "a lot of improvisation," which he believed were all inherent in jazz. At the same time, however, in his comments to *Swing Journal*, while seeking to undoubtedly flatter a number of Japanese jazz musicians, Teagarden celebrated that Japanese jazz musicians "correctly" understood "our music," suggesting that he saw the Japanese jazz scene through the lens of American exceptionalism:

> For some time, [Gene] Krupa, [Louis] Armstrong, [Benny] Goodman and Peanuts Hucko told me that the most wonderful country in the Far East was Japan. I was totally surprised that it was more than I had expected. Our music is correctly understood here. Anyone from America will be surprised. All Japanese jazz men are truly worthy artists. Mr. Fumio Nanri's style sounds exactly like Satchmo, and I am pleased to find that Mr. Muneyoshi Nishiyo's style sounds like my brother Charlie Teagarden ... I can say that Japan is the most mature country in terms of jazz during this long tour.[59]

What is problematic here is his assertion that Japanese musicians' understanding of jazz was correct. To affirm the so-called "correctness" of the Japanese understanding of jazz is only possible if the American understanding of jazz is fixed as the only standard. Maintaining a degree of authenticity in American jazz has the effect of stressing American exceptionalism. This tension (or complementarity) between the universality of jazz and American exceptionalism would later lead some Japanese musicians to explore Japanese-style jazz during the 1960s. Meanwhile, it is enough to say that Japanese musicians could not have fully appreciated Teagarden's flowery compliments as jazz in Japan was consistently seen as being at the lower level of the hierarchy of musical development.

The cases discussed above show that the global dispatching of jazz ambassadors during the 1950s often brought to the fore tensions among not only American government officials and musicians, but even fans and critics outside America. In a similar vein, when the tide of the civil rights movement and the process of decolonization ran its full course in the 1960s, a new set of discussions arose among not only American government officials and musicians, but also critics about the strategic value of jazz. The next chapter elaborates on various jazz discourses using the case study of Africa, also revisiting a number of discursive tensions that arose as they prepared and implemented jazz diplomacy.

Notes

1. For the Soviet cultural offensive, see Frederick Charles Barghoorn, *The Soviet Cultural Offensive: The Role of Cultural Diplomacy in Soviet Foreign Policy* (Princeton: Princeton UP, 1960); Nigel Gould-Davies, "The Logic of Soviet Cultural Diplomacy," *Diplomatic History*, vol.27 no.3, 2003.
2. For recent studies on the US strategy of winning the hearts and minds of people in foreign countries by means of cultural exchanges, see Walter L. Hixson, *Parting the Curtain: Propaganda, Culture, and the Cold War, 1945–1961* (New York: St. Martin's Press, 1997); Takuya Sasaki, "The Eisenhower Administration's Containment Policy and East-West Exchanges, 1955–60," *Rikkyo Hogaku*, vol.56 and 57, 2000 and 2001; Naima Prevots, *Dance for Export: Cultural Diplomacy and the Cold War* (Hanover: Wesleyan UP, 2001); David Caute, *The Dancer Defects: The Struggle for Cultural Supremacy during the Cold War* (Oxford: Oxford UP, 2003); Richmond, *Cultural Exchange and the Cold War*; Richard T. Arndt, *The First Resort of Kings: American Cultural Diplomacy in The Twentieth Century* (Washington, DC: Potomac Books, 2005); Michael L. Krenn, *Fall-out Shelters for the Human Spirit: American Art and the Cold War* (Chapel Hill: University of North Carolina Press, 2005); Victor Rosenberg, *Soviet-American Relations, 1953–1960: Diplomacy and Cultural Exchange during the Eisenhower Presidency* (Jefferson: McFarland, 2005); Nicholas J. Cull, *The Cold War and the United States Information Agency: American Propaganda and Public Diplomacy, 1945–1989* (Cambridge: Cambridge UP, 2008); Giles Scott-Smith, *Networks of Empire: The US State Department's Foreign Leader Program in the Netherlands, France and Britain 1950–1970* (Brussels: Peter Lang, 2008); Andrew J. Falk, *Upstaging the Cold War: American Dissent and Cultural Diplomacy, 1940–1960* (Amherst: University of Massachusetts Press, 2009); Cadra Peterson McDaniel, *American–Soviet Cultural Diplomacy: The Bolshoi Ballet's American Premiere* (Lanham: Lexington Books, 2014); Greg Barnhisel, *Cold War Modernists: Art, Literature, and American Cultural Diplomacy* (New York: Columbia UP, 2015).

3 University of Arkansas Library, Fayetteville, Arkansas, US, Special Collections Division, Bureau of Educational and Cultural Affairs Historical Collection (hereafter CU), Box 47-8, "Cultural Presentations: Objectives and Issues," undated, Box 2-4, "The Cultural Relations Program of the Department of State, 1938–1978," undated.
4 In addition to the conferences at Geneva and Bandung, Davenport notes the Soviet invasion of Hungary and the cultural offensive of Communists into Asia were factors behind the redirection of the American approach. But the 1955 events had a deeper impact on the discovery and the subsequent launch of America's jazz programs. See Davenport, *Jazz Diplomacy*, p.36. For more on the role of music in the American Cold War strategy, see Von Eschen, *Satchmo Blows Up the World*; Danielle Fosler-Lussier, "Cultural Diplomacy as Cultural Globalization: The University of Michigan Jazz Band in Latin America," *Journal of the Society for American Music*, vol.4 issue 1, 2010; Davenport, *Jazz Diplomacy*; Danielle Fosler-Lussier, *Music in America's Cold War Diplomacy* (Berkeley: University of California Press, 2015); Jessica C. E. Gienow-Hecht, *Music and International History in the Twentieth Century* (New York: Berghahn Books, 2015); Simo Mikkonen and Pekka Suutari, *Music, Art and Diplomacy: East-West Cultural Interactions and the Cold War* (London: Routledge, 2015); Emily Abrams Ansari, *The Sound of a Superpower: Musical Americanism and the Cold War* (Oxford: Oxford UP, 2018).
5 Felix Blair Jr., "United States Has Secret Sonic Weapon," *The New York Times*, 6 November 1955.
6 Von Eschen argues the irony of American jazz musicians not being sent by the State Department to Western Europe rather differently – because of the music's popularity in the region. See Von Eschen, *Satchmo Blows Up the World*, p.8.
7 John S. Wilson, "Who is Conover? Only We Ask," *The New York Times Magazine*, 13 September 1959, quoted, for example, in Mark Breckenridge, *"Sounds for Adventurous Listeners": Willis Conover, the Voice of America, and the International Reception of Avant-garde Jazz in the 1960s* (PhD Thesis, University of North Texas, 2012), p.140.
8 James Lester, "Willis of Oz: A Profile of Famed Voice of America Broadcaster Willis Conover," *Central Europe Review*, vol.1 no.5, 1999.
9 Ibid.; Robert McG. Thomas Jr., "Willis Conover, 75, Voice of America Disc Jockey," *The New York Times*, 19 May 1996.
10 Wilson, "Who is Conover?," quoted in Breckenridge, *"Sounds for Adventurous Listeners,"* pp.117–18. See also Ibid., p.143.
11 CU, Box 2-3, "Landmarks in the History of the Cultural Relations Program of the US Department of State 1938 to 1976," undated; Box 47-7, "Handbook for the Cultural Presentations Program of the United States Government," undated; Box 48-11, "Policy and Program Guide – Cultural Presentations Program," 10 June 1964.
12 Dizzy Gillespie and Al Fraser, *To Be or Not to Bop: Memoirs of Dizzy Gillespie* (New York: Da Capo, 1985), p.413.
13 Scott Gac, "Jazz Strategy: Dizzy, Foreign Policy, and Government in 1956," *Americana*, vol.4 issue 1, 2005; Von Eschen, *Satchmo Blows Up the World*, pp.6–7; Benjamin Franklin, *Jazz & Blues Musicians of South Carolina: Interviews with Jabbo, Dizzy, Drink, and Others* (Columbia: University of South Carolina Press, 2008), p.29; Fred Kaplan, "When Ambassadors Had Rhythm," *The New York Times*, 29 June 2008; Davenport, *Jazz Diplomacy*, pp.35–36; Robin D. G. Kelley, *Africa Speaks, America Answers: Modern Jazz in Revolutionary Times* (Cambridge: Harvard UP, 2012), p.3.
14 John Gennari, *Blowin' Hot and Cool: Jazz and Its Critics* (Chicago: University of Chicago Press, 2006), pp.146–53; Mario Dunkel, "Marshall Winslow Stearns and the Politics of Jazz Historiography," *American Music*, vol.30 no.4, 2012, pp.484–89.
15 CU, Box 100-1, "Music Advisory Panel, International Exchange Program, December 20, 1955 4:00 P.M.," undated.

16 NARA, RG 59, CDF 1955–59, Box 103, 032 Gillespie, Dizzy, Dulles to Embassies, 4 April 1956; Gillespie and Fraser, *To Be or Not to Bop*, p.414. Gillespie's tour has been detailed in the existing literature. See for example, Von Eschen, *Satchmo Blows Up the World*, pp.27–43; Davenport, *Jazz Diplomacy*, pp.46–53; Monson, *Freedom Sounds*, pp.113–23; Graham Carr, "Diplomatic Notes: American Musicians and Cold War Politics in the Near and Middle East, 1954–60," *Popular Music History*, vol.1 no.1, 2004; David M. Carletta, "'Those White Guys Are Working for Me': Dizzy Gillespie, Jazz, and the Cultural Politics of the Cold War during the Eisenhower Administration," *International Social Science Review*, vol.82, 2007.

17 NARA, RG 59, CDF 1955–59, Box 103, 032 Gillespie, Dizzy, "Educational Exchange: President's Fund: Dizzy Gillespie and His Orchestra," 19 March 1956. See also Monson, *Freedom Sounds*, pp.115–16.

18 CU, Box 48-4, Schnitzer to International Educational Exchange Service, 10 January 1956; Box 48-26, "International Cultural Exchange Service of the American National Theatre and Academy, Projects to Date," undated; Box 48-11, "Policy and Program Guide – Cultural Presentations Program," 10 June 1964.

19 NARA, RG 59, CDF 1955–59, Box 103, 032 Gillespie, Dizzy, Gallman to Dulles, 29 March 1956; Dulles to Baghdad, 6 April 1956.

20 NARA, RG 59, CDF 1955–59, Box 103, 032 Gillespie, Dizzy, "EE: President's Fund: Dizzy Gillespie Jazz Group," 13 April 1956; "Visit of Dizzy Gillespie and His Band to Turkey," 1 June 1956. For Gillespie's performance in Dacca, see also Davenport, *Jazz Diplomacy*, pp.47–48.

21 NARA, RG 59, CDF 1955–59, Box 103, 032 Gillespie, Dizzy, "Resounding Applause from Turkey – A Critical Essay," *Metronome*, July 1956.

22 NARA, RG 59, CDF 1955–59, Box 103, 032 Gillespie, Dizzy, "Educational Exchange: President's Fund: Report on Dizzy Gillespie Performances in Athens," 4 June 1956; Kaplan, "When Ambassadors Had Rhythm." See also Von Eschen, *Satchmo Blows Up the World*, p.34; Davenport, *Jazz Diplomacy*, pp.49–50.

23 NARA, RG 59, CDF 1955–59, Box 103, 032 Gillespie, Dizzy, "Educational Exchange: Visit of President's Fund/ANTA – Sponsored Jazz Musician Dizzy Gillespie and Band to Yugoslavia," 1 August 1956. See also Davenport, *Jazz Diplomacy*, p.51.

24 NARA, RG 59, CDF 1955–59, Box 103, 032 Gillespie, Dizzy, "Educational Exchange: Visit of President's Fund/ANTA – Sponsored Jazz Musician Dizzy Gillespie and Band to Yugoslavia," 1 August 1956. The US ambassador in Beirut Donald R. Heath also celebrated the racially mixed band for succeeding in its mission by emphasizing the "non-discriminatory aspects of American relations." See NARA, RG 59, CDF 1955–59, Box 103, 032 Gillespie, Dizzy, "Educational Exchange: President's Fund; Dizzy Gillespie and His Band," 18 May 1956.

25 NARA, RG 59, CDF 1955–59, Box 103, 032 Gillespie, Dizzy, "EE: President's Fund: Dizzy Gillespie Jazz Group," 13 April 1956, "Visit of Dizzy Gillespie and His Band to Turkey," 1 June 1956. See also Alyn Shipton, *Groovin' High: The Life of Dizzy Gillespie* (Oxford: Oxford UP, 2001), pp.282–83; Monson, *Freedom Sounds*, p.117; Davenport, *Jazz Diplomacy*, pp.47–49; Fosler-Lussier, *Music in America's Cold War Diplomacy*, p.94.

26 Gillespie and Fraser, *To Be or Not to Bop*, pp.421–22.

27 For their different agendas, see also Von Eschen, *Satchmo Blows Up the World*, pp.34–5; Penny Von Eschen, *Race against Empire: Black Americans and Anti-colonialism, 1937–1957* (Ithaca: Cornell UP, 1997), p.178.

28 Gillespie and Fraser, *To Be or Not to Bop*, pp.414, 421. See also Carletta, "'Those White Guys Are Working for Me'," p.121.

29 Gac, "Jazz Strategy"; Kevin Michael Angelo Strait, *"A Tone Parallel": Jazz Music, Leftist Politics, and the Counter-Minstrel Narrative, 1930–1970* (PhD Thesis, George Washington University, 2010), p.158. See also Gillespie and Fraser, *To Be or Not to Bop*, p.438.

30 NARA, RG 59, CDF 1955–59, Box 103, 032 Gillespie, Dizzy, "Taken from Baltimore News Post, April 10. (UP)," attached to McGlocklin to Herter, 6 May 1957.
31 *Congressional Record (Extensions of Remarks)*, 84th Congress, 2nd Session, vol.102, Part 10 (July 17, 1956 to July 24, 1956), p.13609; Wagnleitner, *Coca-Colonization and the Cold War*, p.212. See also Iain Anderson, *This Is Our Music: Free Jazz, the Sixties, and American Culture* (Philadelphia: University of Pennsylvania Press, 2012), p.42.
32 NARA, RG 59, CDF 1955–59, Box 103, 032 Gillespie, Dizzy, Williamson to Butler, 12 April 1957; Butler to Hill, 17 April 1957; Hill to Butler, 29 April 1957. See also Fosler-Lussier, *Music in America's Cold War Diplomacy*, pp.96–97.
33 Dizzy Gillespie with Ralph Ginzburg, "Jazz is too good for Americans," *Esquire*, June 1957.
34 NARA, RG 59, CDF 1955–59, Box 100, 032 De Paris, Wilbur, "Educational Exchange: President's Fund – Wilbur De Paris Jazz Band," 14 March 1957.
35 NARA, RG 59, CDF 1955–59, Box 100, 032 De Paris, Wilbur, "Cultural Exchange: President's Fund: Wilbur De Paris Visit," 20 May 1957; CU, Box 93-19, "President's Special International Program for Cultural Presentations, Second Semi-Annual Report, January 1 1957 – June 30 1957," undated.
36 NARA, RG 59, CDF 1955–59, Box 100, 032 De Paris, Wilbur, "Educational Exchange: Report on Visit of Wilbur De Paris Jazz Band to East Africa," 15 July 1957.
37 NARA, RG 59, CDF 1955–59, Box 100, 032 De Paris, Wilbur, "Tunisian Tour of Wilbur De Paris Jazz Orchestra," 9 May 1957. For De Paris's African tour in general, see also Monson, *Freedom Sounds*, pp.126, 128; Davenport, *Jazz Diplomacy*, pp.57–59; Fosler-Lussier, *Music in America's Cold War Diplomacy*, p.95.
38 NARA, RG 59, CDF 1955–59, Box 100, 032 De Paris, Wilbur, Moore to Dulles, 17 March 1957; Hill to Moore, 31 May 1957.
39 After Gillespie conducted another official tour in South America from July to August of 1956, six groups assumed the role of jazz ambassadors: Benny Goodman toured several Asian countries from December 1956 to January 1957; Wilbur De Paris toured several African countries from March to May of 1957; the Glenn Miller Orchestra toured Poland and Yugoslavia in April 1957; Dave Brubeck toured Poland, the Middle East and South Asia from March to May of 1958; Woody Herman toured South America in August 1958; and Jack Teagarden toured parts of Asia from September 1958 to January 1959.
40 NARA, RG 59, CDF 1955–59, Box 104, 032 Goodman, Benny, "U Nu Get Itchy Feet Listening to Benny," *The Nation*, 3 January 1957; CU, Box 93-18, "First Semi-Annual Report, President's Special International Program, July 1 1956 – December 31 1956," undated.
41 NARA, RG 59, CDF 1955–59, Box 104, 032 Goodman, Benny, Godley to Dulles, 21 November 1956; Box 88, 032, USIS Phnom Penn to USIA Washington, 3 January 1957. For Goodman's tour in Thailand and Cambodia, see also Von Eschen, *Satchmo Blows Up the World*, pp.44–47; Davenport, *Jazz Diplomacy*, pp.55–56.
42 NARA, RG 59, CDF 1955–59, Box 104, 032 Goodman, Benny, "Benny Goodman Takes Varsity by Storm," *The Nation*, 31 December 1956; "U Nu Get Itchy Feet Listening to Benny," *The Nation*, 3 January 1957; "President's Fund: Visit to Rangoon of Benny Goodman and His Orchestra, December 29, 1956 – January 4, 1957," 11 June 1957.
43 Jiro Kubota and Shoichi Yui, "Goodman ka? Badman ka?," *Swing Journal*, vol.11 no.2, 1957, p.11; Teruo Isono, "Goodman Rainichi no Gakuyabanashi," ibid., p.18.
44 "Goodman Tokyo Koen Snap" *Swing Journal*, vol.11 no.3, 1957, pp.3–5. See also Fumiko Fujita, *America Bunka Gaiko to Nihon: Reisenki no Bunka to Hito no Koryu* (Tokyo: University of Tokyo Press, 2015), pp.183–86.
45 Keiichiro Ebihara, George Kawaguchi, Eiji Kitamura, Munehiro Okuda, Mihiro Sasayama and Shoichi Yui, "Zadankai 'B. Goodman Ensokai' wo Kataru," *Swing*

Journal, vol.11 no.3, 1957, pp.18–20; Fujita, *America Bunka Gaiko to Nihon*, pp.184–85.

46 NARA, RG 59, CDF 1955–59, Box 96, 032 Brubeck, Dave Jazz Quartet, Lightner, Jr. to Flemming, 12 February 1958.
47 NARA, RG 59, CDF 1955–59, Box 96, 032 Brubeck, Dave Jazz Quartet, "Educational Exchange: Report on Dave Brubeck Jazz Quartet in India during Its Tour Under the President's Program and ANTA," 6 June 1958. For Brubeck's tour in India, see also Von Eschen, *Satchmo Blows Up the World*, pp.52–53; Davenport, *Jazz Diplomacy*, pp.76–77.
48 NARA, RG 59, CDF 1955–59, Box 96, 032 Brubeck, Dave Jazz Quartet, "Educational Exchange: Report on Dave Brubeck Jazz Quartet in India during Its Tour Under the President's Program and ANTA," 6 June 1958.
49 Ibid.
50 Ibid.
51 CU, Box 93-21, "President's Special International Program, Fourth Semi-Annual Report," undated; NARA, RG 59, CDF 1955–59, Box 96, 032 Brubeck, Dave Jazz Quartet, "Educational Exchange: Dave Brubeck Quartet's Visit to Dacca," 14 May 1958.
52 NARA, RG 59, CDF 1955–59, Box 126, 032 Teagarden, Jack Sextet, "Educational Exchange: President's Program: Visit of Jack Teagarden Sextet to Bombay Area," 4 February 1959; CU, Box 93-23, "President's Special International Program, Fourth Semi-Annual Report," undated. Davenport only briefly touched upon Teagarden's tour in Davenport, *Jazz Diplomacy*, pp.78–79.
53 NARA, RG 59, CDF 1955–59, Box 126, 032 Teagarden, Jack Sextet, "Cultural Presentations: Jack Teagarden's Visit to Malaya," 31 March 1959.
54 NARA, RG 59, CDF 1955–59, Box 126, 032 Teagarden, Jack Sextet, "Report on Concerts by Jack Teagarden Sextet in Kabul September 26, 27, 28," 16 October 1958; "Cultural Presentations: President's Program: Jack Teagarden Sextet," 6 October 1958.
55 NARA, RG 59, CDF 1955–59, Box 126, 032 Teagarden, Jack Sextet, "President's Fund: Visit to Burma of Jack Teagarden Sextet, November 3–14, 1958," 30 January 1959.
56 NARA, RG 59, CDF 1955–59, Box 126, 032 Teagarden, Jack Sextet, "Educational Exchange: President's Fund: Jack Teagarden in Hong Kong December 28–31, 1958," 26 January 1959.
57 NARA, RG 59, CDF 1955–59, Box 126, 032 Teagarden, Jack Sextet, "Durbrow to Dulles, 2 December 1958, "Cultural Presentations: President's Program – Korean Visit of the Jack Teagarden Sextet," 29 January 1959.
58 NARA, RG 59, CDF 1955–59, Box 126, 032 Teagarden, Jack Sextet, "Cultural Presentation: Jack Teagarden Sextet," 7 May 1959. See also Fujita, *America Bunka Gaiko to Nihon*, pp.187–88.
59 "Jack T Ikko no Enso ha Nihon de Dou Uketoraretaka?" *Swing Journal*, vol.13 no.2, 1959, pp.68–69.

4 The politics behind the selection process

During the turbulent 1960s, the distance between jazz and politics further narrowed. At the global level, as the wave of decolonization reached its highest point, jazz ambassadors found themselves increasingly sent to Africa. Whereas at the domestic level, as the civil rights movement intensified in America, musicians began to express themselves more explicitly, with voices of protest mounting against institutional and day-to-day segregation.[1] American jazz musicians in this decade also had to face the growing popularity of rock music, which was becoming a symbol of counter-culture. These events naturally affected the discourse surrounding jazz diplomacy. The importance here lies in the fact that when jazz's role and interpretation was changing in America, its external value was articulated differently by various agents – such as government officials, musicians and critics.

It is widely known that jazz musicians, through their music, had used their right to protest against the existing system of American democracy since the late 1950s. The Little Rock crisis of 1957 offered just one such example. When nine African American students tried to enter the all-white Central High School and met fierce opposition from segregationists – promoting a call out of the National Guard by the Governor of Arkansas Orval Faubus – these actions provoked fierce criticism, including from Charles Mingus. Mingus harshly condemned the Governor with extraordinarily intense lyrics in "Fables of Faubus." Social protests through jazz continued well into the 1960s. When four African American college students in Greensboro, North Carolina, launched sit-ins in February 1960, which later developed into a large-scale protest movement, Max Roach released the album *We Insist!* with a lunch-counter sit-in photo on the jacket. Subtitled *Freedom Now Suite*, the album's message was abundantly clear. Bolstering Roach's standing as a prominent civil rights activist – joined by Abbey Lincoln who later married Roach – the album contained five impressive tracks, including one dealing with the Sharpeville massacre that occurred near Johannesburg, South Africa, while under apartheid. Immediately following the tragic white supremacist bombing of an African American Baptist church in Birmingham in September 1963, John Coltrane recorded "Alabama," which he later added to the live album *Live at Birdland* as a studio-record track. For these musicians, an ideal democracy should be found in jazz. When jazz was played, Roach asserted, "everybody in the group has the opportunity to speak on it and comment on it through their performance. It's a democratic process, as opposed to most European classical music in which the two most important people are the composer and conductor. They are like the king and queen."[2] Understandably, Roach's *We Insist!* expressed his thirst for democracy and, therefore, was a medium for demanding greater and more concrete change in America. Here jazz was interpreted as a protest against the "real Americana."

As musicologists Ingrid Monson and Eric Porter suggest, some white musicians stressed the discourse of racial integration to reverse the perception commonly held in the American jazz scene, whereby jazz's musical authenticity was guaranteed by being "black." To be color-blind had the effect of relaxing this musical authenticity, negating the musical assets African American musicians were believed to possess. Likewise, the discourse of racial integration functioned to cover up the privileges white musicians held in the music industry, in the sense that problems became defined in terms of an individual's ability or talent, rather than racial factors or the extant social structure. When the Black Power movement of the late 1960s enhanced the appeal of jazz's blackness, this was antithetical to the color-blind "American music" discourse that seemed to have long ignored institutionalized racial discrimination.[3]

The sections of the chapter below review how discursive frictions arose among various actors involved in jazz during the 1960s – notably, frictions over the external, compared with domestic, value of the music. As the existing research on the jazz diplomacy program has documented, government officials and musicians had somewhat different agendas in implementing the jazz tours in Africa. Some of these examples are reviewed here to support the overarching themes of the chapter. Whereas less attention has been placed on certain frictions among government officials and critics that foregrounded during the process of selecting jazz ambassadors. Combining both sets of perspectives will provide a much clearer view of how differently these domestic actors evaluated the strategic value of government-sponsored jazz tours in Africa, and how they at times clashed with one another.

Satchmo, Duke and the external value of jazz

As the original American jazz ambassador – nicknamed by fans "Ambassador Satch" – Louis Armstrong had long been a natural choice for the State Department. American diplomats saw him as the quintessential official jazz ambassador. From Peru, for example, the US embassy ardently expressed its hope to the State Department, as early as February 1956, that his visit would materialize.[4] In addition, the next year in Bucharest, the chief of mission Robert H. Thayer asserted that his tour "would certainly receive sensational reception by people."[5] However, these early hopes did not immediately materialize, as Armstrong's manager wished to prioritize touring domestically, and because of the problematic fingerprinting requirement to which the Soviet bloc countries had protested.

In any event, Armstrong was well-known as someone who strongly criticized the contradictions embedded in the notion of color-blind Americanism.[6] When President Eisenhower initially refused to send troops to Little Rock, Armstrong furiously complained: "The way they are treating my people in the South, the government can go to hell." He lamented that "It's getting so bad, a colored man hasn't got any country." Unsurprisingly, Armstrong publicly refused the alleged plan of the State Department to send him to Moscow. He saw it as ridiculous to represent "America" as a free and democratic nation when southern racial problems had not been solved. Facing overt criticism from America's original jazz ambassador, Secretary of State Dulles complained that racial problems in the south were "ruining our foreign policy."[7] Immediately afterwards, the State Department received a flood of letters criticizing Armstrong's remarks during the Little Rock crisis. Members of Congress and some citizens demanded not only the banning of Armstrong from representing America but punishing him for his critical remarks against the government. Despite previously held high expectations about "Ambassador Satch," the State Department dispassionately responded: "We naturally deplore his recent intemperate remarks which no doubt would be taken into consideration should he apply for Government financial support for foreign tour."[8] Moreover, when other members of Congress and concerned citizens inquired of Dulles about press reports suggesting the US government was planning a Soviet tour by Armstrong, the State Department flatly denied the existence of such a plan. According to the department, the US government "could not initiate arrangements of any kind for exchanges with the Soviet Union until certain procedural questions had been resolved," and any plans for his Soviet tour were "presumably based on private or commercial arrangements."[9]

Nevertheless, Armstrong's South American tour took place shortly afterwards on a commercial basis, providing the State Department with a chance to reconfirm the strategic value of "Ambassador Satch." It was right after the turmoil at Little Rock – during which various Communist countries capitalized on this incident in their anti-American propaganda – when US embassies in South America grew wary of Armstrong's partiality for making critical remarks against the incumbent government. Proving their concerns ill-founded, he showed nothing but professionalism, and focused his efforts on playing his trumpet, undoubtedly gratifying State Department officials. His immense popularity was on show in Argentina, when so many fans crowded into the concert hall that Armstrong was forced to enter the venue wearing a baseball catcher's mask in order to protect his lips. During his stay, he tirelessly visited women's organizations and facilities for disabled children to conduct free performances. A report from the US embassy in Buenos Aires asserted: "no American at the post can remember a warmer or more unrestrained reception given to any American artist."[10]

The State Department's enthusiasm for "Ambassador Satch" came to the fore during his first tour as an official jazz ambassador, when he visited 15 African countries over two months commencing in October 1960. During his stay in Accra, Ghana, he visited President Kwame Nkrumah. And he also participated in the Odwira festival, held in the eastern region of the country, to deepen musical and cultural ties with locals. The embassy assessed in its reporting that Armstrong represented America with "the highest professional competence," while also stressing: "His artistry, his sincerity and his friendliness won friends again here no less than in every other country he has visited over the years."[11]

Arguably, Dakar and Bamako were African capitals where the process of regional decolonization impacted Armstrong's tour itinerary more directly than in Accra or other destinations. In West Africa, after the Sudanese Republic and Senegal, both former French colonies, had formed the Federation of Mali – gaining independence in June 1960 – the Senegalese withdrew from the Federation in August, resulting in a sharp deterioration of relations between the two countries (the Sudanese Republic became the Republic of Mali). Embarrassed with these developments, the US embassies started to raise concerns about the possible effects Armstrong's tour could have on both countries. Decolonization had provided the US government with a chance to expand its influence in Africa. However, it was suddenly forced to consider the exigencies of rising tensions between these newly independent countries just as Armstrong's tour was due to arrive. Sending the band to Senegal's capital Dakar while ignoring Mali's capital Bamako would antagonize the Malians. From the US embassy in Bamako, the acting chargé d'affaires John G. Dean insisted it would be unwise to "appear deliberately to neglect the capital of this newly-independent and fiercely proud country." The performance by one of the world's most famous musicians would definitely produce a powerful "'good will' impact," Dean asserted, but "Failure to include Bamako may have powerful adverse 'bad will' impact."[12] Ultimately, Armstrong had no choice but to visit both newly independent African countries to ensure US diplomatic aims did not suffer.

Although not taken seriously in the existing research, the postwar wave of decolonization stimulated a debate among critics over the utility of the strategic use of jazz. In February 1963, the editor-in-chief of *Down Beat* proposed to the State Department that experienced artists assume a responsibility for managing the jazz ambassadors program. He recommended Duke Ellington and Coleman Hawkins or, if impossible, Ralph Ellison, as possible candidates. Importantly, it was purposefully suggested that African Americans were best placed for this oversight role.[13] To some, if jazz's blackness was to be emphasized, it was both inevitable and natural to send jazz to Africa. However, there was no unanimous opinion among critics and policy-makers on this point. In February 1963, at a meeting of the Advisory Committee on the Arts, which the State Department had established in the late 1950s for seeking advice on its artistic programs – consisting of highly influential members from the American art world – a cautionary note was raised by some members against sending jazz to Africa. The committee's general opinion was that enough jazz groups had performed in Africa to date, and the time was now ripe to send representatives from other musical genres as a means of reaching new audiences. In contrast, many in the State Department believed that sending jazz to Africa "should be continued because it has been so successful," soon bringing it into disagreement with the committee.[14]

Then in April and July 1963, the Music Advisory Panel, whose task was to evaluate particular artists from an artistic standards perspective, discussed who was to be sent to Africa under the Cultural Presentations Program.[15] On this occasion, jazz critic Marshall Stearns referred to the existence of musicians playing both classical music and jazz. Glenn G. Wolfe of the Bureau of Educational and Cultural Affairs (CU) in the State Department, on his part, stressed that "there was a great difference of opinion" about the Advisory Committee on the Arts' stance concerning the view that jazz musicians should not be sent to Africa. Specifically, it was the Africa area specialists in the State Department who were most supportive of continuing to send jazz ambassadors to Africa. Under pressure from the State Department, the committee offered a somewhat compromise solution by suggesting the US government could send a group that would give the Africans some "beat" and "tempo." However, Carleton Sprague Smith, a musicologist and member of the panel, expressed concern at this perceived risky suggestion, noting it could send a message that could be interpreted as: "you are Africans, therefore you like to hear rhythm." As Smith stated, "from a psychological point of view, this might be the worst thing you can do."[16]

During a series of discussions, it became clear that the alternative to jazz was classical music. This was because, firstly, there were groups of political elites who had been educated in Europe and they appreciated classical music. Secondly, as Robert Bauer of the CU suggested in a panel meeting, it was important to demonstrate that "we do not consider Africa as primarily composed of jungle-drummers." He believed this had an advantage of showing African audiences that "we consider them our cultural equals." Thirdly, Bauer emphasized recent precedents in noting that "Germany sent a chamber music group, and the British sent a Shakespearean company." Additionally, another member of the panel hoped that a racially mixed group of chamber musicians could be sent "to demonstrate that interracial units do not stop with the jazz field," thus echoing the philosophy of color-blind Americanism. As a result of these discussions by the panel, there emerged a consensus that striking the right balance as well as flexibility were key prerequisites for any representation of America in Africa. According to Mark Schubart, the former dean of the Juilliard School of Music, if "a popularity contest with other nations" had to be eschewed, they needed to send what they recognized as representing them. And this necessitated sending classical chamber groups even if the audience had to "sit through fifteen minutes of Mozart."[17]

Following these protracted discussions, finally during the 1960s, jazz groups as well as chamber groups were sent to Africa, as there was a prevailing view that jazz could foster ties with Africa somewhat more easily than other forms of music. The minutes of the March 1966 meeting of the Advisory Committee on the Arts suggest that common ground for communicating with people in Africa could be established by folk songs as well as jazz, because "Africans know these art forms." Notably, Committee members admitted that classical music (and ballet) were "not appreciated in Africa and therefore not effective."[18] There was, however, a period when no jazz groups performed on the African continent – from March 1963, when the Cozy Cole jazz review returned from its African tour, to April 1966, when Duke Ellington performed in Senegal.

Even if jazz remained on the list for the Cultural Presentations Program, there was still another question – who should be sent to Africa? This was always a challenging question. A wide variety of names came and went. For example, Josephine Baker, who had once created a great sensation in interwar France with her performance of *La Revue Nègre*, was at times mentioned. But she was out of the question for the State Department, as Baker had been loudly denouncing the US government for ignoring domestic racial problems in her travels around the world. Further, she had been kept under FBI surveillance domestically, and the State Department monitored her activities when she was outside America. At one time, Adam Clayton Powell Jr, the original proponent of the jazz ambassadors program, publicly condemned Baker for distorting the image of racial conditions in America. In another instance, her South American tour was canceled due to her entry visa not being issued under pressure from the State Department. In Cuba, local military police interrogated Baker after the FBI provided them with her dossier, outlining a range of her political activities. Unsurprisingly, Secretary of State Dulles was stubbornly against selecting Baker for the jazz ambassadors program, leading to other less controversial names to be considered.[19]

Duke Ellington was seen as first among equals in official circles, as someone who had both knowledge and ability to represent jazz as a sophisticated art form abroad. Ellington, playing various styles of jazz, had been accepted and adored by generations of jazz followers. While having plenty of experience on the world stage, he was also willing to interact off the stage in more informal settings with local fans. In the context of selecting musicians for the Middle East and Southeast Asia, his name was frequently mentioned as a suitable candidate. The only problem was the high fees associated with his services, which were estimated to be twice as much as Woody Herman and five times as much as Chico Hamilton. However, Herman was unavailable to tour Africa due to his schedule, and Hamilton had problems with his temperament and waning popularity – his band was also negatively seen as having a propensity for going "far out." While there was some apprehension that Ellington could be considered as too "old hat," Marshall Stearns vouched for his success in noting "Duke is the exception of all rules" and "everybody thinks he is the greatest."[20] As a result, and clearly despite the high financial costs involved, Ellington successfully toured the Middle East from September to November 1963.

Allaying their concerns, State Department officials saw Ellington's jazz within their tolerance parameters – and not being too "far out" – and they were, accordingly, confident that he was a safe set of hands as the next American jazz ambassador for Africa. In April 1966, three years after the earlier aforementioned panel meeting when Stearns had firmly proposed Ellington as a suitable candidate, Ellington landed on the continent of Africa. His visit's main purpose was to appear at the First World Festival of Black Arts held in Senegal. Ellington performed at some domestic venues from 4–6 April, with President Léopold Senghor visiting the stadium where he was performing on 6 April. As one of the leading figures of the Négritude movement, which affirmed a sense of pride in having African heritage and a black identity, Senghor had come across jazz during his stay in Paris during the interwar period – which had had an influence on his poetry. Senghor felt a great significance in Ellington's visit from America, where he was aware that the Black Power movement was on the rise. When they personally met two days later, Senghor extolled Ellington's performance at the festival and stated it had been "even greater than I had anticipated." Looking back at the time he spent in Paris as a student in the early 1930s, he told Ellington that his jazz had inspired Senghor to engage in the Négritude movement.[21]

But Ellington was not content with simply emphasizing race. As his autobiography reveals, when he visited countries across South Asia and the Middle East as a jazz ambassador in 1963, Ellington was often asked by local press reporters about his views on racial problems, thus presenting an occasion for him to express his own views. Ellington relativized racial problems at home by responding: "the basis of the whole problem is economic rather than a matter of color." It was Ellington's belief to assert blackness through musical expression, thereby improving the status of African Americans, rather than make direct political statements on race. This belief often caused friction with people who expected him to express more forthright political views on racial problems.[22]

Nonetheless, race was not irrelevant in the course of Ellington's life. In the year before his visit to Senegal, the Pulitzer Prize Advisory Board declined the recommendation of the music jury to award him a special citation. Reportedly, this was because jazz was not taken as seriously as classical music, or because he was an African American musician. In any case, when seeing jazz critic Nat Hentoff immediately after this disappointing news, Ellington complained – perhaps with more than a tinge of regret – that "my kind of music is still without, let us say, official honor at home." While most Americans still put value on classical music, he lamented, jazz was always "like the kind of a man you wouldn't want your daughter to associate with."[23] These insightful observations by one of the biggest jazz names of the twentieth century underscored a distinct aspect of America, a decade after the launch of the jazz ambassadors program.

It was to be four years later when Ellington's birthday party was celebrated at the White House, hosted by President Nixon. By then, jazz had become a diplomatic tool for welcoming heads of sovereign states visiting Washington DC. During the Johnson administration, Dave Brubeck performed a welcome concert for King Hussein of Jordan, while Charlie Byrd and Herbie Mann played before the King of Nepal and Britain's Princess Alexandra respectively. Also, the University of North Texas jazz band pleased King Bhumibol of Thailand when he visited Washington DC in 1967. Among African American musicians, Sarah Vaughan was invited to the formal banquet for Japanese Prime Minister Eisaku Sato to sing a welcome song in January 1965. The plan for Ellington's birthday party was initially conceived by Willis Conover and passed along to Leonard Garment, a special consultant for Richard Nixon. Once a saxophonist in the Woody Herman Orchestra himself, Garment possessed a deep understanding of jazz. On the day of the birthday party for Ellington, Vice President Spiro Agnew welcomed guests with his piano performance of "In a Sentimental Mood" and "Sophisticated Lady," and saxophonist Gerry Mulligan's "Honeysuckle Rose" set a festive tone for the reception. While the atmosphere of this special birthday party has been described in the book's opening chapter, needless to say, it was a uniquely grand event. Notably, three months later, Garment and Conover visited the Soviet Union to participate to the sixth Moscow International Film Festival, where a short documentary film showing the Ellington birthday party was screened to Soviet audiences.[24]

This documentary was produced by the United States Information Agency (USIA), a service organization responsible for presenting American culture abroad with its overseas branch the USIS. It was screened by US embassies and USIA libraries around the world. It was possible to record Ellington's birthday party because a movie camera was brought in for the first time for an event of this kind at the White House. These facts suggest that the Nixon administration wished to make use of the birthday party for public relations purposes. On the one hand, Nixon, who had once summoned well-known cultural figures to the HUAC, must have been familiar with the various connections linking jazz circles with Communism. But on the other, since he was Vice President when jazz started to take on an overtly anti-Communist tone in the Eisenhower administration, it is unlikely that he was ignorant of the political utility of jazz. Faced with the rise of Black Power and frequent occurrences of violence in the late 1960s, as cultural historian Harvey G. Cohen points out, Nixon arguably found a unique opportunity to dispel the image of a divided society by disseminating the image that Nixon and Ellington were on intimate and friendly terms. Against this background, it was likely that filming the birthday party was a political strategy by Nixon, cognizant that he had garnered very few votes in African American communities in the 1968 presidential election.[25] Ellington, therefore, one of a rare cohort of Republican-friendly African American jazz musicians, was ostensibly seen an invaluable political asset for Nixon.

Coleman and the problem of selecting musicians

As mentioned earlier, compared with the friction between jazz musicians and government officials, divergences in opinion between music critics and government officials – in the process of selecting jazz ambassadors – has not been well-documented in the existing literature. However, examining these different perspectives reveals not only what important criteria the State Department used in selecting jazz musicians, but also tells us what aspects of jazz caused concern for government officials in the context of this turbulent decade. In 1964, a subcommittee for jazz and folk music was established in the Musical Advisory Panel of ANTA. After Marshall Stearns passed away in December 1966, music critic John Wilson became chair of the subcommittee; other members of the subcommittee included VOA's Willis Conover, as well as composers Gunther Schuller and Hall Overton. As of early 1967, the following musicians were examples of those who were deemed suitable to play the role of jazz ambassador following on from Duke Ellington:

Cannonball Adderley, Count Basie, Louie Bellson, Art Blakey and the Jazz Messengers, Bob Brookmeyer, Ray Bryant, Ornette Coleman, Don Elliott, Bill Evans, Art Farmer, Bud Freeman, Erroll Garner, Stan Getz, Jimmy Giuffre, Chico Hamilton, Slide Hampton, John Handy, Hampton Hawes, Quincy Jones, Stan Kenton, Gene Krupa, Yusef Lateef, Rod Levitt, Ramsey Lewis, Charles Lloyd, Machito, The Modern Jazz Quartet, Gerry Mulligan, Tito Puente, Max Roach, The Mitchell-Ruff Trio, Mongo Santamaria, Billy Taylor, Clark Terry, Cal Tjader, Randy Weston, Teddy Wilson, and Kai Winding.[26]

In the selection process, the subcommittee emphasized both musical talent and non-musical factors, such as whether the candidate had a personal history of drug abuse. The rating list created by the subcommittee shows that candidates were evaluated from AA to C depending on musical talent. Examples of AA, A and B ratings are shown below.

- Musicians with an AA rating: John Coltrane, Miles Davis (with "personal problems"), Bill Evans, Gil Evans, John Handy and Thelonious Monk.
- Musicians with an A rating: Red Allen, Count Basie (although "many commercial appearances in Europe – may be tired"), Art Blakey and the Jazz Messengers (with "personal problems"), Ornette Coleman (with "personal problems"), Stan Getz, Coleman Hawkins, Thad Jones, Gene Krupa (A for showmanship, B for musicianship), Charles Lloyd, Charles Mingus ("may have personal problems"), The Modern Jazz Quartet (with "personal problems"), Gerry Mulligan, Max Roach, Pee Wee Russell, Horace Silver, Clark Terry, Teddy Wilson and Attila Zoller.
- Musicians with a B rating: Cannonball Adderley, Ray Bryant, Quincy Jones, Stan Kenton, Billy Taylor and Randy Weston.[27]

It appears that "personal problems" did not necessarily preclude musicians from making the AA or A list, as shown by Miles Davis, Art Blakey and the Jazz Messengers, Ornette Coleman, Charles Mingus, and the Modern Jazz Quartet making the cut. Notably, Gene Krupa was rated A for his showmanship, but rated B for his "musicianship." Conversely, Cannonball Adderley was rated B, but he was rated A "in terms of representation," with selectors pointing out he was "An excellent speaker."[28]

Apart from illegal use of drugs, another non-musical factor in selecting musicians was the extent to which musicians criticized the US government. As noted earlier, Josephine Baker had been screened out from the selection process for this reason. Moreover, when Max Roach and Abbey Lincoln toured the Middle East, the subcommittee discussed the possibility of nominating them as jazz ambassadors, but this did not materialize. Their musicality was not the source of the problem. Conover explained the issue as such: "Max Roach is one of the great musicians in America and Abbey Lincoln is a striking performer." However, the subcommittee seemed concerned that "they are capable of speaking out very strongly about the race situation in America, and of making remarks in the foreign press."[29]

In addition, careful attention was paid to ensure jazz was not to be confused with rock music. Due to his intense aversion to rock music, Conover resented the fact there was the "increasing emphasis on bad music just because it is popular." He was especially concerned that the Cultural Presentations Program would reflect "what is happening in music today, such as Janis Joplin, who was on the cover of a recent *Newsweek* magazine [emphasis in original]." For Conover, "Just because a bunch of kids are crazy about these people and they run around the country making a lot of money does not mean we have to send it abroad." In the same vein, Conover believed that rock music, no matter what scales of popularity it reached, did not legitimately represent America nor should it do so. While all the subcommittee members admitted that "in recent years rock has been on the rise and is extending more and more into the jazz field," Conover was the most adamant in stressing that it should have nothing to do with American cultural diplomacy. In a subcommittee meeting, he reiterated his dislike of rock music by remarking: "It should not be presented abroad just because it is happening. We do not send out weeds to show what is happening in a garden."[30]

Lastly, free jazz became a target of intense discussion during the process of selecting jazz musicians for Africa. This style, which aimed at liberating jazz from all musical constraints, stimulated a major controversy in the jazz scene of the 1960s. In September 1967, as a result of a series of internal consultations by the jazz subcommittee, Hugh Masekela and Ornette Coleman were selected as candidates.[31] Of the two, Masekela showed some hesitation in assuming the responsibility due to his pre-arranged touring schedule. Curiously, no contact was made with Coleman, despite being a leading figure in free jazz. This was because, according to a jazz subcommittee member, "various reports had been heard that he was too 'far out' musically for African audiences." To this, it was noted, "Panel members vehemently disagreed." The subcommittee itself gave Coleman a uniformly high evaluation. According to the chair John Wilson, Coleman was "one of the top jazz people in the world today," affecting a "major influence on the mainstream of contemporary jazz." He went on to say that if the State Department problematized his personality or other similar issues around him for nominating him for Africa, "that is all right, but it doesn't make sense to reject anyone on musical grounds." On his part, Gunther Schuller, while admitting that Coleman "had had a violent start in this business and was a controversial figure," confirmed that there was no doubt about his position in the American jazz scene. Conover introduced him as "better known" in Eastern Europe than John Coltrane. Coleman was, Conover insisted, "most accessible," and at the same time "a kind of Messianic type who will make friends, a very original person, a philosopher and a real Christian who will overwhelm with the forcefulness of his personality."[32] The speculation that Coleman would be interested in an African tour also raised the subcommittee members' hopes. Accordingly, the subcommittee unanimously decided to re-recommend him for the position of jazz ambassador. However, the State Department was unyielding and would not concede to sending free-jazz musicians to Africa – of any ilk. "Ornette Coleman has been recommended for sophisticated areas and even Africa, but the Department has turned him down as being too far out." The State Department's concern for Coleman was clearly serious and this was not about to change.[33]

The rise of Black Power, which had been promoting free jazz as "black music," arguably underscored the State Department's wariness of this latest style of jazz. The existence of people who interpreted free jazz as a voice of resistance from the American periphery, such as poet and critic Amiri Baraka (formerly LeRoi Jones), was clearly a key concern for the State Department.[34] They saw sending free jazz to Africa as a double-edged sword – it could potentially backfire as a severe criticism of America in a greater way than it could promote ties with Africa.

Herman, Weston and the problem of the gap in interpretation

While discussions over who to send to Africa continued until the middle of the 1960s, two jazz ambassadors were sent to the region. Their visits provide important perspectives on the problem of evaluating the external value of jazz.

The first was clarinetist (and saxophonist) Woody Herman. Immediately after Duke Ellington's visit to Senegal in early April 1966, he carried out a two-month long African tour with 17 other musicians. Originally he was scheduled to visit the Soviet Union and Eastern Europe but due to the Soviet authorities canceling the visit, an additional African tour starting from Morocco was incorporated into the schedule at the last minute. Herman attracted fans with his swing-style jazz based on blues in his young days, but he also played modern jazz and had gained wide popularity. For the State Department, one crucial purpose behind sending Herman to Africa was to introduce "one of America's notable cultural developments – namely, its contribution to the history and growth of modern jazz."[35]

Soon after the tour started, a problem arose regarding for whom to perform the music. In the three performances at Rabat, Morocco, where Herman exchanged views with Gnawa musicians who played Moroccan folk music rooted in African spiritual traditions, half the audience at a performance and the jam session were white Europeans. This remained the same for the concerts held in Casablanca.[36] The color of the audience, coupled with the fact that Herman was white, gradually became a source of government concern as the tour subsequently went southward to sub-Saharan Africa. In other words, the State Department had to face the problem of race. In Tanzania's capital Dar es Salaam, where the Herman band was forced to play with substitute instruments since the alto saxophone and drum set did not arrive, the audience was generally dominated by governing elites and white Europeans due to the high price of tickets. The performance in Tanga, a city facing the Indian Ocean, also saw predominantly white Europeans (80 percent), while in Mwanza on the shore of Lake Victoria, around half the audience was European.[37] In Uganda, at the performances in the capital city of Kampala, the European audience was about half, and at the southeastern city of Jinja, the African audience was still a minority (40 percent). The scenery changed for a concert held at a university of education. The audience was dominated by local Africans, who were fascinated with the 90-minute performance focusing on the history of jazz. The US ambassador Olcott Deming was delighted that Herman's performance attracted "sizable African audiences," compared with the "Soviet Variety Show" that had once performed in front of primarily "white and Asian audiences." According to Deming, a pianist sent from the British Council "performed for largely a European group," while a string quartet from France and a singer from West Germany entertained "merely a handful of Africans."[38] The notable points of his reporting were two-fold – not only that America was faced with increasing competition from other Western countries in the field of cultural diplomacy, but also that the State Department was extremely sensitive to the racial makeup of African audiences.

There was a reason behind this concern. At the end of April, the Associated Press reported that audiences for Herman's performances in Morocco, Tanzania and Uganda were mostly made up of white Europeans. Somewhat irked at this story, the State Department immediately ordered the US embassies in these countries to fact-check the story, soon discovering the Associated Press had been incorrect in its initial reporting. Following this incident, the State Department issued a policy directive to its missions stating how to deal with news agencies. In this official guidance, the color-blind discourse regarding audience composition was reaffirmed, stipulating that the Cultural Presentations Program was "open to all audiences without regard to race, creed, or color."[39] Although this document problematized the ratio of Africans in attendance and sought to address it forthrightly, the problem was not completely solved. In Leopoldville, the Democratic Republic of the Congo, many Africans gathered for the American jazz performance at a local university, but the performance at a local zoo mainly attracted white Europeans. The four performances in the city of Elisabethville in Katanga province were free of charge, in order to increase the ratio of Africans in the audience, but it turned out that most of the audience were white Europeans except for the governor Godefroid Munongo – who was rumored to be involved in the assassination of local political rival Patrice Lumumba six years previously – and some of his supporters.[40]

Despite the initial objectives around sending Herman to Africa, some American officials even doubted the aesthetic sense of Africans, and thereby jazz's strategic advantage on the continent – a serious problem in the context of evaluating the external value of the music as a tool of American cultural diplomacy. The US consul in Elisabethville, Arthur T. Tienken, expressed some skepticism in noting that "modern American jazz is not readily understood by the mass of African listeners." Therefore, according to Tienken, if the State Department hoped to reach the "heart and minds of the mass of Africans, it will have to, at least here, look for other means." His reporting went on to say that the Congolese, who responded with eyes instead of ears, were excited by the movement of Herman on the stage, as well as flashing lights and a saxophonist's stepping instead of modern jazz, and therefore, they would be probably more interested in performances by magicians or dancers. For Tienken, as most of the Congolese people usually had little in the way of entertainment, they were not prepared "to accept such sophisticated cultural fare at this point in time."[41] An escort officer, who attended all Herman's performances, suggested sending a small combo for a variety show in the future, because the more Herman moved around the stage, the more the audience became excited, and because "straight orchestra playing and solo work does not have a visual impact and the audience tires sooner than it should."[42] Therefore, Herman's African tour was testimony to the existence of orientalistic views about Africa in the minds of some State Department officials in the mid-1960s. Significantly, these views were in marked contrast to what the well-known musicologist had warned while sitting on the Music Advisory Panel three years earlier – that is, sending an entertainment group "might be the worst thing you can do."[43]

If the Herman tour reignited the debate about the strategic value of jazz in Africa, as well as the persistent notion of color-blind Americanism among State Department officials, the African tour by pianist Randy Weston problematized once again the gap in American perceptions over the external value of jazz. For three months from January 1967, Weston visited 27 cities in 14 countries located mainly in West Africa. The main goal of his tour for the State Department was to "show that American jazz has evolved from African roots." Unlike the case of Herman, the promotion of jazz emphasizing African-ness was manifest in the composition of the band. The six foot eight inch-tall pianist Weston led the band, which also included trumpeter Ray Copeland, tenor saxophonist Clifford Jordan, bassist Bill Wood, drummer Ed Blackwell and the African drummer Chief Bey: they were all African Americans.[44]

Weston was a natural choice for the State Department. He had visited Nigeria twice in 1961 and 1963 to perform and to present a lecture for the American Society for African Culture. There he was strongly impressed with the diversity of African music when co-starring with local musicians. His deep personal interest in African culture and music was widely known, as evidenced by his albums *Uhuru Afrika* (1960) and *African Cookbook* (1964). Often participating in workshops at the United Nations (UN) Jazz Society, established by UN officials in 1959, he had been inspired by a young scholar from Tanganyika who advocated the possibility of making Swahili a common language for Africa, which later led Weston to compose a song about Uhuru (Uhuru means freedom in Swahili).[45]

For Weston, therefore, jazz was more than a music for representing "America." He was conscious of a more transnational and lively relationship between jazz and African music. Prior to departure, he explained to State Department officials his own philosophy of music by categorizing his songs into five groups – "Africa," "Children," "Nature," "Spiritual" and "Portraits of People." Among these, Weston described his songs categorized in "Africa" as part of himself and his music. "African Cookbook," "Congolese Children," "A Night in Mbari" and "Blues to Africa," for instance, used African rhythm, arranged African music, or were composed in retrospect based on his previous stay in Nigeria. In particular, he specified "African Cookbook" as symbolizing his thinking on the influence of African music on his own jazz style.[46]

During the tour, "African Cookbook" became useful for emphasizing the musical and cultural ties between jazz and Africa. Later, Weston recalled that his African tour "was a very successful one" not least because, he believed, there was a "real rapport established with our audiences."[47] In Mali, after "African Cookbook" was played at the climax of the performance, inviting a thunderous audience reaction, young fans rushed over to the stage and then to his dressing room asking for his autograph.[48] When Weston appeared at the Ghana Arts Festival and the University of Ghana, the final number, "African Cookbook," continued for 45 minutes, with the audience mesmerized until the end.[49] His performance in Gabon was another good example of a strong bond formed between his band and the audience. At an informal concert held for cabinet members of the ruling party, the Minister of Public Works referred to members of the Weston band as "our brothers." The atmosphere was best depicted by a local daily newspaper that reported: "It was an evening of authentic jazz, recreated at its source, with an African rhythm which at times was soft as a moan, and at other times was violent or trembling like a mob, and born of a magic tamtam." The reporting by US ambassador David M. Bane acknowledged this as proof that the State Department's original goal of identifying America with Africa had been achieved, which in reality contrasted very sharply with Weston's interpretation of the tour.[50]

The contrasting interpretations regarding the external value of Weston's African tour were also apparent in remarks by US ambassadors stationed across the region. First of all, Weston's search for the origin of jazz in Africa was generally overlooked by State Department officials, deemed somewhat unimportant at best in their minds. During his stay in Dakar, the US ambassador earnestly asked Weston at a reception why he would not perform in a racially mixed band. According to an escort officer in attendance, this "strange observation" created "a few delicate moments," obviously embarrassing Weston.[51] Secondly, there was a hint of orientalism in some embassy officials' perceptions of Africa. The US ambassador in Niger assessed Weston's musical ability most favorably, but believed that "This sophisticated jazz, although perhaps derived from African sounds or rhythms, is too advanced and cerebral to be meaningful to many Africans." Moreover, like during the Herman tour, this ambassador advocated the use of variety shows – including rock music, balloon arts, puppet shows and jugglers – as having a greater impact on local Africans. Probably with Weston and his sometimes "far out" performances in mind – despite his being no fan of avant-garde jazz – the official complained that over-confident and independent-minded musicians tended not to change their program according to the audience's interests. When Weston's manager heard these complaints from US embassy officials, she angrily retorted that these comments were nothing short of "colonialist."[52]

It was rather the African local press that showed a solid understanding of Weston's jazz. *Le Journal d'Égypte* introduced Weston as determined to preserve the purity of jazz. According to the press, he turned to its roots "in order to safeguard its authenticity." The press also praised his music as sprung out of "pure jazz" that was characterized by "the permanent and fundamental dualism between tension and relaxation." Regarding the concert program, which could reportedly lose an audience's attention – a notable criticism by US diplomats – there was distinct sympathy in that they saw Weston's search for authentic jazz as being "pursued without any concession – or playing down – to the public."[53] In addition, the Algerian government newspaper *El Moudjahid* supported the incorporation in Weston's repertoire of "many pieces composed with Africa in mind, often based directly on African melodies collected during his extensive tours." In this sense, Weston, according to the newspaper, followed the same course Charlie Parker, Dizzy Gillespie, Art Blakey and Max Roach had taken earlier.[54] Furthermore, *An Nasr* also explicitly approved of Weston's attempts to play many numbers which had an African origin.[55]

Put differently, the local press in Africa shared much the same interpretation of jazz as Weston did, and certainly understood it better than the State Department officials. They simultaneously represented and appreciated Weston's ideas on jazz. Indeed, Weston himself problematized this gap in interpretation between inside and outside America when he stressed: "it would not only be expedient to utilize this music fully, but it might also help jazz gain the stature and acceptance on its native soil – the United States, where it is not really accepted as a creative art form – while it was being used to further goodwill abroad." His dissatisfaction with the social standing of jazz in America was obvious. He complained that rarely was jazz played at an arts center like the Lincoln Center, with his sentiment shown below.

> I feel that I should emphasize this lack of acceptance very strongly, because although jazz is included in the State Department Cultural Presentations program, that is the one exception to a general rule whereby jazz is *not* included as part of the normally accepted cultural life in this country.
> [emphasis in original]

Importantly, for Weston, jazz's external value was closely intertwined with its domestic social value. Weston expected that with the State Department continuing to use jazz as a central pillar of America's externally focused cultural diplomacy, this would inevitably lead to an improvement in the status of jazz inside America.[56]

His comments revisited the decade-old question regarding what "America" actually meant in the jazz ambassadors program. Weston's interpretation of jazz was closely related to his expectation for social change in his home country. Questioned in Algiers by "two twenty-year olds" why he could play jazz as an African American when mass slaughter was occurring in Vietnam, he retorted:

> War, man, is a drag. There isn't just one Vietnam – there are lots of them, we have them in Mississippi, in Alabama and in the North. We're not just mouthing about them – we're trying to do something about them. You can't just mouth – you've got to *do* something – are *you*?
> [emphasis in original]

Weston arguably uttered the word "we" as a means of associating violence in Vietnam with the ongoing Black Power struggle at home. In this vein, Weston

80 *The politics behind the selection process*

hoped to position jazz not as a tool of diplomacy per se but as a tool for promoting social change, as well as a catalyst to narrow the gap between American ideals and reality.[57]

When understanding that Weston's interpretation of jazz contained a sense of criticism directed at American reality, it becomes possible to find the same critical discourse of jazz outside America. It was an alternative discourse to the color-blind Americanism officials worked hard to promulgate abroad in its cultural diplomacy programs. In postwar France, with the social position of jazz somewhat higher than in America, jazz eventually took on an anti-American tone. In West Germany, where a process of making a clean break with the past through national reconstruction saw the commencement of its own jazz ambassadors program, jazz's American-ness became arguably diluted on the global stage. A search for a national jazz style was also found in postwar Japan. The next chapter explores the role of such de-Americanized jazz discourses, which conveniently provide us with a set of fresh perspectives that are implicitly or explicitly critical of the roots of jazz.

Notes

1 Recent studies have argued the relationship between the Cold War and the civil rights movement. See for example, Brenda Gayle Plummer, *Rising Wind: Black Americans and U.S. Foreign Affairs, 1935–1960* (Chapel Hill: University of North Carolina Press, 1996); Mary L. Dudziak, *Cold War Civil Rights: Race and the Image of American Democracy* (Princeton: Princeton UP, 2000); Azza Salama Layton, *International Politics and Civil Rights Policies in the United States, 1941–1960* (Cambridge: Cambridge UP, 2000); Thomas Borstelmann, *The Cold War and the Color Line: American Race Relations in the Global Arena* (Cambridge: Harvard UP, 2003); Brenda Gayle Plummer (ed.), *Window on Freedom: Race, Civil Rights, and Foreign Affairs, 1945–1988* (Chapel Hill: University of North Carolina Press, 2003).
2 Paul F. Berliner, *Thinking in Jazz: The Infinite Art of Improvisation* (Chicago: University of Chicago Press, 1994), p.417, quoted in Jennifer Fay, "'That's Jazz Made in Germany!': Hallo, Fräulein! and the Limits of Democratic Pedagogy," *Cinema Journal*, vol.44 no.1, 2004, p.13.
3 Ingrid Monson, *Saying Something: Jazz Improvisation and Interaction* (Chicago: Chicago UP, 1996), pp.199–203; Eric Porter, *What Is This Thing Called Jazz?: African American Musicians as Artists, Critics, and Activists* (Berkeley: University of California Press, 2002), p.110.
4 NARA, RG 59, CDF 1955–59, Box 93, 032 Armstrong, Louis, "Educational Exchange: President's Fund: Louis Armstrong's Band," 29 February 1956.
5 NARA, RG 59, CDF 1955–59, Box 93, 032 Armstrong, Louis, Thayer to Dulles, 19 July 1957.
6 Charles Hersch details the festivity in the life philosophy and music of Armstrong, which also contained a revolutionary element for subverting the existing segregated order. See Charles Hersch, "Poisoning Their Coffee: Louis Armstrong and Civil Rights," *Polity*, vol.34 no.3, 2002.
7 US Department of State (ed.), *FRUS, 1955–1957, Volume IX, Foreign Economic Policy; Foreign Information Program* (Washington, DC: Government Printing Office, 1987), p.613; "Memorandum of a Telephone Conversation Between the Secretary of State and the Attorney General (Brownell), Washington, September 24, 1957, 2:15 p.m.," 24 September 1957; Kaplan, "When Ambassadors Had Rhythm"; Dudziak,

Cold War Civil Rights, pp.130–40; Jeff Woods, *Black Struggle, Red Scare: Segregation and Anti-Communism in the South, 1948–1968* (Baton Rouge: Louisiana State UP, 2003), pp.68–69. See also Von Eschen, *Satchmo Blows Up the World*, pp.63–64; Davenport, *Jazz Diplomacy*, pp.63–66.

8 NARA, RG 59, CDF 1955–59, Box 93, 032 Armstrong, Louis, Murphy to Kane, 21 September 1957; Highland II to Morton, 26 September 1957.

9 NARA, RG 59, CDF 1955–59, Box 93, 032 Armstrong, Louis, Case to Hoghland II, 14 October 1957; Meagher to Ziegler, 30 October 1957.

10 NARA, RG 59, CDF 1955–59, Box 93, 032 Armstrong, Louis, "Visit of Louis Armstrong to Buenos Aires," 21 November 1957; "Visit of Louis (Satchmo) Armstrong to Brazil," 5 December 1957; "Educational Exchange: Visit of Louis (Satchmo) Armstrong to Brazil," 20 December 1957. For Armstrong's tour in South America, see also Von Eschen, *Satchmo Blows Up the World*, p.65.

11 NARA, RG 59, CDF 1960–63, Box 28, 032 Armstrong, Louis Band, "Cultural Presentations: Pepsi-Cola Brought Us Louis Armstrong," 19 October 1960. For Armstrong's African tour in general, see also Von Eschen, *Satchmo Blows Up the World*, pp.67–73; Davenport, *Jazz Diplomacy*, pp.85–86. It should be noted, however, that later in 1963, the State Department official Glenn G. Wolfe questioned Armstrong's external value in forming ties with people in some parts of Africa during a meeting of the Music Advisory Panel. According to Wolfe, "In Central Africa we have an area that knows nothing but the beat, rhythm and missionary hymns. They feel we adapted jazz from their music so this becomes extremely popular in that area. The fact that we sent them Louis Armstrong was a great compliment and they came by the thousands to see him, but then they walked away. His music did not mean anything to them." CU, Box 100-23, "U.S. Department of State, Bureau of Educational and Cultural Affairs, Office of Cultural Presentations, Music Panel Meeting, Wednesday, July 24, 1963, 10:30 A.M. – New York City," undated.

12 NARA, RG 59, CDF 1960–63, Box 28, 032 Armstrong, Louis Band, Dean to Harter, 22 October 1960.

13 CU, Box 47-21, Demicheal to Battle, 25 February 1963.

14 CU, Box 100-6, "Music Advisory Panel Meeting, International Cultural Exchange Service of ANTA, March 26, 1963–2:30 P.M.," undated.

15 For the different role the Advisory Committee on the Arts and the Music Advisory Panel of ANTA played, see Danielle Fosler-Lussier, *Music in America's Cold War Diplomacy*, pp.9–10. For more on ANTA and the Music Advisory Panel, see Emily Abrams Ansari, "Shaping the Policies of Cold War Musical Diplomacy: An Epistemic Community of American Composers," *Diplomatic History*, vol.36 no.1, 2012.

16 CU, Box 100-23, "U.S. Department of State, Bureau of Educational and Cultural Affairs, Office of Cultural Presentations, Music Panel Meeting, Wednesday, April 24, 1963, 10:00 A.M. – Washington, D.C.," undated; "U.S. Department of State, Bureau of Educational and Cultural Affairs, Office of Cultural Presentations, Music Panel Meeting, Wednesday, July 24, 1963, 10:30 A.M. – New York City," undated.

17 Ibid. See also Davenport, *Jazz Diplomacy*, pp.98–99.

18 CU, Box 95-16, "Summary of Minutes of Meeting Held in Washington, D.C., March 16, 1966," undated.

19 NARA, RG 59, CDF 1955–59, Box 94, 032 Baker, Josephine, Dulles to the American Embassy, Paris, 4 November 1958; Dudziak, *Cold War Civil Rights*, pp.67–77.

20 CU, Box 100-23, "U.S. Department of State, Bureau of Educational and Cultural Affairs, Office of Cultural Presentations, Music Panel Meeting, Wednesday, April 24, 1963, 10:00 A.M. – Washington, D.C.," undated. See also CU, Box 49-15, "Cultural Presentations Plan, FY 1966," undated.

21 CU, Box 50-17, "A Brief Documentary Report on United States Participation in the First World Festival of Negro Arts," August 1966; Box 61-7, "Duke Ellington, Africa, March 31 – April 9, 1966," undated; Cook to Rusk, 12 April 1966; Jeremy

F. Lane, *Jazz and Machine-Age Imperialism: Music, "Race," and Intellectuals in France, 1918–1945* (Ann Arbor: University of Michigan Press, 2013), pp.111–25. For Ellington's performance in Senegal, see also Von Eschen, *Satchmo Blows Up the World*, pp.150–60.
22 Edward Kennedy Ellington, *Music Is My Mistress* (New York: Da Capo, 1976), pp.308–9, 338–39. See also Von Eschen, *Satchmo Blows Up the World*, pp.123–35.
23 Nat Hentoff, "This Cat Needs Not Pulitzer Prize," *The New York Times Magazine*, 12 September 1965, reproduced in Mark Tucker (ed.), *The Duke Ellington Reader* (Oxford: Oxford UP, 1995), p.363; Harvey G. Cohen, *Duke Ellington's America* (Chicago: University of Chicago Press, 2011), pp.494–96.
24 Leonard Garment, *Crazy Rhythm: From Brooklyn and Jazz to Nixon's White House, Watergate, and Beyond* (Cambridge: Da Capo Press, 2001), pp.171–79; Leonard Garment, "Music; A New Revelation from the Nixon White House," *The New York Times*, 25 August 2002.
25 Cohen, *Duke Ellington's America*, pp.508–9.
26 CU, Box 100-26, "Jazz and Fork Unites Approved but not Sent Abroad under the Cultural Presentations Program," undated.
27 CU, Box 47-27, "Summary of Minutes of Meeting Held in New York, N.Y., December 12, 1966," undated.
28 Ibid.
29 CU, Box 101-4, "Sub-Panel on Falk Music and Jazz, Wednesday, May 21, 1969, Washington D.C. 10:30 A.M.," undated.
30 Ibid.; CU, Box 101-3, "Sub-Committee on Falk Music and Jazz, Tuesday, Monday, April 29, 1968 10:00 A.M. Washington D.C.," undated.
31 Masekela, born in South Africa and moved to America after the Sharpeville massacre in 1960, played both in Africa and America. For the South African jazz scene under the apartheid era, see Gwen Ansell, *Soweto Blues: Jazz, Popular Music, and Politics in South Africa* (London: Bloomsbury Academic, 2004).
32 CU, Box 101-3, "Sub-Committee on Jazz Meeting, Wednesday, August 30, 1967 – New York City," undated.
33 CU, Box 101-4, "Sub-Panel on Falk Music and Jazz, Wednesday, May 27, 1970, 9:45 A.M., Washington D.C.," undated; Box 101-3, "Sub-Committee on Jazz, Friday, May 12, 1967, 3:00 P.M. – New York City," undated. John Coltrane was selected as a candidate for an East Asia tour by the subcommittee as well as the Advisory Committee, but it never materialized due to his death on 17 July 1967.
34 LeRoi Jones, *Blues People: Negro Music in White America* (New York: William Morrow, 1963). See also Anderson, *This Is Our Music*, pp.93–121.
35 CU, Box 66-10, "Educational and Cultural Exchange: Cultural Presentations: Visit of Woody Herman and His Orchestra," 1 June 1966.
36 CU, Box 66-10, AmEmbassy Rabat to SecState WashDC, 28 April 1966; USIS Rabat to USIA Washington, 11 May 1966; AmConsul Elisabethville to SecState WashDC, 28 April 1966.
37 CU, Box 66-10, Sudrow to Ellison, 16 and 18 April 1966; AmConsul Elisabethville to SecState WashDC, 28 April 1966.
38 CU, Box 66-10, AmEmbassy Kampala to SecState WashDC, 28 April 1966; "Educational and Cultural Exchange: Cultural Presentations: Visit of Woody Herman and His Orchestra," 1 June 1966.
39 CU, Box 66-10, Ellison to Frankel and Howland, 10 May 1966; "AP Story on Woody Herman in Africa," 27 April 1966; Lisa Davenport, "Jazz and the Cold War," in Darlene Clark Hine and Jacqueline McLeod (eds.), *Crossing Boundaries: Comparative History of Black People in Diaspora* (Bloomington: Indiana UP, 2001), p.294. For the audience problem in Herman's African tour, see also Von Eschen, *Satchmo Blows Up the World*, pp.169–70.
40 CU, Box 66-10, AmConsul Elisabethville to Department of State, 3 May 1966.

41 CU, Box 66-10, American Embassy Leopoldville to Department of State, 26 May 1966; AmConsul Elisabethville to Department of State, 3 May 1966.
42 CU, Box 66-10, Sudrow to Ellison, 29 April 1966. See also Von Eschen, *Satchmo Blows Up the World*, pp.169.
43 CU, Box 100-23, "U.S. Department of State, Bureau of Educational and Cultural Affairs, Office of Cultural Presentations, Music Panel Meeting, Wednesday, July 24, 1963, 10:30 A.M. – New York City," undated.
44 CU, Box 49-2, "Annual Report of the Cultural Presentations Program, Department of State for the Year July 1, 1966 to June 30, 1967," January 1968.
45 Kelley, *Africa Speaks, America Answers*, pp.55–70, 78–79.
46 CU, Box 84-25, "Background Material on Compositions to Be Used in Regular Concerts – Randy Weston," 6 December 1966.
47 CU, Box 85-3, "Report from Randy Weston on State Department Tour of West and North Africa (1/16/67–4/11/67)," undated.
48 CU, Box 85-3, AmEmbassy Bamako to Department of State/CU, 22 February 1967.
49 CU, Box 85-3, AmEmbassy, Accra to Department of State, 1 June 1967.
50 CU, Box 85-3, "Report from Randy Weston on State Department Tour of West and North Africa (1/16/67–4/11/67)," undated; AmEmbassy, Libreville to Department of State, 5 June 1967.
51 CU, Box 84-25, Hirsch to Ellison, 22 January 1967.
52 CU, Box 85-1, AmEmbassy Niamey to Department of State, 11 February 1967; Georgia Griggs, "With Randy Weston in Africa," *Down Beat*, vol.34 no.14, 13 July 1967. See also Von Eschen, *Satchmo Blows Up the World*, pp.172–74; Kelley, *Africa Speaks, America Answers*, pp.81, 86–88.
53 CU, Box 85-3, "A Climate of Pure Jazz with the Randy Weston Sextet," *Le Journal d'Egypte*, translated, 3 April 1967.
54 CU, Box 84-26, "Randy Weston in Algiers," *El Moudjahid*, translated, 4 April 1967.
55 CU, Box 84-26, "African Jazz – Something New!," *An Nasr*, translated, 4 April 1967.
56 CU, Box 85-3, "Report from Randy Weston on State Department Tour of West and North Africa (1/16/67–4/11/67)," undated.
57 CU, Box 84-26, AmEmbassy Algiers to Department of State, 13 April 1967. In her analysis of Weston's African tour, Von Eschen argues that Weston's usage of "we" refers to ordinary people who were doing something to oppose the war. See Von Eschen, *Satchmo Blows Up the World*, pp.170–76, especially pp.175–76. Still, Von Eschen stresses that for some people freedom was an aspiration and not what had been achieved. See ibid., p.71. See also Kelley, *Africa Speaks, America Answers*, p.6.

5 Anti-Americanism in the Western jazz discourse

After Europe was liberated from Nazi occupation, "America" flowed into Europe on an unprecedented scale. The devastation brought by the Second World War facilitated a sharp increase in the American presence there. However, it also strengthened in some corners of Europe a grass-roots opposition to Americanization, which itself had existed since the eighteenth century. Thus, while the owner of *Life* and *Time* magazines Henry Luce described the twentieth century as the American century in 1941, it was also the century of anti-Americanism.[1] Western Europe relied on America for its reconstruction and security as an "empire by invitation," best manifested in the Marshall Plan (the Europe Recovery Program) and the North Atlantic Treaty. But in the socio-cultural arena, America was seen differently, as an "uninvited empire."[2]

Some leftist Western intellectuals shared with the Soviet propagandists a typical view of America as a depraved capitalist state devoid of culture. In order to win the cultural Cold War, America needed a weapon for publicizing its accomplishments in such fields as modern art, performing arts and music. Thus, to take an example, 13,000 people and US$129 million was spent in 1953 on winning the hearts and minds of mostly intellectuals in Western Europe.[3] In this context, the US government engaged in a range of covert cultural operations. A good example was the Congress for Cultural Freedom (CCF). The CCF was a CIA-funded organization and was headquartered in Paris. With prominent philosophers – such as Bertrand Russell, Karl Jaspers and Benedetto Croce – as honorary presidents, the CCF mobilized intellectuals and cultural figures in promoting social and cultural ties among people in the Western world through exhibitions, music festivals and other similar events. It also emphasized that Western intellectual and cultural freedom was superior to socialist realism. Of various events the CCF organized, one of the largest was the Masterpieces of the Twentieth Century festival, which took place in 1952. It was a magnificent art festival held in Paris, where ballet, opera, and classical music concerts were carried out for a full month. The festival was under the direction of the CCF's executive secretary Nicolas Nabokov, an accomplished composer and immigrant from Russia. The anti-Communist character of the festival was shown when Nabokov strongly urged an orchestra to play two pieces – one was "Finlandia" by Jean Sibelius, then referred to as a symbol of courage and resistance, and the other was "Lady Macbeth of the Mtsensk

District" by Dmitri Shostakovich, which had been condemned earlier by the Soviet authorities as bourgeois and decadent.[4]

During this period of the cultural Cold War, it was an unexpected win for the US government when young Texan pianist Van Cliburn took first prize at the Tchaikovsky Competition in Moscow in April 1958. Shortly after, a congratulatory message from President Eisenhower was delivered to Cliburn.[5] Cliburn could certainly boast of being popular in Western Europe. Immediately after his win at the Competition, Cliburn's Paris performance was held at the Palais de Chaillot. One public affairs officer in the US embassy in France reported with excitement that the kind of ovation that was normally given to Soviet troupes was this time given to an American for probably the first time in history. Cliburn also appeared at the Brussels World's Fair with pianist Byron Janis and violinist Isaac Stern. More than satisfied with his popularity, John Clifford Folger, the US ambassador in Belgium, admired him as possessing great flair and éclat. However, Cliburn's reputation offstage was less than stellar, with the ambassador sometimes at a loss with the problems caused by this "very young and a very high-strung" musician. At one time Cliburn demanded to play Rachmaninov rather than Tchaikovsky, and at another time he insisted on staying in the best suite in the Metropol hotel for him and his friends.[6] The US ambassador to Japan Douglas MacArthur II did not miss noticing this high-profile example of American high culture, urging Dulles to consider him performing in Japan. There was a sense of caution in the ambassador's mind that the Soviet cultural delegations to Japan overwhelmed those from the Western countries in terms of both quality and quantity. In Japan at that time, performances by American cultural delegations were relatively few compared with those by Soviet cultural figures such as David Oistrakh, Lev Oborin and the Leningrad Philharmonic Orchestra. Thus, America was on the defensive in the cultural Cold War in Japan. For MacArthur, Cliburn's performance would produce "tremendous success" with minimal expense. His Japan tour did not materialize for some time, but finally took place in 1966.[7]

In comparative terms, more American classical orchestras visited postwar Western Europe than anywhere in the world under the Cultural Presentations Program. These classical orchestras were tasked with selling the image that America was contributing to the world in the field of high culture. Instead, Western Europe rarely had a chance to directly see official American jazz ambassadors. This was because of the already high popularity of jazz, and the frequent commercial tours by well-known American jazz musicians. Curiously, however, this was the same place where critical jazz discourse emerged questioning the legitimacy of America as the sole claimant to the ownership of jazz. What is discussed below is how countries in the West saw this unique jazz discourse and how identity politics defined the meaning of the music.

"America" in the postwar jazz discourse in Western Europe

Though not formal jazz ambassadors, Norman Granz and the JATP troupe started their European tour in 1952. During their performances, however, the ideas of American freedom and democracy, which were believed to be embodied in the jazz ambassadors program of the 1950s, were not necessarily accepted by Europeans as such. A good example is a concert held in the Sistina Theater in Rome in June 1958, where musicians including Dizzy Gillespie, Stan Getz, Coleman Hawkins, Herb Ellis, Lou Levy, Max Bennett, Ray Brown, Roy Eldridge, Sonny Stitt, Pete Johnson and Joe Turner appeared. To such a high-quality performance littered with jazz stars, the audience reacted with mixed emotions of pure excitement, as well as a degree of disillusionment. The performance itself, although beginning one hour behind schedule, saw enthusiastic applause from fans at its conclusion. And yet, when fans requested an encore, Granz ignored this request and waited for silence, simply sitting on a chair on the stage. Responding to their demand for an encore, Gillespie played a short solo twice, but then the curtain came down and the concert abruptly ended. The unsatisfied audience, who had purchased these high-priced tickets, could only leave the theater with much frustration. According to *Il Tempo*, a local paper, Granz provocatively remarked that "The Roman public is stupid" and "You will have no more jazz concerts in Italy, because I am jazz," triggering a wave of local criticism. Locals were reportedly antagonized by "the hysterical American impresario," who was "absolutely ignorant of any rules of stage courtesy." When official jazz ambassadors were playing their part in the world representing "America," a reviewer of *Il Tempo* paid attention to "the value of jazz as an effective propaganda weapon, which when misused may become counter-productive." Ultimately, Granz became recognized as "an unworthy representative" of America. One week later, when Sarah Vaughan appeared at the same theater, many vacant seats were noticeable. This was seen by a local newspaper as the result of Granz's irresponsible behavior.[8]

In his conduct and remarks in Italy, we could observe a paternalistic pride in America as the roots of jazz. Nevertheless, fans and critics had not necessarily accepted "America" in jazz, contrary to the expectations held by the State Department. Indeed, there were various alternative interpretations as to what jazz represented in postwar Europe. And especially in France, where jazz fans were confident that they were appreciating jazz before Americans were, jazz came to function as a means of expressing criticisms against America, alongside empathy with African Americans.

In the country where nearly half of the public investment for the first five-year plan for reconstruction and modernization, the Monnet Plan, was financed under the Marshall Plan, America's economic presence could be hardly denied. Ironically, however, France was also the same country where criticism of the Marshall Plan was strongest. According to historian Tony Judt, only 38 percent of adults believed that America's reconstruction assistance was not a serious threat to France's independence in 1947. Even in the mid-1950s, barely one-third of adults had heard of the Marshall Plan, while 64 percent of them felt that the reconstruction assistance from America was a "bad" influence.[9] Among the many American products in Europe, Coca-Cola was arguably the most iconic American product, and thus a prominent target of hostility in postwar France. In 1947, the Coca-Cola Company started to build factories in Western Europe and expand its market share. When *Le Monde* reported that sales targets in France in 1950 amounted to 240 million bottles, the editorial declared that this problem had become "the Danzig of European culture," and deep concerns over "Coca-Colonization" spread widely across society.[10]

Although it seems to contradict such grass-roots sentiments about American culture, jazz was widely accepted in postwar France. For instance, the Festival International de Jazz was held in Paris in May 1949, which American musicians such as Kenny Clarke, Miles Davis, Charlie Parker, Sidney Bechet and Max Roach attended. The fact that an international jazz festival was organized in Paris, and not in an American city, symbolized the standing and importance of Paris as a hub of postwar global jazz. Indeed, large jazz festivals in America only took place after 1954, when the Newport Jazz Festival started. Curiously, relatively little was reported in America about the jazz festival in Paris. The *New York Times* covered Benny Goodman's London performances at around the same time as the festival in Paris was occurring, but the fact that many African American musicians were participating at the festival was not reported at all. This highlighted a significant gap over the perceived standing of African American musicians in the respective jazz scenes of France and America.[11]

One factor that encouraged the favorable interpretation of jazz in postwar France was empathy for African American musicians. In contrast to the concept of color-blind Americanism, jazz was interpreted in France as originating in the struggle for the abolition of segregation. While jazz's Frenchification advanced in the interwar years as detailed earlier, both fans and critics appreciated the contribution and originality of African American musicians in the development of jazz. Following the end of the war, fans, especially intellectuals, deepened their empathy with the segregated people of America, and took a firm stand against American racial problems. Although not all sympathized with Communism, they were usually close to leftist groups and ideals, and did not hide their anti-American attitudes in the books and articles they published. In this context, the jazz discourse in France turned into an intellectual weapon by which to criticize America. For example, the Jim Crow laws, lynching incidents involving African Americans, and the civil rights movement, all became themes that jazz magazines and radio programs frequently reported on inside France. *Jazz Hot* highlighted Louis Armstrong's criticism of President Eisenhower during the Little Rock crisis. The same journal accused the New York city police of initiating a "brutal attack" when Miles Davis's cabaret card was revoked by the police. Other journals reported on poor financial rewards for talented African American musicians, as well as lost revenue over concert cancelations for the Brubeck quartet because its membership included African American bassist Eugene Wright. The arrest of Granz and his musicians by the Houston city police, dubbed "the enemies of freedom between blacks and whites" by jazz fans, was also widely reported. Therefore, as in America during the civil rights era, jazz in France became part of a protest movement that appealed for justice from outside America.[12] But for white American jazz musicians, to recognize African American musicians as the true creators and practitioners of jazz was to effectively reverse the logic of Jim Crow. During his European tour with the JATP musicians, Granz was puzzled by this idea of "reverse racism."[13] For Granz, assuming that legitimacy of African American jazz musicians came about simply because of skin color, actually equated to practicing the ideas of Jim Crow.

It is well-known that Jean-Paul Sartre and Simone de Beauvoir accepted jazz as embodying Existentialist thought, while criticizing America through *Les Temps modernes*. In Sartre's *Nausea*, an important role was given to jazz recordings for rescuing the protagonist, who felt nauseated when he understood the bare existence of things. Boris Vian was one who was at the intellectual and cultural center of Saint-Germain-des-Prés, introducing Charlie Parker and Miles Davis – then visiting the Festival International de Jazz – to Sartre. In his hardboiled novel *I Spit on Your Graves*, written in 1946, Vian criticized racial segregation in America through his compassionate phrases and sentences about jazz. Above all, for Vian, jazz was not "American music" promoting racial integration, but a weapon for suppressed people to employ, and only in that sense could jazz be a music for freedom. Jazz must never be interpreted as embodying American values – jazz had to be a possession of the weak, in this line of thought.[14]

It is important that jazz, born at the periphery of America, was here understood as a symbol of protest, because this enabled the French to compare the postwar standing of France in global politics with that of African Americans in America. This is to say that empathy for African Americans was not unrelated to postwar France society's self-recognition of its relative standing in a global arena. When the new hegemon was exercising its global influence as the guarantor for Western defense and reconstruction, France was facing harsh realities over its unceremonious withdrawal from its colonial empire. The fact that Charles de Gaulle pursued *grandeur* of France after returning to power in 1958 should be understood as a symbolic act of protest in response to the new global reality facing France as a former great power in relative decline. Although the political positions of jazz fans and de Gaulle were obviously opposite, they shared frustrations about the different roles given to France and America in the postwar world.

Imperial nostalgia

If, behind the jazz discourse of postwar France, there was a domestic consciousness of still being a great power – most vividly revealed in the Suez crisis of 1956 – the situation was similar in another declining empire, Britain.[15] As superpower relations started to define global politics from the late 1940s, Britain's role in the world had also declined, manifestly shown by the Suez crisis. Important in this context is the fact that the revival of trad jazz (New Orleans jazz) reached its high point in Britain at around the same time as these geopolitical realities were being acknowledged. When modern jazz was setting the trend in the American jazz scene following the rise of bebop, British society saw a new trend that had been seen once before during the interwar period. In one sense, what the trad jazz revival reflected in Britain was a reminiscence of a past empire, in which jazz performed an analgesic role, when faced with the reality of terminal imperial decline. Still, it would be insufficient to simply point out that a retreat from empire was behind the British jazz scene of the 1950s, without also discussing the role of political activism and politics more broadly. Jazz, like in France, was a fellow traveler of the political left.

Although the anti-American tone in postwar British society is believed to have been relatively modest compared to other West European countries, there was nonetheless an aversion to the American Cold War strategy, as well as some skepticism toward capitalism among Britain's leftist politicians and intellectuals. In his essay, published in the American literary quarterly *Partisan Review*, George Orwell critically remarked that there was no future in capitalism, while lamenting that the construction of the Socialist United States of Europe was almost unforeseen. Regarding culture, Orwell expressed concern over "how deep the American influence has already gone." Writer J. B. Priestley, on his part, condemned the society around him that, in his eyes, had been dominated by mass advertising, terming it "Admass." Whereas Richard Hoggart, author of *The Uses of Literacy: Aspects of Working-Class Life*, was critical that working-class culture was being lost to large inflows of American culture. Meanwhile, in the 1950s, a group of writers and playwrights, called the Angry Young Men, began to pay attention to working-class life, denying modernist literature and poetry as highbrow. It is quite suggestive that some of the leading figures among them, such as Kingsley Amis and Philip Larkin, loved jazz. The point here is that it was trad jazz rather than modern jazz that they liked to listen to. Therefore, it is no coincidence that in John Osborne's play *Look Back in Anger*, written in 1956, the protagonist played trad jazz on his trumpet.[16] Eric Hobsbawm's *The Jazz Scene*, published in 1959, was also an attempt to re-read jazz in the context of Marxist orthodoxy.[17]

In this regard, the relationship between the Campaign for Nuclear Disarmament (CND) and jazz is symbolic. The first British thermonuclear bombs were tested in 1957. In the same year, the British government decided to deploy 60 Thor medium-range nuclear missiles in East Anglia to keep up with the nuclear arms race that was playing out between the superpowers. Following changes in the political environment around nuclear weapons at both domestic and international levels, a large march took place from central London to Aldermaston, where Britain's main nuclear research facilities were located. The Aldermaston March coincided with the birth of the CND, with both events enjoying sympathetic support from the British Labour Party. This anti-nuclear peace movement was imbued with performances by various jazz bands. Besides the CND's posters, publicity booklets and badges were omnipresent at the many sites where jazz festivals were being held.[18]

The coexistence of conservativeness and progressiveness in the trad jazz revival in postwar Britain revealed two things – what Britain had lost in the postwar world and the difficulty it had in coping with that reality. As historian A. J. P. Taylor recalls, the CND was able to take the moral high ground by creating some distance in its ideology between nuclear weapons and America. However, in the vain expectation that Britain could still maintain its global influence as a major power by being morally right, Taylor later lamented, "Ironically we were the last Imperialists."[19]

To psychologically compensate for lost or declining national power is a motif repeated in the history of global politics when a declining power faces a rising power. Harold Macmillan, later becoming Prime Minister after the Suez crisis, told Richard Crossman, a future Labour Party heavyweight, in 1943 when they were at the Allied Forces Headquarters (AFHQ) in Algiers:

> We, my dear Crossman, are Greeks in this American Empire. You will find the Americans much as the Greeks found the Romans – great big, vulgar, bustling people, more vigorous than we are and also more idle, with more unspoiled virtues, but also more corrupt. We must run AFHQ as the Greek slaves ran the operations of the Emperor Claudius.[20]

Comparing the wisdom of ancient Greece to contemporary Europe, on the one hand, and the Roman Empire to America on the other, was an analogy popular among European intellectuals. After staying in America for four months at the time of the Truman Doctrine in 1947, Simone de Beauvoir published the travelogue *America Day by Day*, which also contained descriptions about jazz. But the following is her description about America's "adolescence" that fascinated as well as disappointed her:

> Adolescence is precisely the passage from the given world of childhood to adult existence, where everything must be built and conquered – a passage that is often effected only through a difficult crisis. I think that the majority of adolescents in America do not make it; and this is what gives a certain truth to the otherwise superficial slogan "Americans are just big children." Their tragedy is precisely that they are *not* children, that they have adult responsibilities, an adult existence, but they continue to cling to a ready-made, opaque universe, like that of childhood.
>
> [emphasis in original][21]

Even though the rise of America led to a decline in the global status of Europe, for intellectuals, this did not necessarily mean compromising its longstanding moral and cultural heights. As the Greeks thought about the Romans, they regarded America as "the Romans of our time." This "Athenian complex" was a mindset by which to supplement the lost political, military and economic power with cultural power on which to criticize America.[22]

In the postwar British jazz scene, some insisted on the obligation to nurture jazz as parents in place of the "big children" who could not support the music appropriately. From lofty cultural heights, therefore, Britain was positioned as the guardian of the memory of jazz's roots. Jazz was beyond America's possession in the context of the peculiar perspective of the Greek = "adult" and the Roman = "big children," which Macmillan and de Beauvoir recalled in their descriptions of America. Ultimately, the British music magazine *Melody Maker* published several articles suggesting that the roots of jazz could be found in the Commonwealth, thus denying America's position as the sole owner of this music.[23]

Faced with a relative decline in their geopolitical standing in postwar global politics, the postwar jazz scenes of both former empires tried to project, in a critical tone, the reality of America just around the same time when the State Department began disseminating the image of the new hegemon as free and democratic through its jazz ambassadors. Although jazz in the former empires did not necessarily demand global democracy, the tone was still discernible that jazz in both countries reflected a sense of nostalgia, in search of a more decentralized world. And in that sense, the music was antithetical to the world where America sought to reign as the world's only sovereign.

Overcoming the past

If jazz became a symbolic icon of anti-Americanism in former empires, jazz in defeated countries following the Second World War – primarily West Germany and Japan – connoted different meanings. Of the two, jazz in West Germany first needed to overcome and expunge its past image as associated with its dire Nazi history.

The West German jazz scene saw a revival after the war, and soon blossomed in big cities such as Berlin, Munich and Frankfurt, as detailed by Michael H. Kater. In Berlin, some of those who had played jazz before the war formed the swing combo, the Berlin All Stars. Among them was Coco Schumann, an Auschwitz survivor who had been forced to play jazz at the Theresienstadt camp as a member of the Ghetto Swingers. In Munich, Fritz Brocksieper, the drummer in Josef Goebbels's band, Charlie And His Orchestra, also resumed his musical activities. During the occupation period, local musicians played music upon request from Americans at the American military officers' club, with jazz numbers a popular choice. Radio stations also started to broadcast jazz following the war. The American Forces Network (AFN), the radio network catering to American military personnel, broadcast popular jazz and attracted German listeners as well. Local West German radio stations, on their part, began to play jazz right after the end of the war, with Joachim Berendt, critic and producer, from Southwest German Broadcasting, and Dietrich Schulz-Köhn, former German Air Force Lieutenant dubbed Dr. Jazz, from Northwest German Broadcasting, driving this jazz revival.[24]

However, it would be incorrect to assume these developments were coordinated and intentionally sought to promote certain policies inside the area under American occupation. For example, the AFN basically targeted American audiences stationed in the occupation zone. Whereas, in the Amerika Haus, established with the aim of introducing American culture, jazz performances were rare, although classical music recitals were organized. American officials themselves saw jazz as popular, but did not place a high value on this music.[25]

German intellectuals were the same. Believing to have succeeded in building high levels of spiritually enriching *Kultur* in their own society, they tended to oppose the notion of *Zivilisation*, seeing this as a concept underpinning a culturally vacuous American society. In their imagination, in America, materialistic life was guaranteed, but society's spiritual and cultural aspects were lacking. America was often portrayed as a society colonized by commercialism, superficial, and having poor-quality products, as well as crass popular culture – as opposed to "serious" art. As mentioned earlier, philosopher Theodor Adorno called jazz an artificially produced folk song, criticizing the music as lacking creativity. In addition, the weekly magazine *Der Spiegel* depicted bebop as a chaotic music with grotesque improvisation that ignored harmony and stressed only rhythm. Moreover, there was confusion between jazz and rock music, a genre seen in no uncertain terms as uncivilized. Although associated with juvenile delinquency, sexual abandonment and violent images of scandalous films – such as *The Wild One* and *Rock Around the Clock* featuring Bill Haley – somewhat surprisingly, rock music was broadcast on AFN more frequently than jazz until the mid-1950s. And last but not least, prejudice against black music remained, as exemplified in an excerpt from a travelogue report on America at the time that depicted jazz as nothing more than "primitive Negro dances."[26]

Against this context, critic Joachim Berendt's contribution to changing the social status of jazz in West Germany was considerable. As the author of the seminal publication *The Jazz Book*, which was published in 1952 in German and then translated into many languages, he strenuously attempted to repudiate societal prejudice toward jazz. To enhance the status of the music to the same level as classical music, Berendt endeavored to separate jazz from commercialism – long associated with American culture – as well as from rock and dance music in order to refute the suite of criticisms led by Adorno against the "culture industry." Berendt tirelessly sought to reinterpret the nature of jazz by comparing the history of jazz to that of classical music from baroque to the contemporary. This enabled him to reintroduce the music in an intellectual manner. Accordingly, a particular emphasis was placed on cool jazz. Developed from bebop but more intelligent and restrained, this style was played by many white musicians, paving the way for a revamping and reinvention of the image of jazz while at the same time associating the music with notions of modernity. Keeping its distance from the image of Halbstarke – the juvenile groups inspired by *The Wild One* and *Rock Around the Clock* – a realignment of jazz, thus drawing it closer to the basic tenets of classical music, soon saw it find its rightful place in the conservative society of the Adenauer period.[27]

Berendt's attempt had a distinct philosophical advantage. The fact that jazz was suppressed during the Nazi period was a convenient historical detail that he could effectively harness to gain support for its anti-totalitarian character. "Dictators don't swing" was a catchphrase that could be harnessed in stressing the incompatibility between dictatorship and jazz aesthetics, therefore providing West

German society with an effective foundation for emphasizing its differences with East Germany. In this sense, overcoming criticisms of jazz in West Germany became a moral obligation. Although it is possible to detect a strategic aspect of selling jazz here, the social status of jazz drastically improved as it became seen as a music embodying the new Germany. As the acceptance of jazz in West German society advanced, the institutionalization of the music also progressed – even being taught as a formal subject in West Germany's higher education system.[28]

Meanwhile, the reality of West Germany as a divided country remained the same well into the 1960s. Or more precisely, that reality became deep-rooted after August 1961 following the construction of the Berlin Wall, which served to isolate West Berlin inside East Germany. The consolidation of a divided Germany further raised the profile and social value of jazz. West Berlin, now surrounded by the wall, saw itself as an important beacon of the West and a vital messenger for propagating the Western way of life and showing its cultural superiority to the East. Mayor of West Berlin, Willy Brandt, who would later practice *Ostpolitik* under the idea of "change through rapprochement" as Chancellor from 1969, was among many of those who were profoundly affected by the reality of the newly built wall. Shortly afterwards, he recruited Nicolas Nabokov, a composer and executive secretary of the CIA-funded CCF, as advisor to the arts festival in West Berlin. At the same time, Nabokov asked Berendt to assume the role of art director for the Berliner Jazztage, to be held as part of a major annual arts festival commencing in 1964. This jazz festival was eventually carried out as an independent project, and even attracted musicians from Eastern Europe. For Berendt, who had long believed in the role of jazz for publicizing the openness of West Germany, the participation of musicians from Communist countries meant more than just cultural exchange.[29]

The Berliner Jazztage festival functioned as a venue for interconnecting the West German jazz scene with the global jazz scene. In 1965, the "Hideo Shiraki Quintet and Three Koto Girls" were invited from Japan. The quintet played "Sakura Sakura" and "Matsuri-no-Genso" from their album *Sakura Sakura*, which had been recorded at a studio in Berlin just before the festival. When Berendt visited Japan two years earlier, he had been deeply impressed by local attempts to fuse Japanese traditional music with Western music. It was an amazing experience for him to see the way clarinetist Tony Scott co-starred with *koto* player Shinichi Yuize. Hideo Shiraki was another musician who impressed Berendt with his musicality. Ostensibly, these experiences led him to invite Shiraki to the Berliner Jazztage. The following year, Stan Getz and Astrud Gilberto, who had recently released *Getz/Gilberto* with João Gilberto and launched the Bossa Nova boom in America, also performed their numbers at this event. In 1967, the Indonesian All Stars visited the festival from Indonesia, where the Suharto regime was undertaking a strident anti-Communist line following the fall of the Sukarno regime after the September 30 incident of 1965.[30] While staying in West Berlin, the members of the band recorded the album *Djanger Bali*, which included jazz renditions of Indonesian folk songs such as "Burung Kakatua."

Throughout the 1960s, jazz in West Germany served as a means to publicize internationally its new national identity. This necessitated jazz to break away from the past and go beyond "American music" at the same time. Therefore, when jazz's blackness began to be emphasized in America along with the rise of Black Power, Berendt recognized this move as an extension of the peculiar understanding of culture during the Nazi period (i.e. cultural essentialism), and felt a need to distance these trends from his own idealized image of more open and multicultural jazz in West Germany.[31]

In a similar way that the German jazz scene was relatively unaffected during the occupation, American occupation policies in Japan also failed to give a special place to jazz. Though it is certainly true that NHK – Japan's national broadcaster – under the control of General Headquarters, the Supreme Commander for the Allied Powers (GHQ/SCAP), did broadcast jazz. The program *New Pacific Hour* had started broadcasting as early as autumn 1945, featuring the New Pacific Orchestra led by saxophonist Shin Matsumoto, who had once played jazz for a radio program during the war. Other members in the orchestra included Hisashi Moriyama, Francisco "Kiko" Reyes and Raymond Conde.[32] Notably, Japanese musicians were also hired to play swing at American military officers' clubs during the occupation. In addition to Hiroshi Watanabe and Fumio Nanri, who had been popular since before the war, Nobuo Hara, Toshiko Akiyoshi, Sadao Watanabe and George Kawaguchi soon became vibrant figures in the postwar Japanese jazz scene. However, strictly speaking, the officers' clubs were considered off-limits to most Japanese citizens. In the same vein, although jazz was certainly played at facilities operated by the Recreation and Amusement Association (RAA, also called the Special Comfort Facility Association), which had been established by the Japanese government to provide entertainment for American forces, as well as at cabarets run by Japanese, neither of these venues were under GHQ's absolute control.[33] Therefore, while jazz was needed as an outlet for recreation in Japan during the occupation period, the connection between jazz and American occupation policies was tenuous. Considering that the position of jazz as "American music" had not had a solid foundation in early Cold War America, it is safe to draw the conclusion that jazz did not have a special place in American occupation policies in Japan.[34]

After the San Francisco Peace Treaty took effect in April 1952, Japanese society started to be re-acquainted with jazz more broadly. The Gene Krupa Trio and Louis Armstrong both visited Japan in this same year, while Oscar Peterson, Ella Fitzgerald, Roy Eldridge, Benny Carter as well as Krupa conducted the JATP tour for the first time in Japan in 1953, which led to an "unprecedented jazz boom" across metropolitan Japan. However, the level of understanding of jazz among the Japanese public was quite ambiguous. Thus, dance music imported from America was recognized, in general, as jazz. Critic Shoichi Yui depicted what actually happened in the early 1950s as an "imported entertainment boom," in which jazz was only one of many popular new avenues of entertainment and music.[35] The boundary between jazz and other musical genres was too vague to label it as "American music." As examined by Mike

Molasky, historian on the postwar Japanese jazz scene, the popular understanding of jazz in Japan at the time could be understood through the films *Drunken Angel* (1948) and *Man Who Causes a Storm* (1957). In both films, jazz was treated as rough and lowbrow, seen as occupying a lower cultural position and social status than classical music. Whereas immediately after the latter film was released, Louis Malle's *Ascenseur pour l'échafaud* (1958) received high acclaim among Japanese intellectuals, with its impressive improvisation by Miles Davis. Effectively using modern jazz, as well as sophisticated imagery and cinematography, the film triggered some changes in the popular understanding of jazz in Japan. As Molasky points out, jazz in the late 1950s was seen as a hybrid music of sorts – being associated simultaneously in the public's mind with both popular and highbrow images.[36]

The 1960s Japanese jazz scene saw the emergence of a new discourse regarding the social standing of the music. This was not irrelevant to the series of changes surrounding the American jazz scene occurring at the same time. Domestic socio-political developments, as exemplified by the radicalization of the student movement in the years leading up 1968, narrowed the distance between Japan's university student population and jazz. In an era when the university entrance rate was around the 10 percent range, students were seen as elites, but some of them projected themselves as part of the repressed, thereby associating themselves with the ideology of Black Power, while also appealing for solidarity with the Third World.[37]

Around this time, Amiri Baraka's *Blues People* became globally acclaimed. In France, students as well as intellectuals raised their abstract expectations to Maoism while listening to free jazz. Philosophical jazz criticisms based on the thoughts of Roland Barthes, Jacques Derrida, Michel Foucault, Pierre Bourdieu, Louis Althusser and others spread widely, and the social position of jazz was frequently discussed in these circles. A typical example was one critic's article "Le Nouveau jazz et la réalité américaine" – detailing the civil rights movement – interpreting the free-jazz aesthetics and the riot in Watts, Los Angeles in 1965, through a reading of Frantz Fanon's *The Wretched of the Earth*, a seminal work in postcolonial criticism.[38]

Although the jazz scenes of France and Japan had not been exactly the same, they became closer once Japanese fans and critics started to pay attention to the social condition of African Americans in American society. Still, unlike France where its declining global standing and paucity of influence in global affairs overlapped with the poor social standing of African Americans, many jazz discourses in Japan stressed the need for promoting ties between the Japanese and "colored people," as it was believed they had both been at one point ruled by white people. These criticisms were influenced by the ongoing conflict in Vietnam and the decolonization process in Africa.[39] "Blackness" in Japanese jazz discourse was conspicuous at the World Jazz Festival held at Tokyo, Osaka, Kyoto, Nagoya and Sapporo in 1964. Many stars, including Miles Davis, Wynton Kelly, J. J. Johnson, Clark Terry, Gene Krupa, Paul Chambers, Red

Nichols, Sonny Stitt and Carmen McRae, participated in this festival, appearing alongside Japanese jazz musicians such as Toshiko Akiyoshi, Hidehiko Matsumoto, and Nobuo Hara and His Sharps & Flats. In a panel discussion with Leonard Feather, who once had caused a controversy in *Down Beat* by carrying out the so-called blindfold test to insist that race had no basis in determining the quality of a jazz performance, Feather denied racial factors existed in jazz based on his long-held conviction of color-blindness. This highlighted a key difference with the Japanese panelists he was appearing with, who believed that jazz and race were indivisible.[40]

As the jazz discourse advocating solidarity with "colored people" in America, Asia and Africa attracted social attention, abstract ideas like "freedom," "revolution," "anarchy" and "destruction" began to appear frequently in jazz journals. Critical pieces by better-known critics of the day – Hisato Aikura and Masaaki Hiraoka – employed such provocative titles as "Is Solidarity with Black Jazz Possible?," "An Introduction to the Jazz Revolution" and "Theoretical Fundamentals of the Jazz Revolution." Just a sample of these titles suggests that critics at the time were alive to the social and political issues in the Third World as well as racial problems in America. In one of Hiraoka's more critical works, "Jazz Declaration," in which he recognized jazz as in the process of permanent revolution, he writes: "Deep in society, in the unfathomable part of our consciousness, in the core of trees and stones, and in the core of apples, only jazz can set off an explosive device." These were testimonies that, at least among critics, social expectations for jazz were quite high – not simply as a genre of music to appreciate, but as a medium through which to stimulate concrete social action. The Nobel Prize-winning novelist Kenzaburo Oe, one of many Japanese artists inspired by Hobsbawm's *The Jazz Scene*, focused on this "element of protest" in his essay "Resisting Jazz." He was highly critical of some Japanese jazz fans who in his eyes were indifferent to the political nature and undertones of jazz.[41]

The jazz discourse during this decade sheds light on how Japanese critics and followers of jazz tried to overcome elements of Japan's unfortunate recent past. They focused their critical energies on "imperialism" or "new colonialism," to use the terminology of leftist groups of the day. At the same time, the jazz discourse of this era contained an implicit criticism of America. It provided fans and critics, who were surrounded in their everyday lives by strong American influences, with a medium to express their objections to that reality through the glorification of black people, and using the noble savage concept. Then, what jazz critics really had at their disposal was a discursive weapon with which to initiate protest against American policies from moral and cultural heights.[42] If so, the composition of these arguments was similar to those drawn upon by Macmillan and de Beauvoir. In that sense, the concept of "black people" was not merely a strategic discourse necessary for criticizing America, but it represented a version of the Japanese "Athenian complex."

In search of alternative jazz ambassadors programs

The American jazz ambassadors program did not target Western Europe. But it was reported on in detail by the local media, with critics broadly divided in their reviews. *Jazz Hot*, for instance, covered the program in a positive light, praising Gillespie's tour and highlighting a letter it received from Quincy Jones who had accompanied Gillespie as a fellow band member. However, there were some jazz fans who were critical of the American Cold War strategy, and this cohort was mainly found in the French Communist Party. They complained that jazz should not be used for anti-Communist propaganda campaigns. Overall, however, many fans and critics appreciated the US government for finally acknowledging the immense cultural value of jazz.[43]

However, this was not the entire story. In July 1957, when cultural delegations visited Moscow from around the world to attend the sixth World Festival of Youth and Students, there were also jazz musicians from France. Following the festival, Michel Legrand led the Soviet tour, performing around 20 times across various cities including Moscow, Leningrad and Kiev. In Leningrad, about 110,000 fans attended his concerts, astounding and delighting the French musicians with a rapturous welcome. Notably, this highly positive welcome was five years before Benny Goodman's groundbreaking Soviet tour in 1962.[44]

More remarkable was the French jazz ambassador tours to parts of Africa, while decolonization on this continent was still taking place. As if searching for a new identity, jazz was being disseminated from an empire in decline as a part of its own culture. In the early 1960s, French jazz musicians, including Stéphane Grappelli appeared in the Semaine du Jazz festival in Algeria, while other musicians performed at the Festival de Jazz in Morocco. Clarinetist Maxim Saury, supported by the French Ministry of Cooperation, toured six West African countries (Senegal, Republic of the Congo, Côte d'Ivoire, Togo, Dahomey and Cameroon) for 25 days as a French jazz ambassador. As Saury himself later explained in an interview for a popular journal, his function had been "cultural propaganda." Clearly, jazz was being at this time projected as a part of French music, while at the same time promoting ties with former French colonies. Although this was a rare occasion, the French jazz ambassadors program was initiated with governmental support – with jazz performances by French musicians continuing in Africa under the support of various cultural centers and radio stations. At some jazz clubs established in Dakar, French as well as local musicians played together, thus keeping at least the semblance of a pro-French atmosphere in Senegal. Similarly, a jazz club was established in Tunisia under Tunisian government sponsorship. Furthermore, the state-owned radio station started to broadcast jazz programs, and a local jazz festival was also organized, in which Saury, Grappelli and Kenny Clarke enthusiastically participated. Crucially, this set of events was facilitated by jazz fans who had once lived in France during the colonial period and had had deep experience with this music.[45]

If French jazz was a catalyst through which to nurture ties with the former colonies, the case of West Germany shows how jazz became a means of externally propagating the country's new national identity, while also serving to overcome the past. At least for Joachim Berendt, it was necessary to give jazz a role in representing the country abroad, and thereby consolidate jazz culture inside West Germany. For this purpose, and partly because of his old friendship with Marshall Stearns who had accompanied Dizzy Gillespie's 1956 tour, Berendt kept a close eye on the American jazz ambassadors program. Stearns's success in raising the status of jazz by using the music as a diplomatic weapon in America's Cold War strategy had motivated Berendt to follow suit. As one of those who was convinced that "dictators don't swing," projecting West Germany as a peace-loving and anti-fascist country – unlike the Nazi regime or East Germany – took on a special meaning. Still, unlike Stearns, it was imperative for Berendt to overcome jazz's association with Americanism before he embarked on this project.[46]

An opportunity came as early as 1957, when a number of West German jazz musicians – including the Joki Freund quintet, Emil and Albert Mangelsdorff, and the Spree City Stompers – visited the jazz festival being held in Sopot, Poland. The proponent for this visit was Berendt. Although memories of the last war were still fresh, they were nonetheless warmly welcomed by local fans – much more so than Berendt had expected.[47] Six years later, another jazz concert was held at the Salle Pleyel in Paris, supported by the Goethe Institut, the cultural center widely promoting German language and culture. The French audience greeted them with cheers, and was especially excited to hear "Autumn Leaves," originally composed for Chanson. The success of the Paris performance changed many of the conservative voices in the West German government, culminating in the launch of their own jazz ambassadors program the following year. As the first jazz ambassadors, a quintet led by Albert Mangelsdorff carried out a tour to Asia and the Middle East under the support of the Goethe Institut – a series of concerts that ran over 65 days from January to March of 1964. In a similar way as Stearns had accompanied Gillespie, this time Berendt accompanied the West German inaugural jazz ambassadors tour.[48]

According to Berendt, when he first proposed sending jazz musicians overseas, the idea was received with a sense of collective official shock. For the West Germans, who had had significant experience sending classical orchestras abroad over the years, the notion that the Goethe Institut would send jazz musicians abroad representing the West German identity was unimaginable. However, local branches of the Institut in Asia and South America had somberly reported that their local chamber music events always saw the same audiences at each event. Along with a call from one local branch to "send us a jazz band for once!," what in effect greatly assisted Berendt in his cause was an ardent request from Thailand's King Bhumibol – a keen alto saxophonist. The King clearly wanted West Germany to seriously consider organizing a series of jazz concerts for his country.[49]

West Germany's first jazz musicians tour to Asia and the Middle East covered key strategic countries such as Iraq, India, Thailand and Japan, seeking to put forward a modern, democratic and anti-fascist image of West Germany. In India, the theme song of the film *Pather Panchali*, composed by sitarist Ravi Shankar, was arranged for jazz, and in Thailand, Mangelsdorff played numbers composed by the King himself. A jam session with the King of Thailand's band was also organized, wherein improvisation of the folk song "Nau Djay Ramwong" sent the local audience into a frenzy. According to Berendt, the song was played in a style reminiscent of John Coltrane's "My Favorite Things." The jazz renditions of "Planting Rice" and "Sakura Sakura" were also performed in the Philippines and Japan respectively to entertain local audiences. As these renditions indicate, jazz was in a more advantageous position, in comparison to classical music, for conveniently arranging local and traditional music, and thereby successfully capturing the audience's hearts and minds.[50]

While the Mangelsdorff band's reinterpretation of folk songs from various parts of the world excited local jazz fans, in contrast, playing German folk songs was usually carefully avoided, as in many cases they had been associated with the folk ideology used by the Nazi regime. Almost the only exception was "Es sungen drei Engel," which was used in the opera *Mathis der Maler* by Paul Hindemith, a composer labeled as "degenerate" by the Nazi regime for producing so-called atonal modernist music. The premiere of the symphony *Mathis der Maler* by Wilhelm Furtwängler and the Berlin Philharmonic caused a sensation at the time, and eventually the Nazi regime banned the opera, prompting Furtwängler to pen an open letter stridently defending Hindemith as an artist. Known as the Hindemith Case, the incident was now very convenient for West Germany, which was aiming to break away from the unpleasant past. A jazz rendition of "Es sungen drei Engel" was highly suitable for stressing the democratic nature of the country.[51]

Jazz ambassadors from West Germany interacted successfully with local jazz fans in each country, much in the same way American jazz ambassadors did. But what they played was not interpreted as "American music." Local press reporting tended to interpret it as "German jazz" or "Frankfurt jazz." The *Evening News* in Manila reported that in the same way as automobiles were made in West Germany, "German jazz is a highly finished, a reputable product worthy of export anywhere." The *Indian Express* in New Delhi opined that "Jazz made in Germany is no mere cliché. It is jazz with a distinctive character." It even declared: "it is certainly not American." The aim of Berendt to dilute jazz's blackness and American-ness was, therefore, markedly successful on this tour. After the tour, saxophonist Klaus Doldinger commenced another tour across various nations in Asia, Africa and South America. Albert Mangelsdorff, on his part, formed the German All Stars to visit several Asian countries again. And eventually, in February 1967, the Mangelsdorff quintet conducted a tour of America and Canada. The Canadian newspaper, the *Globe and Mail*, wrote that jazz was "no more an exclusively American art form," which must have pleased the Goethe Institut. Similarly, at the time of the South American tour, the Brazilian daily the *Jornal do Brasil* declared that it was "no longer the Americans who are bringing the quintessence of the art form with them; it is the Germans."[52]

On the part of Japanese musicians, an attempt was made during this same period to construct a version of Japanese jazz, which necessitated them to transcend jazz's black origins and its American-ness – all at the same time. The simplest answer was to focus on traditional folk songs. Thereby, Japanese musicians were able to attract a wider global audience for their unique music. In 1964, Tony Scott released *Music for Zen Meditation* with *koto* virtuoso Shinichi Yuize and *shakuhachi* player Hozan Yamamoto. In 1967, Yamamoto as well as Nobuo Hara and His Sharps & Flats participated in the Newport Jazz Festival, where they played the traditional songs "Sakura Sakura" and "Awa Dance." Another good example was the case of Hideo Shiraki, who played "Sakura Sakura" and "Matsuri-no-Genso" at the Berliner Jazztage.[53]

If color-blind Americanism had the effect of diluting the privilege of "being black" in the American jazz scene, Japanese jazz was able to enhance its presence through propagating its ethnic sensitivity. However, this meant that Japanese jazz leaned towards essentialism, something Berendt had complained about. Critic Shoichi Yui, who depicted the zeitgeist of the period as "jazz nationalism" and a "departure from America," was discontent with simply playing folk songs with a distinctive jazz rhythm or using traditional musical instruments. In light of the fact that "jazzing" traditional folk songs like "Yagi-Bushi" or "Soran-Bushi" had failed in prewar Japan, he said: "They may have all been Japanese-Western compromises, but they have never been 'Japanese'." Japanese musicians – such as Toshiko Akiyoshi, Terumasa Hino, Masabumi Kikuchi, Masahiko Sato, Masahiko Togashi and Sadao Watanabe – were not necessarily uniform in the types of music they liked to play. Their search for Japanese jazz continued even after the Japan-US Security Treaty was extended in 1970 and the protest movements targeting the treaty faded away.[54]

When an emancipation from American jazz was being discussed in Europe with the rise of free jazz, Japanese musicians increased their international presence with their own interpretation of jazz.[55] Representing Japanese jazz, Terumasa Hino's quintet and the Masahiko Sato trio participated in the Berliner Jazztage in 1971, and the Yosuke Yamashita trio participated in the same festival in 1974. Further examples of Japanese jazz musicians appearing on the international stage in the years up to 1970 included Toshiko Akiyoshi (1957 and 1958), Sadao Watanabe (1968 and 1970) and Masabumi Kikuchi (1970), who all successfully participated in the Newport Jazz Festival, while Hidehiko Matsumoto performed at the Monterey Jazz Festival in California (1964), and Sadao Watanabe played at the Downbeat Jazz Festival in Chicago (1965). Outside America, the Mitsuaki Kanno quintet appeared at the Ljubljana Jazz Festival in Yugoslavia, as well as the Budapest Jazz Festival in Hungary in 1969, where the quintet won a gold medal for its performance of "Shisendo-no-Aki." In 1970, the Sadao Watanabe quartet performed at jazz festivals in Yugoslavia, Poland

and Switzerland. At the Montreux Jazz Festival in Switzerland, the audience was so electrified by the solo performance of "Tokyo Suite" that a great hush fell over the concert hall.[56] Musicians outside America continued to contribute in their own ways to the construction of unique jazz through such public and high-profile performances seen as these.

When the Osaka World Expo was held in 1970, Berendt oversaw a jazz festival for this event. For this purpose, he organized the European Jazz All Stars, who were composed of such musicians as Albert Mangelsdorff, Belgian-born pianist Francy Boland, Danish bassist Niels Pedersen and French violinist Jean-Luc Ponty.[57] From the Japanese side, Toshiko Akiyoshi, Terumasa Hino, Sadao Watanabe, and Nobuo Hara and His Sharps & Flats participated in the festival. The Indonesian All Stars also performed on this occasion. There was great significance here in that jazz promoted transnational communication between Asia and Europe at the Expo, whose main theme was "Progress and Humanity for Mankind." Following the decade when an "emancipation" of jazz from America was debated in Europe, such transnational exchanges were facilitated via the music, yet without the country of its roots. In the sense that jazz developed as a genre outside America – while connecting musicians and fans from various countries – what the Osaka Expo effectively represented was the "progress and harmony of jazz." But still the question remained as to whether, and in what sense, jazz in other parts of the world found room for upholding emancipation from authority, be it American jazz or a government-controlled version. The next chapter explores how jazz was represented in the Soviet Union and how the Soviet authorities struggled in their efforts to dilute jazz's American-ness.

Notes

1 Richard Pells, *Not Like Us: How Europeans Have Loved, Hated, and Transformed American Culture since World War II* (New York: Basic Books, 1998), p.156.
2 For the argument of "empire by invitation," see Geir Lundestad, *The United States and Western Europe since 1945: From "Empire" by Invitation to Transatlantic Drift* (Oxford: Oxford UP, 2005).
3 Ellwood, *The Shock of America*, pp.345–46, 372–74; Tony Judt, *Postwar: A History of Europe Since 1945* (London: Penguin Books, 2005), p.233.
4 Giles Scott-Smith, "The 'Masterpieces of the Twentieth Century' Festival and the Congress for Cultural Freedom: Origins and Consolidation 1947–52," *Intelligence and National Security*, vol.15 no.1, 2000, pp.122–36; Ian Wellens, *Music on the Frontline: Nicolas Nabokov's Struggle against Communism and Middlebrow Culture* (London: Routledge, 2002), p.105. For recent studies on American covert operations, see Scott Lucas, *Freedom's War: The American Crusade against the Soviet Union* (New York: New York UP, 1999); Gregory Mitrovich, *Undermining the Kremlin: America's Strategy to Subvert the Soviet Bloc, 1947–1956* (Ithaca: Cornell UP, 2000); Frances Stonor Saunders, *The Cultural Cold War: The CIA and the World of Arts and Letters* (New York: New Press, 2000); Volker R. Berghahn, *America and the Intellectual Cold Wars in Europe: Shepard Stone Between Philanthropy, Academy, and Diplomacy* (Princeton: Princeton UP, 2001); Giles Scott-Smith, *The Politics of Apolitical Culture: The Congress for Cultural Freedom and the Political Economy of American Hegemony 1945–1955* (London: Routledge,

102 Anti-Americanism in the Western jazz discourse

2002); Hugh Wilford, *The CIA, the British Left and the Cold War: Calling the Tune?* (London: Routledge, 2003); Hans Krabbendam and Giles Scott-Smith (eds.), *The Cultural Cold War in Western Europe, 1945–60* (London: Routledge, 2004); Helen Laville and Hugh Wilford (eds.) *The US Government, Citizen Groups and the Cold War: The State-Private Network* (London: Routledge, 2006); Kenneth Osgood, *Total Cold War: Eisenhower's Secret Propaganda Battle at Home and Abroad* (Lawrence: UP of Kansas, 2008); Hugh Wilford, *The Mighty Wurlitzer: How the CIA Played America* (Cambridge: Harvard UP, 2008); Giles Scott-Smith, *Western Anti-Communism and the Interdoc Network: Cold War Internationale* (London: Palgrave Macmillan, 2012); Sarah Miller Harris, *The CIA and the Congress for Cultural Freedom in the Early Cold War: The Limits of Making Common Cause* (London: Routledge, 2016).

5 "Cablegram to Llewellyn E. Thompson, Ambassador to the U.S.S.R., Concerning Awards to Van Cliburn and Other American Musicians," 17 April 1958, in Dwight D. Eisenhower, *Public Papers of the Presidents of the United States: Dwight D. Eisenhower, 1958* (Washington, DC: Government Printing Office, 1959), p.324.

6 NARA, RG 59, CDF 1955–59, Box 98, 032 Cliburn, Van, "Van Cliburn in Paris," 29 July 1958; "Visit to Belgium of Van Cliburn," 27 August 1958; Sarah Nilsen, *Projecting America, 1958: Film and Cultural Diplomacy at the Brussels World's Fair* (Jefferson: McFarland, 2011), p.135.

7 NARA, RG 59, CDF 1955–59, Box 98, 032 Cliburn, Van, MacArthur to Dulles, 16 June 1958. It should be noted that Cliburn's victory at the competition was interpreted differently among the Soviet authorities, fans, American people and Cliburn himself. See Nigel Cliff, *Moscow Nights: The Van Cliburn Story-How One Man and His Piano Transformed the Cold War* (New York: Harper, 2016).

8 NARA, RG 59, CDF 1955–59, Box 108, 032 Jazz at the Philharmonic, "'Jazz at the Philharmonic' Concert Presented by Norman Granz," 26 June 1958.

9 Judt, *Postwar*, pp.96–97, 220. See also Archie Brown, *The Rise and Fall of Communism* (London: Bodley Head, 2009), p.118. For the publicity and cultural sides of the Marshall Plan, See Brian A. McKenzie, *Remaking France: Americanization, Public Diplomacy, and the Marshall Plan* (New York: Berghahn Books, 2005).

10 Judt, *Postwar*, p.221. See also Richard F. Kuisel, *Seducing the French: The Dilemma of Americanization* (Berkeley: University of California Press, 1997), pp.52–69.

11 Rashida Kamilah Braggs, *"American" Jazz: Traversing Race and Nation in Postwar France* (PhD Thesis, Northwestern University, 2006), pp.88–90, 102. Festival International de Jazz in 1949 was organized by Charles Delaunay who often clashed with Hugues Panassié over how to evaluate bebop. The views of Panassié and those close to him, dubbed "moldy figs," stressed the importance of New Orleans jazz rather than modern jazz. See also Braggs, *Jazz Diasporas*, pp.41–42.

12 However, it should be pointed out there was racial discrimination within French society as well. See Elizabeth Vihlen, "Jammin' on the Champs-Elysées: Jazz, France, and the 1950s," in Reinhold Wagnleitner and Elaine Tyler May (eds.), *"Here, There and Everywhere": The Foreign Politics of American Popular Culture* (Hanover: UP of New England, 2000), pp.151–55; Elizabeth Vihlen McGregor, *Jazz and Postwar French Identity: Improvising the Nation* (Lanham: Lexington Books, 2016), pp.80–117.

13 Hershorn, *Norman Granz*, p.164.

14 Ludovic Tournès, "La réinterprétation du jazz: un phénomène de contreaméricanisation dans la France d'après-guerre (1945–1960)," *Revue française d'études américaines*, vol.5, 2001, pp.75–81; Tournes, *New Orleans sur Seine*, pp.197–99, 310–15; Colin W. Nettelbeck, *Dancing with De Beauvoire: Jazz and the French* (Melbourne: Melbourne UP, 2004), pp.129–39, 146–61; Schweitzer, "Irresponsibly Engage," pp.80–88. Jean Paul Sartre (trans. Lloyd Alexander), *Nausea*

(New York: New Directions, 2013); Boris Vian (trans. Boris Vian and Milton Rosenthal), *I Spit on Your Graves* (Los Angeles: TamTam Books, 2013).
15 Yoichi Kibata, *Shihai no Daisho: Eiteikoku Hokai to Teikoku Ishiki* (Tokyo: University of Tokyo Press, 1987).
16 Hugh Wilford, "Britain: In Between," in Alexander Stephan (ed.), *Americanization of Europe: Culture, Diplomacy, and Anti-Americanism after 1945* (New York: Berghahn Books, 2007), pp.29–32; Ellwood, *The Shock of America*, p.341; Newton, *The Jazz Scene*, pp.252–53.
17 Philip Bounds, "From Folk to Jazz: Eric Hobsbawm, British Communism and Cultural Studies," *Critique: Journal of Socialist Theory*, vol.40 no.4, 2012, pp.583–91.
18 George McKay, *Circular Breathing: The Cultural Politics of Jazz in Britain* (Durham: Duke UP, 2005), pp.55–59.
19 A. J. P. Taylor, *A Personal History* (London: Hamilton Press, 1983), p.227, quoted in Dominic Sandbrook, *Never Had It So Good: A History of Britain from Suez to the Beatles* (London: Little, Brown, 2005), p.252. See also McKay, *Circular Breathing*, pp.66–68.
20 Anthony Sampson, *Macmillan: A Study in Ambiguity* (London: Allen Lane, 1967), p.61, quoted in N. Ashton, *Kennedy, Macmillan and the Cold War: The Irony of Interdependence* (London: Palgrave Macmillan, 2002), p.6.
21 Simone de Beauvoir (trans. Carol Cosman), *America Day by Day* (Berkeley: University of California Press, 2000), p.313.
22 For more on the "Athenian complex," and the family metaphor in the context of the discourse of America, see Pells, *Not Like Us*, pp.160–61; G. H. Joost Baarsen, "'Sucking on [America's] Tit': Metaphorical Dimensions of the Family in Conservative American Discourses on Europe," *Traversea*, vol.3, 2013, p.49, fn.4.
23 Hilary Moore, *Inside British Jazz: Crossing Borders of Race, Nation and Class* (London: Routledge, 2007), pp.53–65.
24 Michael H. Kater, "New Democracy and Alternative Culture: Jazz in West Germany after the Second World War," *Australian Journal of Politics and History*, vol.52 no.2, 2006, pp.174–78.
25 Poiger, *Jazz, Rock, and Rebels*, p.39.
26 Kater, "New Democracy and Alternative Culture," pp.179–84.
27 Poiger, *Jazz, Rock, and Rebels*, pp.138–41, 164–65, 210–11; Andrew Wright Hurley, *The Return of Jazz: Joachim-Ernst Berendt and West German Cultural Change* (New York: Berghahn Books, 2009), pp.38–39.
28 Hurley, *The Return of Jazz*, pp.20, 49.
29 Elizabeth Janik, *Recomposing German Music: Politics and Musical Tradition in Cold War Berlin* (Leiden: Brill, 2005), p.257; Hurley, *The Return of Jazz*, pp.79–83.
30 Joachim Ernst Berendt, "Jazz in Japan," *Down Beat*, vol.29 no.30, 6 December 1962; Hurley, *The Return of Jazz*, pp.170–76, 180, 199–204. For the Indonesian jazz scene of the time, see Andrew McGraw, "The Ambivalent Freedoms of Indonesian Jazz," *Jazz Perspectives*, vol.6 no.3, 2012.
31 Hurley, *The Return of Jazz*, pp.209–11.
32 Atkins, *Blue Nippon*, p.172; Uchida, *Nihon no Jazz-shi*, pp.160–61.
33 Mamoru Toya, *Shinchugun Club kara Kayokyoku he: Sengo Nihon Popular Ongaku no Reimeiki* (Tokyo: Misuzu Shobo, 2005), pp.7, 9, 17–20. A rating system ranging from Special A to D was introduced for groups that wished to play at military officers' clubs. The referees included critics and musicians such as Kobun Nogawa, Kyosuke Kami, Shigeya Kikuchi, Takashi Tsunoda, Takio Niki, Shin Matsumoto, Koichi Mine (Dick Mine), and Hiroshi Watanabe. Uchida, *Nihon no Jazz-shi*, pp.173–75. When considering the development of jazz in postwar Japan, Japanese American Jimmy Araki cannot be ignored. During his stay in Japan as a member of the Occupation Forces, he spread bebop to Japan through extensive musical exchanges with Japanese jazz musicians. Satoko Akio, *Swing Japan:*

Nikkei Beigunhei Jimmy Araki to Senryo no Kioku (Tokyo: Shinchosha, 2012), pp.147–94.

34 Yusuke Torii, "Sengo Nihon niokeru Beikoku no Kohobunka Katsudo to Jazz: Osaka CIE Toshokan/America Bunka Center no Jirei wo Chushin ni," *Setsunan Journal of English Education*, vol.4, 2010, pp.84–88, 99–101. It should be noted, however, that the Japanese jazz historian E. Taylor Atkins points out that "there is ample circumstantial evidence" to show that the Civil Information and Educational Section (CIE) of GHQ/SCAP believed it was possible to democratize Japan through jazz. There were some cases where the CIE library planned or supported jazz record concerts. Still, this does not mean that jazz was intentionally chosen as a strategy. Rather, popular jazz records were lent to citizens as part of a policy to increase the number of library users. See Ibid.; Atkins, *Blue Nippon*, pp.172–74.

35 Atkins, *Blue Nippon*, pp.184–86.

36 Mike Molasky, *Sengo Nihon no Jazz Bunka* (Tokyo: Seidosha, 2005), pp.61–86. *Drunken Angel* describes the relationship between a young gangster (played by Toshiro Mifune) and a poor doctor (played by Takashi Shimura), in which jazz (or a jazz-like music) functions as a background music representing a "darkness" such as a black market or gambling. In *Man Who Causes a Storm* Yujiro Ishihara played a young man who dreamed of becoming a jazz drummer but his hand was wounded in a fight. Here also, jazz is situated on the "dark" side, compared with classical music that is always depicted as being on the "elegant" side. See Ibid. See also Atkins, *Blue Nippon*, p.191.

37 Atkins, *Blue Nippon*, pp.236–37.

38 LeRoi Jones, *Blues People*; Frantz Fanon (trans. Constance Farrington), *The Wretched of the Earth* (New York: Grove Press, 1963); Tournes, *New Orleans sur Seine*, pp.387–98; Tad Shull, "East Meets West at Jazz Hot: Maoism, Race, and Revolution in French Jazz Criticism," *Jazz Perspectives*, vol.8 no.1, 2014; Perchard, *After Django*, pp.162–70. For more on French intellectuals during the 1960s, see Richard Wolin, *The Wind from the East: French Intellectuals, the Cultural Revolution, and the Legacy of the 1960s* (Princeton: Princeton UP, 2010).

39 As an extreme example, Japanese dramatist Shuji Terayama called the Japanese "Yellow Negro." See Atkins, *Blue Nippon*, pp.250–52.

40 Leonard Feather, "Tokyo Blues," *Down Beat*, vol.31 no.25, 10 September 1964; Torii, *Swing Ideology*, pp.177–80.

41 Masaaki Hiraoka, "Jazz Sengen," *Jazz Hihyo*, vol.1, 1967, p.14; Molasky, *Sengo Nihon no Jazz Bunka*, pp.160–88, 243–45; Torii, *Swing Ideology*, pp.195–210. Like France in the same era, Hiraoka referred to Fanon when he talked about the "revolutionality" in jazz. See Masaaki Hiraoka, "Frantz Fanon no Bop Kakumei Rikai," *Jazz Hihyo*, vol.20, 1975, pp.52–60.

42 For "blackness" in the Japanese jazz discourse, see also Torii, *Swing Ideology*, pp.203–19. For the French jazz scene of the same period, see Eric Drott, "Free Jazz and the French Critic," *Journal of the American Musicological Society*, vol.61 no.3, 2008, p.562.

43 McGregor, *Jazz and Postwar French Identity*, pp.137–40.

44 Ibid., pp.141–44.

45 Ibid., pp.205–6, 216–17, 220–29.

46 Mario Dunkel, "Jazz Made in Germany and the Transatlantic Beginnings of Jazz Diplomacy," in Rebekah Ahrendt, Mark Ferraguto, Damien Mahiet (eds.), *Music and Diplomacy from the Early Modern Era to the Present* (London: Palgrave Macmillan, 2014), pp.148, 152.

47 Hatschek, "The Impact of American Jazz Diplomacy in Poland During the Cold War Era," p.267.

48 Hurley, *The Return of Jazz*, pp.54–55; Dunkel, "Jazz Made in Germany and the Transatlantic Beginnings of Jazz Diplomacy," pp.153–58.

49 Joachim E. Berendt, "Teutonic Tour," *Down Beat*, vol.31 no.25, 10 September 1964.
50 Ibid.; Hurley, *The Return of Jazz*, pp.158–60; Dunkel, "Jazz Made in Germany and the Transatlantic Beginnings of Jazz Diplomacy," pp.158–60.
51 Hurley, *The Return of Jazz*, pp.94–95, 101–2.
52 Berendt, "Teutonic Tour"; Hurley, *The Return of Jazz*, pp.158–60; Dunkel, "Jazz Made in Germany and the Transatlantic Beginnings of Jazz Diplomacy," pp.158–65.
53 Uchida, *Nihon no Jazz-shi*, pp.326–32.
54 Shoichi Yui, "Nihon teki Jazz," *Jazz Hihyo*, vol.6, 1969, p.28; Atkins, *Blue Nippon*, pp.238–56.
55 For free jazz in Europe, see Mike Heffley, *Northern Sun, Southern Moon: Europe's Reinvention of Jazz* (New Haven: Yale UP, 2005); Akio Hoshino, *Europe Jazz Ogon Jidai* (Tokyo: Seidosha, 2009); Kazue Yokoi, *Avant-Garde Jazz: Europe Free no Kiseki* (Tokyo: Michitani, 2011).
56 Uchida, *Nihon no Jazz-shi*, pp.326–32.
57 Hurley, *The Return of Jazz*, p.176.

6 Containing the Soviet jazz scene

During October 1957, when the aftershock of the Little Rock crisis was still reverberating across America, the Soviet Union launched its first artificial satellite, *Sputnik I*, initiating a subsequent space race. The successful satellite launch demonstrated to the world that the Soviet Union had succeeded in developing an intercontinental ballistic missile that could reach the American mainland. Less than four years later, in January 1961, the Soviet Union succeeded in launching a manned spaceflight, *Vostok II*, into space. Against this historical Cold War backdrop, it is no wonder the Soviet leadership felt Communism was a superior economic and technological model to American capitalism.

Held between the two events, the July 1959 American National Exhibition at Moscow's Sokolniki Park – immortalized through Vice President Nixon's controversial "Kitchen Debate" incident with the Soviet leader Nikita Khrushchev – became well-known as a venue for introducing American culture to the people of the Soviet Union. But the American image in the Soviet Union was multilayered and complex. Khrushchev's explanation of why he had agreed to hold an exhibition allowing millions of Soviet citizens to see American products, suggests he held an image of America as both an adversary and a model for Soviet development. To the East German Communist leader Walter Ulbricht, he said: "We want to turn the exhibit against the Americans. We will tell our people: look, this is what the richest country of capitalism has achieved in one hundred years. Socialism will give us the opportunity to achieve this significantly faster."[1]

The Soviet leaders were searching for boundaries in their cultural "thaw" with the West. On the one hand, the atmosphere of de-Stalinization helped advance the relatively open cultural policies of the Khrushchev period. Shortly following the Cuban missile crisis, Aleksandr Solzhenitsyn's *One Day in the Life of Ivan Denisovich* – describing the inhumane conditions of the Soviet gulag system – was published in the literary journal *Novy Mir*, the official organ of the Soviet writers' union. On the other hand, shortly after the novel was published, Khrushchev became furious when he visited an exhibition of abstract paintings, seemingly because the work failed to conform with socialist realism. He disparaged the art as being drawn with a "donkey's tail" (Donkey's Tail was a group of Russian avant-garde artists around 1910).[2]

Where does jazz fit into this snapshot of Soviet Cold War history? Before the American exhibition, jazz critic Marshall Stearns struggled to organize jazz concert tours to Moscow. He brought bureaucrats from the Soviet Ministry of Culture, who were visiting America to discuss the American National Exhibition with American officials, to Duke Ellington's concert to convince them jazz should also be incorporated into the exhibition as a representation of American culture. But Stearns's attempts failed. He later lamented: "It was like trying to explain a transistor to a cave man."[3] Still, the popularity of jazz among the Soviet people was evident by what they asked American officials at the exhibition in Moscow. Out of the 20 most frequently asked questions, three were directly related to jazz. Such queries included broad questions about the origins of American jazz and how jazz was developing in America. More specific questions included, for instance: "How old is Louis Armstrong?"[4]

Soviet society of the 1960s gradually saw a more accommodating policy toward jazz. The Komsomol, facing considerable demand to provide cultural products to young people in the hope they would support Communism in the future, established and actively managed jazz cafes in the 1960s, as a way of reaching out to this generation. Therefore, although Soviet authorities controlled "parasites" like the youth counterculture stilyagi, jazz became a tool by which to increase contact with young people, while they still kept state control over the domestic jazz scene. This arrangement made it possible to be a good Soviet citizen and also a jazz fan. Jazz cafes were also important places in terms of refocusing young people's attention away from rock music.[5] The control of the domestic jazz scene, although not suitably addressed in the existing literature on jazz diplomacy, is nonetheless the best approach through which to understand jazz's precarious standing in the Soviet Union of the 1960s and early 1970s. Through reinvestigating four American jazz ambassadors, the following sections show how the Soviet authorities rationalized jazz tours from America, and also look at the means they employed to control the American musicians' interactions with Soviet citizens.

Goodman and the Soviet jazz scene

When Benny Goodman landed on Soviet soil in 1962, it was the result of his strenuous "selling efforts" – successfully convincing the State Department he should travel to the Soviet Union as an American jazz ambassador. As early as August 1955, he had appealed to Charles Bohlen, the US ambassador to the Soviet Union, to support his band's Soviet tour in view of the Soviet people's love of music. Goodman, an advocate of racial integration since the 1930s, understood more than anyone else why the State Department needed a policy for projecting America as a country striving to overcome its racial problems. He personally believed he could demonstrate to Soviet society how American democracy was working through a series of performances by a racially mixed band. Since Goodman's parents were Jewish immigrants from the former Russian empire, the Soviet tour perhaps had a special meaning for him. At this time, Bohlen and the State

Department were initially supportive of his proposal and asked him to organize a detailed travel itinerary, as well as a list of names for his accompanying orchestra.[6] But the plan failed to progress any further, presumably because of the lack of a formal cultural agreement between two countries that would provide the diplomatic underpinnings for this tour. However, the combination of two events – the cancellation of Louis Armstrong's Soviet tour in the wake of the Little Rock crisis, and the 1958 signing of the US-Soviet Cultural Exchange Agreement – immediately gave new impetus to Goodman's earlier proposal.

Goodman's Soviet jazz tour lasted about six weeks, from May to July 1962. It attracted enormous public attention both inside and outside the country. According to Terrence F. Catherman, cultural attaché to the US embassy in Moscow, the total audience figure, in 30 performances, was 176,680. Goodman traveled through the entire Soviet Union, not only major cities such as Moscow and Leningrad, but also regional hub cities like Sochi, Tashkent and Tbilisi. Prior to the Soviet tour, Goodman himself selected a number of leading musicians to form a special band in preparation for this tour. These members included well-known musicians, such as alto saxophonist Phil Woods, tenor saxophonist Zoot Sims, trombonist Jimmy Knepper, pianist Teddy Wilson, bassist Bill Crow, drummer Mel Lewis, vibraphonist Victor Feldman and guitarist Turk Van Lake.[7]

His band consisting of 18 musicians arrived at Sheremetyevo Airport in Moscow on the evening of 28 May 1962, accompanied by a full NBC camera crew. By this time, there had already been many journalists from both sides of the Cold War ideological divide reporting on this historical spectacle. However, the tour was beset with troubles from the beginning. When observing a Soviet army sports facility that had been assigned as the concert hall on the way from the airport to the city center, Goodman grew irritated at the prospect of performing in this "gymnasium." Misunderstanding the "dingy" side entrance as the main gate, he walked back to the waiting car and insisted that "he would rest" rather than play at this grimy looking hall. Although the Soviet authorities were successful in persuading Goodman to continue as scheduled, the troubles on the first day did not end there. After dinner, Goodman's assistant discovered the schedule for the band differed from that of the Soviet agency Goskonsert, which was tasked with managing the tour. The Soviet officials had a schedule showing two symphony concerts in Tbilisi and Kiev, which Goodman had not been aware of. This sparked a heated dispute between Goodman and Goskonsert. The final crisis on the first day after arriving in the Soviet Union occurred when one of Goodman's musicians choked on a chicken bone over dinner and was rushed to a local hospital by ambulance. Goodman, now exhausted and somewhat shaken over this series of events in Moscow, shut himself in his hotel room, and without talking to anyone, reportedly took four sleeping tablets to put it all behind him.[8]

During the tour, Goodman's personality was frequently more of a problem than Soviet officialdom. Catherman reported that in Moscow, Goodman abruptly canceled an event where he was scheduled to meet local jazz musicians and fans. Similarly, an invitation from the Moscow Conservatory, which was accepted by the US embassy under the direction of the State Department, was willfully ignored by Goodman. However, some unplanned yet successful meetings also occurred on this tour, when they suited Goodman. An unscheduled meeting at the House of Soviet Composers to exchange ideas and discuss jazz was organized while in country, resulting in Aram Khachaturian, Tikhon Khrennikov and several promising young Soviet jazz composers having cordial discussions with Goodman. While Goodman regretted that Dmitri Shostakovich – his favorite composer – did not attend this meeting, he was delighted when Khachaturian promised to compose a special piece of jazz for him. These incidents showed that while the Soviet authorities were rarely prepared to compromise on the pre-arranged schedule and rules, they nonetheless were forced to yield to a highly persistent Goodman on more than one occasion. For instance, concessions were made to Goodman – who even personally visited the Ministry of Culture – in regards to reducing the total number of performances, canceling classical performances, and permitting television recording. Backstage at one performance even saw Goodman suggest he might discontinue the tour when he discovered that the Sochi authorities had stopped recording his performance, ostensibly due to improper documentation held by the recording team – a problem American embassy officials did not tell Goodman about until the end of the performance. Only after embassy officials apologized to the furious Goodman the next morning, admitting it had been inappropriate, and gaining formal permission from Moscow in the afternoon for future recordings, was the problem finally resolved to his satisfaction. Ultimately, it was also Goodman's uncooperative attitude during the tour that led the NBC crew to return home after his Tashkent performance.[9]

Trouble also occurred between the NBC camera crew and the Soviet authorities during Goodman's tour. The presence of the crew apparently "completely bewildered and almost paralyzed" the Soviets as the camera crew failed to arrange formal permission for recording beforehand. Although recording or reporting on the performances had been flatly refused by the Soviet authorities, the Americans refused to budge from their demands. Fortunately, five minutes before the first day's performance was to commence, the Soviet authorities gave official permission for television news coverage to occur. Unfortunately, the American television crew carrying the heavy equipment failed to arrive in time to record the arrival of Khrushchev and his wife, First Deputy Premiere Anastas Mikoyan, or Alexei Kosygin. In any event, the recorded images of this event were out of focus and of poor quality.[10]

The reaction of Soviet audiences varied. The official organ of the Soviet Communist Party, *Pravda*, reported performances by "one of the best American jazz bands." However, somewhat more coolly, Catherman described the audience's reaction only as "mild enthusiasm," due to the presence of Khrushchev and other Soviet officials in the hall who attended the performance to give "a hard-eyed evaluation" of American jazz.[11] In Tbilisi, performances were not sold out. The audience's reaction was polite but rather cool in most cases, according to Catherman. Nonetheless, at the last performance, the blare of whistling, stomping and shouting by the audience created a carnivalesque atmosphere, it was reported. In Sochi, the audience's reaction was "puzzlingly mild," and applause often faded away quickly after each number – Catherman reported there was "practically no whistling or shouting" and there were some empty seats. In Tashkent, the audience was mostly apathetic to the tour and only polite applause could be heard even after sizzling-hot numbers were performed, while some solo numbers received no applause. In contrast, Leningrad was one of the cities where Goodman's band was warmly welcomed by excited local fans. Here the band members also enjoyed local culture by attending performances of the Igor Moiseyev Dance Company and the Leningrad Ballet. During this stage of the tour, Moiseyev, his wife, his artistic director and several dancers visited Goodman backstage after one performance. Following the final Leningrad performance, the audience did not want to leave Winter Stadium. They kept stomping their feet, clapping and whistling, while demanding an encore, finally resulting in Goodman returning to the stage in casual clothes to play a solo number. Back in Moscow, the final stop on his Soviet tour, there was an informal meeting with several members of the Moscow State Symphony Orchestra, where Goodman played a solo performance and gave the orchestra members a trumpet, a clarinet and two flutes as gifts.[12]

Although the mere fact that the Soviet authorities even accepted the Goodman tour symbolized some positive changes occurring inside the Soviet jazz scene at this time, the severe constraints on Soviet society nonetheless overshadowed the tour. In Sochi, the chairman and several members of a local jazz club, who were talking with trumpeter Joe Newman in front of their hotel, were arrested by police, while all the records or books the band distributed to local fans were confiscated by authorities. Reportedly, some fans had received a prior warning from local plain-clothes police officers to stay away from the band. In Tashkent, fans who wanted to meet with the band were harassed by the police, while officials associated with members of the local philharmonic society stood at the back of the theater checking passes and monitoring the band, thus preventing any fans going surreptitiously backstage to meet with band members. In Leningrad, while the performance itself was reportedly very successful, there was a repressive atmosphere around them. Fans who visited the hotel where the band was staying were sparse, and instead, sought out low-profile clandestine meetings with the band in local parks out of sight of local police. A Soviet musician was explicitly warned by the police to not "see too much" of Woods.[13]

Against this repressive and controlling context, it is therefore imperative to consider the rationale behind the Soviet acceptance of the Goodman tour. On this point, Catherman's reporting provides a clue. He concluded that Goodman was a "safe" bet because he was a competent classical musician. Moreover, Goodman's tour was part of a package under which it was agreed to exchange cultural delegations for performances in each country, including the New York City Ballet and the Robert Shaw Chorale from America – while on the Soviet side this arrangement involved the Bolshoi Theatre Orchestra, the Leningrad Philharmonic Orchestra and the Ukrainian Dance Ensemble. Curiously, this cultural exchange arrangement suggests Goodman's jazz was treated as part of

American high culture by the Soviets. By the time Goodman performed his jazz concert in Moscow, the New York Philharmonic, the American Ballet Theater and the Juilliard String Quartet – all fine examples of American high culture – had already performed in the grandest Soviet concert halls. For officials in the American embassy in Moscow, it was disappointing there had been no classical concerts by Goodman in support of the jazz component of the tour.[14]

His signature "classical" style of jazz caused some discord between Goodman and the fans on the one hand – and also within the band on the other. As scholars have subsequently revealed, this friction centered on the question of what style of jazz should be played. During each performance, Goodman remained loyal to swing – reminiscent of jazz orchestras of the 1930s – which disappointed some fans who had come to listen to modern jazz. Through *Music USA*, they were highly familiar with popular American jazz. On one occasion, trombonist Willie Dennis was left "open-mouthed" in surprise when asked by local jazz fans in Sochi about the latest jazz rankings on *Down Beat*, about which he did not know. To put it differently, while Goodman was a "safe" bet for both the US and Soviet governments due to his musical pedigree, some fans who wanted to hear modern jazz came away dissatisfied. The problem as to which style – swing or modern jazz – should be performed during the Soviet tour soon became a point of contention within Goodman's band. Goodman boasted upon arrival in Moscow he could pick and choose the best musicians in the business for his band, yet unlike the "King of Swing" himself, many of these band members were leading modern jazz musicians. These younger musicians were generally dissatisfied with the repertoire, seeing it as limiting the audience's exposure to real jazz and failing to show them the latest developments in American jazz. "If I had known we were going to play music like this I would not have come," Mel Lewis complained, adding that Goodman's music was "older than what the Russians are entitled to hear." Goodman answered these criticisms by saying that the Russians were not prepared for "progressive jazz." Instead he preferred to play "Sing Sing Sing" or "Caravan," which were typical numbers found in swing-era repertoires. While Goodman did not want his swing – a symbol of himself – to be infected by modernistic renditions performed by younger band members, the modernists in his band felt they were being "cheated" in failing to represent real American jazz.[15]

Reflecting these simmering disagreements, when the tour arrived in Sochi, Goodman told Jimmy Knepper to go back home. Earlier, during the first set of Moscow performances, Goodman had been displeased by Knepper's modern solo play, seeing it as objectionable at the time. This incident created ongoing friction between them for the duration of the Soviet tour. Goodman also raised the ire of other band members. During one rehearsal, Goodman insulted Phil Woods's musical abilities with "some slurring remark" – he also tried to bring a substitute saxophonist from America. These provocative attitudes frequently provoked angry reactions from the other band members as well. When some of the band members held a late-night party in a hotel room directly above Goodman's room, they loudly discussed his various faults in unflattering terms and even shouted: "The King is dead." Although he was unsuccessful, the next day

Goodman attempted to cut the number of band members to a workable minimum number in order for the tour to continue, and then send the rest home. Following this spike in acrimony, however, internal tensions receded, albeit on the back of heightened morale because the band had suddenly discovered they all shared anti-Goodman feelings.[16] Following the Soviet tour, Goodman released the album *Benny Goodman in Moscow* from RCA Victor, which was based on live recordings of the Russian performances. Notably, at around the same time, the anti-Goodman band members who had toured the Soviet Union with him – including Zoot Sims, Phil Woods, Bill Crow, Willie Dennis and Mel Lewis – also released an album based on this experience titled *Jazz Mission to Moscow* from Colpix Records.

The standing of jazz in Soviet society at the time of the Goodman tour was probably best illustrated by reactions made by the Soviet leader himself in a discussion with the Moscow-based American ambassador. When Khrushchev met the ambassador Llewellyn Thompson, he praised the musical competence of the band, yet also informed Thompson that "he did not dance and did not understand jazz."[17] In contrast, critic Leonard Feather, who accompanied Benny Goodman on his Soviet tour, pointed out on *Down Beat* that the "fruit is no longer forbidden," after witnessing photos of Vladimir Lenin and saxophonist Cannonball Adderley hanging on a wall side by side in the living room of a local musician's apartment.[18] Taken together, these comments suggest that while the official ban on jazz had been removed, Soviet officialdom was reluctant to completely lower its guard with the music – exemplified by attempts by authorities to limit interactions between the Goodman band members and local fans during the tour. Therefore, although the existing literature highlights that a "Pandora's box had been opened" in the early 1960s in Soviet society, it would be more accurate to note that the Soviet authorities expanded significant resources to ensure that jazz would not be socially disruptive.[19]

Hines and US-Soviet relations of the mid-1960s

Although Goodman's Soviet tour experienced its share of difficulties, the State Department could not ignore the extant local popularity of jazz in this country. Expectations grew in American official circles to further promote the acceptance of jazz, a music which was clearly gaining increased legitimacy in Soviet society. Therefore, to provide a "stimulating experience" to the Soviets, the State Department accelerated the search for the next jazz ambassador.[20]

Meanwhile, a new kind of official jazz discourse began to appear at a meeting of the Union of Soviet Composers held in the autumn of 1962. Attended by renowned composers, the meeting saw jazz stridently criticized by some key musical figures, including the general secretary Tikhon Khrennikov. But these criticisms were strongly refuted, notably by Dmitri Shostakovich, Alexander Tsfasman and Leonid Utesov, among others. There were also pro-jazz voices calling for a change in the derogatory label of jazz as "vulgar music," as it had once been described by Maxim Gorky and repeated by several other cultural figures. At this meeting a consensus was reached on the need for the Union to lead jazz in an "approved direction," which in reality meant the construction of "Soviet jazz." Much in the same way as Michel Legrand fused French traditional music with jazz, it was now recognized that jazz had to be de-Americanized by fusing it with traditional Soviet music.[21] Behind this notion was the recognition that there was a tension between the social demand for jazz – especially among young people – and the need for the Soviet authorities to contain the local jazz scene. After the Goodman tour, Khrushchev reportedly said: "I don't like jazz. When I hear jazz, it's as if I had gas on the stomach. I used to think it was static when I heard it on the radio." But domestically, the popularity of jazz had been steadily increasing since the sixth World Festival of Youth and Students in 1957.[22]

At the end of the Khrushchev era, there were some signs of improvement in US-Soviet relations – the so-called little détente – manifesting in agreement to establish a Hot Line and the Partial Test Ban Treaty signed by both countries in 1963. However, as the tempo of the Vietnam War increased with sustained large-scale US bombing campaigns of North Vietnam, any prospect of a dramatic improvement in bilateral relations soon dimmed. Nonetheless, the Consular Treaty, the first bilateral treaty between the two superpowers, was concluded in 1964, and the Civil Air Transport Agreement was achieved in 1966. For the new Soviet leader Leonid Brezhnev, who was facing an intensification of the Sino–Soviet conflict at this time, any unnecessary confrontation with America was undesirable. Amid limited signs of improvement in political relations, both countries were mildly supportive of cultural exchanges, which ostensibly played an adjunct and complementary function within their broader bilateral relationship.

Against this context, Earl Hines, the "father of modern jazz piano," was seen as a suitable candidate to become the next American jazz ambassador to the Soviet Union, following in the recent footsteps of Goodman. With a highly distinctive way of playing a solo, Hines played no avant-garde jazz, although his "trumpet style" piano playing once seemed avant-garde. After he played with Louis Armstrong during the 1920s, he contributed to popularizing swing and bebop. During the 1950s, he successfully led a Dixieland jazz band. Although his popularity faded in the early 1960s, it was not too long before he was "rediscovered" by a jazz critic in the mid-1960s. Importantly, the Soviet authorities failed to foresee the excited reaction Hines would cause during the course of his Soviet tour. Later at a meeting of the Advisory Committee on the Arts, Richard Davis, working for the USIA, recollected that during the negotiations with the Soviets on sending an American jazz band, "they didn't know who Earl Hines was, and they were extremely leery; they said, 'what is this?'"[23]

Hines toured the Soviet Union from July to August of 1966. It was a tour that comprised his various repertoires that reflected the diverse styles of jazz he had played over the previous four decades. Although most of the solo performances were played by Hines, unlike Goodman, he gave the other seven members ample opportunities to express themselves freely during these performances. He also maintained a high degree of flexibility through constantly changing the repertoire and the pace of each performance, in accordance with each audience's musical preferences and their level of understanding of jazz. In the eyes of the American ambassador Foy D. Kohler, the band's internal harmony was perfectly maintained. The individual charm and talents of each band member were also appreciated throughout the Soviet tour. Drummer Oliver Jackson and trumpeter Harold Johnson's keen sense of humor was invaluable when the other band members' spirits became low during the long journey, while bassist Bill Pemberton always kept their luggage orderly so it allowed them to be punctual for their performances and appointments. Saxophonist Budd Johnson, who was in charge of musical arrangements, paid great attention to the quality of the performances, and vocalist Clea Bradford created a sensation with her beauty and musical skill. Of critical importance, Hines knew exactly what showmanship was and behaved like a "Fatha" to the band, even under trying conditions such as when numerous members lost significant body weight through sweating profusely during their hot summertime performances. Unsurprisingly, the respect Hines received from his fellow musicians fostered genuine harmony and friendship within the band.[24]

Performance conditions in the Soviet Union were far from ideal and differed greatly from what the band had expected. For instance, concert-standard pianos were hard to come by at their pre-arranged venues, and they were frequently missing keys and pedals, and were generally deemed unsatisfactory by the band. Temperatures occasionally exceeding 104° Fahrenheit (40° Celsius) also extracted a heavy toll on the band. Living standards differed greatly to what was considered normal in America. Everyday items like cigarettes, whiskey, razors, soap and pens proved difficult to purchase, much to the band's annoyance. With news in English in short supply, the band would have been completely isolated from the world outside the Soviet Union without a shortwave radio. Even in the best big city hotels requests for room service were met with blank stares, and rooms providing "all comforts" had sub-standard bathrooms that would hardly meet basic hygiene standards in America. Understandably, dressing rooms, lighting and concert hall acoustic facilities were well below what the band was accustomed to, after playing at venues such as New York's Broadway. Other annoyances included Hines's stage costume not even arriving in Tbilisi, and the American souvenirs that were intended to be handed out along the tour going permanently missing prior to the tour even commencing.[25]

The audiences were much more diverse than during Goodman's tour, according to Kohler, ranging "from the uninitiated, struggling to understand what is going on, to the very 'hep', who inquire why we don't send Charlie Mingus or John Coltrane rather than old timers like Earl Hines." During Hines's tour, the performances in Kiev, the first stop of the tour, were arguably the most important and accomplished. An audience numbering around 10,000 people gathered every night inside a sports arena that was packed out one hour before each performance started. Unsurprisingly these passionate jazz lovers enthusiastically applauded every number after it was played. When performances ended, fans rushed to the front of the stage and noisily requested an encore from the band, which on one occasion sparked a melee between fans and sturdy ushers who tried to prevent them reaching the stage. Oliver Jackson, who managed to borrow a drum kit from local drummers because his own set had failed to arrive, performed well in these performances, despite using borrowed equipment. Fans also expressed their appreciation to the US government for sending Hines on this tour, questioning embassy officials as to why there were so few American jazz bands touring the Soviet Union. The next city on Hines's tour was Tbilisi, which initially showed much less enthusiasm for his music than Kiev had, as seen by the audience's cool response to difficult pieces, and their indifference to loose tempo music. However, they warmed up greatly when Hines changed the repertoire to include joyful pieces, Kohler reported. The audience "applauded thunderously" and showed their appreciation by stamping their feet – the night reached a high point when Clea Bradford appeared on the stage and the concert hall in unison demanded an encore. The reaction of the audience in Yerevan was favorable too.[26]

Following these performances, the audience's understanding of jazz as seen in Kiev and Tbilisi tapered off dramatically. For instance, during performances in Makhachkala, they seemed to be struggling to understand what they were listening to, and there was very little applause. In a city where an opportunity to see foreigners was infrequent, people were not sure how to respond to the visiting Americans. Few students or crowds wished to meet with the band or seek autographs. According to Kohler, the band seemed to be akin to a "circus" for the audience. Nevertheless, the fatigued members were able to recover their vigor in Pyatigorsk and Kislovodsk, both health resort cities in the Caucasus region. In Pyatigorsk, the band was welcomed with enthusiastic cheers from an audience tightly packed into a local venue, but who knew very little, if anything, about Hines. Two performances in the local amphitheater were followed by additional performances at an outdoor stadium in Kislovodsk. Hines's performance schedule in Krasnodar coincided with that of the Moscow State Symphony Orchestra, while they discovered first-hand, somewhat regrettably, that an outdoor hall refurbished from an old tennis stadium was patently unsuitable for a jazz concert.[27]

Similar to the Goodman tour, the reaction of the Soviet authorities was cautious and guarded. After the Hines band received enthusiastic reactions from audiences in Kiev and Tbilisi, the Soviet authorities decided to cancel the pre-scheduled performances for Moscow and Leningrad. This cancelation for the two most culturally significant cities was a blow to the State Department. Although no reason was given, Kohler did at least attempt to portray this outcome in a somewhat positive light, concluding that "The Soviet people may be ill-informed but they are not stupid, and a great number of people got the message in this instance." The point Kohler was trying to make was the timing of the cancellation, which came about shortly following the successful performances held in Kiev and Tbilisi. In other words, American officials speculated that if the Moscow and Leningrad performances had gone ahead, they would have been even more successful. This meant Hines's tour had raised some serious concerns for the authorities. For them, permitting the Hines band to go ahead carried reasonable risks. Understandably, many fans who had pinned their hopes on watching these jazz performances were critical of the Soviet authorities' decision to abruptly cancel this leg of the tour. With these in mind, Kohler reported that the Soviet government's loss of face over this decision had been a very high price to pay.[28]

A distinct wariness by Soviet officialdom soon crept into their interactions with the American jazz musicians, particularly in cases when band members interacted with local Soviet jazz fans, and the band undertook social activities outside their performances. Hines sought unofficial exchanges with fans and musicians but they were sporadic and largely unsuccessful. He was questioned by local officials as soon as they saw him seeking to make contact with local fans and was duly reprimanded. In Kislovodsk, band members reportedly enjoyed cognac and conversation at a restaurant away from the hotel with several members from the Moscow Philharmonic Orchestra, which had just returned from touring America and were doing performances in the same region. But most of the orchestra members refrained from meeting Hines for the fear of punishment by the authorities. Still, dedicated fans always tried to find a chance to personally meet the band members without being detected by authorities. In Sukhumi, the concert hall was overflowing with eager jazz fans who were eager to meet the band personally. Following the performance, ardent students who had come from Leningrad took the band to a nearby beach and restaurant, and even to their apartments, allowing the band members to temporarily evade surveillance by Soviet officials and interact with local people in an unscripted way. In Batumi, the final stop of the tour, hundreds of fans unable to enter the Summer Theater gathered around the theater's exit – as well as the tour bus – in the hope of a brief encounter with one of the visiting American jazz musicians, and possibly acquiring even an autograph.[29]

Kohler felt optimistic about the popularity of jazz in the Soviet Union and expressed confidence that Hines's tour had had a positive impact on Soviet society for several reasons. The most notable of which was excellent attendance numbers. There were many instances during the tour when audience numbers exceeded 10,000 people and crowds overflowed regularly from concert venues, despite limited publicity and promotion. Moreover, many fans had traveled from distant locations. Some had even headed to Tbilisi on the expectation of getting tickets following the Kiev performance. The difference between jazz and rock music was highlighted through these performances, and the band demonstrated a closeness between jazz and classical music. People who had anticipated jeans and electric guitars encountered instead band members who had been educated in classical music and played with advanced musical techniques and skill. Furthermore, the interest the members showed in classical and folk music at the various places they visited, and their attempts to acquire records and scores of Soviet composers, had created a good impression with local people. Finally, that saxophonist Bob Donovan had studied at the Juilliard School of Music – as well as the fact that bassist Bill Pemberton and trumpeter Harold Johnson had studied under Russian-born musicians – were also aspects that had sparked the interest of local people during the tour.[30]

The marked change in the official Soviet posture towards the Hines tour showed the ambivalent standing of jazz in 1960s Soviet society. The initial ignorance of Hines and his music by Soviet officials, miscalculating he was a "safe" bet, instead became a headache for authorities due to the immense popularity of the tour, which resulted in the abrupt cancellation of arguably two of the most important scheduled performances on the last leg of the tour. Nonetheless, the official Soviet position settled into one characterized by tolerating but controlling the local jazz scene. Jazz could be played and appreciated only within the established tolerance limits as set by authorities. This was further exemplified in subsequent visits by eminent American jazz figures who went on to tour the Soviet Union after the Hines tour.

Mulligan, America's informal jazz ambassador

After Hines finished his controversial Soviet tour, discussion continued both in the jazz subcommittee of the Musical Advisory Panel of ANTA and at the Advisory Committee on the Arts about who was most appropriate to become the next jazz ambassador to be sent to the Soviet Union. Upon request by Roy E. Larsen, the committee chair, at the April 1967 meeting, Guy E. Coriden of the State Department proposed several prominent jazz figures who might be suitable. They included Cannonball Adderley, Art Blakey, Dave Brubeck, John Coltrane, Bud Freeman, Dizzy Gillespie, Gene Krupa, Charles Lloyd, the Modern Jazz Quartet, Thelonious Monk, Gerry Mulligan, Clark Terry and Teddy Wilson, among others. Specifically, he also proposed sending someone who could "touch the fringe of the atonal music of Cecil Taylor, Ornette Coleman et al." Not that avant-garde jazz was believed to be attractive to Soviet audiences, but the point was that the musicians were expected to have the capacity to play diverse styles of jazz on tour, in order to represent the real America.[31] Peter Mennin, President of the Juilliard School of Music and an influential committee member, was one who openly complained about being overly cautious with the Soviets. "What disturbed me on the Russian issue was jazz," he said. "The opinion was put forth that we have leadership in this field and yet the comment was made that we should not send anything too 'far out'." Nevertheless, the more cautious viewpoint tended to prevail in this debate. Larsen insisted that "There is a political consideration. If we went too far out, the Russian jazz people would lose face."[32] As in the case of targeting Africa through jazz diplomacy, the problem of who to send to the Soviet Union was not easily solved.

Of the many possible candidates, Gerry Mulligan became the next American jazz musician to perform in the Soviet Union after Hines. In July 1967, he conducted a jam session with local musicians in front of a crowd of 150 people at the jazz cafe the Molodezhnoe, operated by the Komsomol and located on Moscow's busy Gorky Street. The film *Up the Down Staircase*, in which Mulligan's wife, the actress Sandy Dennis, appeared, was shown at the Moscow International Film Festival, and Mulligan accompanied her to this showing. Thus, to be precise Mulligan was not the official jazz ambassador sent by the State Department, but was there in an unofficial capacity to attend the film festival. Rumors of Mulligan's visit had spread in advance by some fans, but initially they were not taken seriously because the director of the film was Robert Mulligan – not the eminent jazz figure sharing the same surname. When later Gerry Mulligan visited Moscow, an American embassy official took him and his wife to the Molodezhnoe to consult with the cafe's management in the hope of organizing an impromptu jam session.[33]

For one and a half hours in the early evening of 14 July, Mulligan played with the KM Quartet, the Molodezhnoe's resident band, who were accomplished musicians in their own right. The performance took place in front of 150 musicians and their friends, going well past 11 o'clock at night – the usual closing time for the Molodezhnoe. The next day, another jam session was held at a large apartment of a local architect, where Mulligan enthusiastically listened to the KM Quartet perform again, and was surprised at their detailed knowledge of his music. Tellingly, Llewellyn Thompson, Moscow's US ambassador, reported that "it seems fair to state that a wide audience of Soviet jazz enthusiasts will get to hear Mulligan jazz secondhand."[34]

The Molodezhnoe, as the designated official space to play and appreciate jazz, provides a clue as to how jazz was interpreted and represented in Soviet society. The head of the cafe who was responsible for managing the Molodezhnoe was receptive to local musicians' activities. Still, as symbolizing the Communist Party's "containment policy" of jazz, he strongly urged local musicians to stop talking to the US embassy officer in private, and asked the officer to make arrangements through him instead. In particular, it was believed to be problematic if local musicians tried "to play like Coltrane." In any case, they did not have the musical capacity to do so, but it showed that avant-garde jazz had become a specific target of official criticism. In this peculiar Soviet jazz scene of the 1960s, this embassy officer heard a report from a local musician about the presence of a "police musician" who was from Moskonsert, Goskonsert's local branch. Allegedly, he was based at officially sanctioned jazz venues for monitoring purposes. According to Thompson's reporting, local musicians would occasionally ask that guests from the West should "be particularly careful in their conversation because there were 'others present'." In most cases, it was impossible to identify these "others" inside the jazz cafes, according to local musicians. Still, one trumpeter in the cafe was identified by other musicians as an "official musician," and these same sources suggested it was possible that one pianist "takes more than music from the musicians." After all, jazz cafes were limited spaces authorized by the state to host local jazz performances, but they were contained and controlled by Soviet officialdom in order to manage musicians and fans. Certainly, the American officer did note that what looked like a militia car was monitoring local musicians near the venue where the second jam session was to take place. For the local Soviet musicians, while it was a once in a lifetime experience to play with professional American musicians, avoiding confrontation and arrest by local authorities also had to be achieved at all costs – resulting in considerable precautions being taken in any interactions with visiting Americans.[35]

In this politically acceptable but constrained jazz scene, musicians were constantly restraining themselves, conscious they were under the watchful eye of the authorities. Soviet officials showed some tolerance towards jazz, but freedom of musical expression that would be otherwise represented through jazz was not a given. Thus the limits of creative expression had to be explored by the musicians themselves. The situation was the same for those who ran the Molodezhnoe. The following remark indicated the subtle yet awkward position of the head of the cafe:

> Of course he can have some of the photographs. What could possibly be wrong with that? How can there be any question? There are no problems. But please come to me about everything. If anything went wrong, well, you know yourself ...

The freedom that jazz should embody was too abstract in the Soviet Union. One bassist commented about his experience of co-starring with Mulligan, which for him was real but fictional at the same time, in the following way:

> I know this didn't really happen and has only been written in science fiction and that you are not really here, but it is still very nice for us.[36]

Still, the fact that the Komsomol even allowed a jazz scene to flourish was in itself a historical milestone for Soviet jazz. Jazz festivals in the 1960s started to appear in various Russian cities, first in Moscow and Leningrad in 1962, and then expanded to other regional cities such as Riga and Novosibirsk. Prominent Soviet jazz figures like Alexander Tsfasman participated as jury at these festivals, with most of the musical pieces either created by members of the Union of Soviet Composers, or were numbers clearly inspired by Russian folk songs. This indicated an explicit intention by the authorities to make jazz "Sovietized." Furthermore, from 1965 onwards the state-owned record company Melodiya began producing jazz records.[37]

In this context, the 1967 International Jazz Festival held at Tallinn has been frequently referred to as one of the most important events in the Soviet jazz scene during the 1960s. The highlight of this festival was the appearance of the quartet led by tenor saxophonist Charles Lloyd. Consisting of Lloyd, pianist Keith Jarrett, bassist Ron McClure and drummer Jack DeJohnette, the quartet won the "Jazz Artist of the Year" as hosted by *Down Beat* in the same year. When the quartet members arrived in Tallinn, the local authorities, who had tolerated their appearance at the festival until that time, suddenly began to show signs of being difficult. Despite permission initially being granted, it was discovered upon arrival in Tallinn that Lloyd's quartet was not allowed to perform at the festival. Oddly, however, after some waiting the authorities relented and they could participate. When the quartet appeared on stage the excited audience "exploded," while the festival's officials tried to restrain the audience by shouting: "We are not children. Please sit down!" Although this riotous response puzzled the authorities, Lloyd was impressed with the solid eight and a half-minute ovation by the audience to such an extent he felt, "I can't describe it in words." The festival was reported by the world's press as a major successful jazz event held in the Soviet Union. Later Lloyd released the album *Charles Lloyd in the Soviet Union* reflecting his time performing in Tallinn.[38]

Compared with the festival in Tallinn, the authorities' treatment of Willis Conover revealed the awkward position jazz held in 1960s Soviet society. Conover, who accompanied the quartet in Tallinn, then visited Moscow and held a film screening event at the US embassy featuring a documentary of sorts of the American jazz scene. Already, following Benny Goodman's Soviet tour, Catherman had suggested sending Conover as a lecturer to the Soviet Union to speak on jazz. He thought the Soviet authorities might accept Conover, "given the respectability which jazz now seems to enjoy."[39] And yet, the increasing respectability of jazz in Soviet society had not eased the caution shown by the Soviet authorities, who were still wary of its explicit association with America. According to historian Rüdiger Ritter, the Komsomol asked local musicians who showed an interest in attending the embassy event to practice self-restraint, and instead invited them to an alternative event at the officially sanctioned jazz cafe the Siniaia Ptitsa, which was intentionally scheduled for the same evening as the Conover event. It also warned those people visiting the embassy that they would not be allowed to participate in future international jazz festivals, and would also be banned from traveling abroad. For musicians who wished to continue to actively participate in the Soviet jazz scene the option was obvious. Saxophonist Alexey Kozlov explained his disappointment to Conover, saying: "You will soon leave us to go home, but we have to live here." Conover simply replied: "I understand." In Kozlov's heart he undoubtedly felt a sense of betrayal, as probably did many of the musicians who went to the Siniaia Ptitsa that evening, only finding a degree of respite in vodka. Somewhat unsurprisingly, many of the same musicians who visited the embassy that evening later decided to leave their home country and emigrate to the West.[40]

As the visits by Mulligan and Conover suggest, while jazz was becoming increasingly legitimized during the 1960s as a part of the official Soviet culture, it was still an awkward fit in Soviet society in light of what had been represented by this music. In this context, the next jazz ambassador to the Soviet Union provides us with another example of how jazz and Americanism had to be deconstructed for the Soviet authorities, even as the dawn of détente became visible.

Ellington, jazz and America

After the Czech crisis, improving relations with America became an urgent priority for the Soviet government. Asserting in his inaugural speech that the world was now in an era of negotiation – against the backdrop of Sino–Soviet conflict – Richard Nixon also saw an advantage to commencing the Strategic Arms Limitation Talks (SALT) with his Soviet counterpart. In these new signs of improvement in the broader US-Soviet relationship, a new jazz ambassador was selected to travel to the Soviet Union. In September 1971, Duke Ellington was sent to Moscow. Already 72 years old but still a star in the global jazz scene, Ellington was a legendary figure and a living symbol of "Take the A

Train" – the popular theme song of *Music USA*. He had a busy month-long schedule in the Soviet Union, including seeing the Bolshoi Ballet perform in response to an invitation on the first day of his arrival, while during his 22-plus performances he drew a total audience of over 120,000 people.[41]

Jazz in Soviet society was still under the authorities' control, and musicians did not enjoy complete musical freedom. Meanwhile, there remained an unsated desire among jazz fans for authentic American jazz. In this respect, Ellington was a highly suitable choice for the Soviet authorities, local media and fans. First of all, for the authorities making strenuous efforts to mitigate the negative image of the Soviet Union caused by the Czech crisis, they saw Ellington as having a useful role to play. As suggested by Boris H. Klosson, the American chargé d'affaires in Moscow, they could show the world their "open-mindedness" by receiving Ellington without really worrying about the effects avant-garde jazz musicians could potentially have on Soviet society. Secondly, with the death of Louis Armstrong in July 1971, Ellington had subsequently reached the status of a "mythical figure" in the global jazz scene, according to Klosson. This enabled the Soviet media to review his performances without too much concern about how this would be construed by local authorities. Finally, for fans, who "waited for his arrival in the USSR with something akin to anticipation of the Second Coming," the 72-year-old Ellington was simply seen as a living jazz legend. When he arrived at Sheremetyevo Airport in Moscow, one fan among the teeming crowd reportedly shouted: "We've been waiting for you for centuries." In Leningrad, one of the fans, who came from Moscow hoping to get a glimpse of Ellington or even acquire a rare ticket, excitedly told embassy officials: "Do you know what it means to Soviet jazz lovers for Duke Ellington's band to play here. It's like believing in a religion for years and then coming face-to-face with God and his prophets. It's fantastic!" As was found later, the age composition of the audiences suggested that there were more fans in their thirties and forties than younger people, for whom rock music was more attractive. The former liked the old repertoires that were classic Ellington, rather than more modern numbers. And certainly, Ellington's repertoire during this tour mostly consisted of numbers from the 1920s and 1930s.[42] His performance was such that Joseph A. Presel, a State Department official tasked with managing the visit, expressed his unconcealed disaffection at this "old-fashioned repertoire." In his mind Ellington had willfully "ignored the educative function of his visit."[43] These observations indicate that Ellington was a clearly a "safe" bet.

Scholars hold the view that the timing of Ellington's tour – following the announcement of Nixon's historical visit to Moscow the next year – and his personal relationship with Nixon himself were key factors behind Ellington's favorable treatment by officials in the Soviet Union.[44] But it should be stressed that as seen in the previous sections, jazz had been reinterpreted by Soviet officialdom so that the music in reality no longer posed a serious threat to Communist ideology. In this context, more focus should be placed on the gap in the interpretation of jazz between Americans and Soviet authorities, which manifested itself during the last stage of Ellington's tour.

Ellington's first performance was in Leningrad, where he was welcomed by local fans soon after he stepped off the Aeroflot flight. At the airport, fans enthusiastically waved their welcome banners, and musicians of a local Dixieland jazz band played an improvised version of "Basin Street Blues." During the performance at Oktyabr Hall, familiar pieces such as "It Don't Mean a Thing," "Misty," "I Can't Get Started" and "Perdido" were played in front of excited Soviet jazz aficionados. According to embassy reporting, the audience "went wild" at their favorites like "Satin Doll" and "Black and Tan Fantasy," and "exploded" upon the opening two notes of "Take the A Train" and "Mood Indigo." They obviously also liked the Russian folk song number "Ochi Chernye (Dark Eyes)" played by tenor saxophonist Paul Gonsalves in one of their last numbers. Fascinated by the "magic" Ellington made, the Leningraders did not allow a single performance to finish on time or without demanding an encore. The final performance in Leningrad saw encores alone last 90 minutes, and even after the performance finally ended, fans would not leave the hall, and instead stayed on clapping rhythmically chanting "Duke, Duke."[45]

Contrary to Leningrad, the jazz scene in Minsk was limited. There were no welcoming fans upon arrival, nor were there any scalpers touting their business. However, as opposed to cool silence, each of the five performances ended with great excitement from the audience. With their enthusiasm sparked with "Caravan," "Satin Doll" and "Sophisticated Lady," the audience reacted with especially loud cheers to "Take the A Train." In Kiev there was a similar reaction. Although the keyboard of the piano was damaged, and the air conditioner was broken, Ellington was eager to leave this place with a good impression because this was where his favorite composer, Nikolai Rimsky-Korsakov, was born. According to Presel, somewhat humorously, some local police officers in attendance at the hall turned out to be from the Ukrainian band of the Ministry of Internal Affairs who were unable to procure tickets, so they effectively sneaked into the show in uniform pretending to be on-duty police officers. In Rostov-na-Donu, trumpeter Harold Johnson played "Hello Dolly" and "Mack the Knife" à la Louis Armstrong, receiving a warm and enthusiastic reaction from fans.[46]

And finally, the "A train" arrived in Moscow, the final city on Ellington's Soviet tour. The first performance lasted for four hours with "encore following encore." Ellington, clearly pleased with the warm welcome, caught drummer Rufus Jones after leaving the stage and responded to the audience's high expectations by saying "Come on Rufus, let's play some more!" Despite high ticket prices by local standards, fans traveled from as far as Odessa, Riga and Yakutsk to see Ellington in Moscow. Not everyone could enter the concert hall though, and a fan who had attended his performances in Leningrad told a US embassy officer in Moscow with obviously mixed feelings: "I should be satisfied with that, but I came to Moscow anyway. I knew tickets would be hard to get, so even if I don't get to attend another concert, at least I will have been closer to Duke Ellington and his wonderful music for just a little longer." For a young fan who rushed from Yakutsk and bought a ticket from a scalper for four times the original price, "This only happens once in a lifetime." He continued, "You cannot imagine the impression that Ellington makes on a Soviet audience."[47]

In Moscow, four performances were planned at first. However, the capacity of the concert hall, the Estrada Theater, was so small that even the Union of Moscow Composers was only allocated a few tickets. There was growing dissatisfaction among fans over this predicament. The Moscow Jazz Club head Alexei Batashev angrily asked "Who got all the tickets?" As a result, a widespread rumor took hold that only a small number of tickets were sold at the decision of the Central Committee of the Communist Party, and the rest were circulated to party bureaucrats. Night lines of fans seeking tickets in areas around the hall were harassed by militia. In the eyes of Klosson, it was obvious that something had to be done to ease the mounting pressure from the public to acquire tickets. In an unprecedented move by Soviet authorities they asked Ellington to put on extra performances to satisfy this fervent demand from the public. Initially proposed were two matinee performances at the same hall, but the US embassy, after consulting with the State Department, asked for performances at the Palace of Sports, which had a capacity about eight times larger than the Estrada Theater. Although the Soviet side declared this was "Impossible" because they were laying ice for ice hockey games, the embassy urged them to simply "Melt the ice." When the US embassy told Soviet officials that it was reluctant to grant any more performances in Moscow, the ice in the ice hockey stadium suddenly "melted." After some unforeseen complications at the end of Ellington's tour, Klosson declared that the entire tour had been "a smash hit."[48]

From the viewpoint of American officials, the Ellington tour was full of unusual and unexpected events. At a jazz session at the House of Friendship in Moscow, Ellington heard his "Take the A Train" played by local musicians, including Alexey Kozlov. Soon tenor saxophonist Gonsalves, trombonist Malcolm Taylor, trumpeter Eddie Preston and several others joined this Soviet-led musical performance in an impromptu jam session. Following this unusual performance, the piece "My Love" was performed, which was a new number Ellington had especially composed for this tour. This rather remarkable and collaborative impromptu US-Soviet jazz performance reached new heights when Ellington performed playing the Russian balalaika, which had been given to him as a gift that same day.[49] However, the most exceptional part of the Soviet tour occurred in an unofficial interaction with local musicians in Leningrad, which would later become known as the "big scandal in Leningrad." Two members of the local jazz club, the Kamerton, had requested through unofficial channels to have a secret jam session with the visiting Americans, with the message discreetly received by Mercer Ellington, Duke's son, who enthusiastically accepted the invitation. Since the event was kept quiet and the authorities purposely not informed, the audience was limited to 150 enthusiastic fans, who packed into the Komsomol-supported local jazz club, the Byeliye Nochi. Ten members of Ellington's tour group participated in this session, as well as a small number of local musicians. Fans who were unable to squeeze themselves into the club crowded around its windows to catch Johnny Coles's hot flugelhorn and the powerful blues of Nell Brookshire. The host of this performance was the Kamerton, which had supported Goodman's 1962 performances at the University of Leningrad. The Kamerton held monthly jazz concerts – while in June each year they played host to an all-night floating jazz party on a local pleasure boat. When the Komsomol Committee inevitably heard about the scandal, they quickly punished the Kamerton by canceling the monthly concerts for one year on the grounds it had not been consulted about the joint session with Ellington's band.[50]

As this scandal suggests, fans could not enjoy unrestricted interactions with Ellington or his band. Like his predecessors had experienced during earlier tours, the authorities sought to keep social contact to a minimum with the American musicians, while any interactions were monitored closely. In Leningrad, local police were stationed in the aisle leading up to the stage to prevent any off-script interactions with the American band, while the authorities also sent an interpreter to accompany the Americans, thus enabling a degree of control over the band's activities and communication with local jazz fans. In Minsk, even at rehearsal when there were few people around, the lobby leading to the stage was flooded with "goons." When the American embassy's escort officer asked whether the Soviet security agency, the Komitet Gosudarstvennoy Bezopasnosti (KGB; Committee for State Security), were part of the entrance guards, the Goskonsert escort officer somewhat unconvincingly denied this was the case.[51]

This contrasted with how Ellington's Soviet tour was treated in local press coverage – what the State Department termed "royal carpet treatment."[52] Highly positive coverage of the visiting band appeared soon after performances started. Immediately after the performance at Leningrad, the Komsomol organ *Komsomolskaya Pravda* reported, "the likes of Toscanini, Stokowski, Ormandy and Weil have all been enraptured by Ellington's music, thus establishing the Duke's credentials even among readers not familiar with the jazz scene as a whole."[53] On the day Ellington left Moscow, after completing the Soviet tour, the usually staid *Pravda* featured an article about Ellington and his band titled "Orchestra of Virtuosos." It wrote with an almost sentimental tone that "The time for parting has come."[54] It was a rare example of *Pravda* positively reporting on an American performing arts group touring the Soviet Union, let alone reporting its activities in such an enthusiastic tone. Similarly, Ellington received high praise in the article titled "'Caravan' comes to Moscow" published in *Sovetskaya Kultura*, while an even more upbeat article in *Sovetskaya Rossiya* titled "Duke Ellington: I Love You" surprised both the band members and the State Department officials by the degree of its warmth.[55]

In examining why these reviews and public messaging were so favorable, we can discern why the Soviet authorities agreed to Ellington's substantial month-long series of concerts. During the tour, despite receiving positive treatment by the press, Ellington was sometimes frustrated with the gap in how jazz was interpreted. Ellington was a pianist, composer and band leader. Once asked whether his music was jazz, he replied: "Louis Armstrong played Louis Armstrong. Sidney Bechet played Sidney Bechet. Gerry Mulligan plays Gerry Mulligan." His philosophy was clear – he hated being pigeon-holed into a specific category of music.[56] This view of music was manifest in a discussion he had with the chair of the Ukrainian Composer Union during the Soviet tour. When the chair suggested that unique African American social conditions had helped create Ellington's music, and proffered that Ellington was a "successful Negro musician and composer," the American became furious at these attempts to impose an identity on him. According to Ellington, his music was not a product of his environment but was the result of nothing short of his raw talent and ability. Klosson described this tense exchange as a difference between a "self-styled rugged individualist of the American music world" and composers "who had made their careers rocking no boats in the sea of socialist realism."[57]

In interviews with Soviet newspapers as well as television and radio stations, Ellington felt that there was a tendency to emphasize skin color. *Sovetskaya Rossiya* introduced Ellington's music as "rooted in the folk arts of African and American negroes," while a local newspaper in Leningrad reported that his music helped the Soviets to understand "the soul of the Negro people."[58] Whereas the newspaper *Sovetskaya Kultura*, while praising his accomplishments in improving the rights of African Americans, explained that Ellington "fired his first salvo at racism as long as 50 years ago, when he traveled to the southern states of America with his 'Negritude'." The paper also touched upon the close relationship between him and Martin Luther King and opined that Ellington created "his own music on the structural basis of a Negro melos."[59] According to the weekly magazine *Nedelya*, his Soviet tour "brought the many voices of the Negro ghetto, the quickened pulse and hard breathing of its inhabitants, the screaming silence of poverty, and the mad rhythms of festive occasions."[60] In addition, Minsk's local newspaper reported how his music skillfully and extensively used "material of the musical epos of American Negroes – the blues."[61] The emphasis on Ellington's skin color in Soviet media underscores the fact that jazz was interpreted in the Soviet Union not as a symbol of Americanism or even as American culture per se, which in turn had enabled Soviet officialdom to consent to Ellington's tour.[62]

Ellington was clearly uncomfortable being labeled a successful "black" composer. According to Presel's reporting, Ellington emphasized that he was awarded the Presidential Medal of Freedom, the highest award for civilians – which made him, more than anything, an "American" composer. However, Soviet journalists appeared unable to understand these nuances, nor his sentiment when he said he had no interest in skin color.[63] It must have seemed inconsistent that the musician who had composed such pieces as "Black and Tan Fantasy" and "A Tone Parallel to Harlem" – and was widely seen as the founder of "Negro music" – had no interest in being treated as an African American. On this, as Harvey G. Cohen points out, Ellington never allowed others in general, and especially Communists as a staunch anti-Communist himself, to attack America by using race. While Ellington had produced a lot of music reflective of African American culture since the 1920s, ultimately he had confidence in American democracy rather than highlighting racial factors when representing his home country outside America.

Therefore, when sensing the critical tone against America by the Soviets, he put race aside and acted as an American.[64]

Here, the logic of racial integration that had upended American society during the 1960s was reinterpreted yet again in a new light by Ellington, as America's best-known jazz ambassador. When American jazz ambassadors began to travel the world in the mid-1950s at the request of the US government, what accompanied them on these tours was the notion of color-blind Americanism, which stressed racial integration and harmony. When in the 1960s, the civil rights movement began gaining momentum – and decolonization was also advancing around the developing world – the portrayal of American jazz as color-conscious began to emerge. Ellington, while touring the Soviet Union, was an American more than an African American, and was a musician who identified his music with freedom and democracy, stubbornly refusing to acknowledge to his interlocutors that his music was defined by the color of his skin.

When Ellington passed away on 24 May 1974, Nixon, then in the midst of the Watergate scandal, offered his condolences and issued a public statement praising the life of "America's foremost composer" for his "wit, taste, intelligence and elegance."[65] However, as discussed above, Nixon's interpretation of jazz as America's foremost culture contrasted with the official Soviet interpretation, which was determined to emphasize that jazz was not the exclusive property of Americanism. As the result of effectively controlling the domestic jazz scene, the Soviet Communist Party succeeded in gradually making jazz less threatening to – and compatible with – official Communist ideology. Furthermore, this ideological gap in the interpretation of jazz enabled the Soviet authorities to accept four American jazz ambassadors without worrying too much about jazz's association with Americanism. Nevertheless, as the descriptions of each of the four American musicians' experiences reveal, unsupervised interactions between jazz ambassadors and local jazz fans were largely forbidden, with authorities taking great pains to restrict and regulate these social and personal interactions. Then, to what extent can the same be said of Eastern Europe, a region where jazz's unique development helped promote a transnational exchange of musicians and their ideas? The next chapter elaborates on what jazz meant in this particular geographical region following the cultural "thaw" initiated in the Soviet Union.

Notes

1 Zubok, *A Failed Empire*, pp.174–76.
2 Ibid., pp.171, 189; Brown, *The Rise and Fall of Communism*, pp.254–55, 262–63. Only three years before, Russian poet Boris Pasternak and his 1957 novel *Doctor Zhivago*, depicting the Russian Revolution in a way deviating from socialist realism, had had a markedly different experience. Despite Pasternak winning the Nobel Prize for Literature, he was forced to decline the prize under heavy political pressure at home. *Doctor Zhivago* was eventually published in Italy. For this process and the CIA involvement in publishing this novel, see Paolo Mancosu, *Inside the Zhivago Storm: The Editorial Adventures of Pasternak's Masterpiece* (Milan:

Feltrinelli, 2013); Peter Finn and Petra Couvee, *The Zhivago Affair: The Kremlin, the CIA, and the Battle over a Forbidden Book* (London: Harvill Secker, 2014).
3 "The Reds and Dr. Stearns," *Down Beat*, vol.26 no.14, 9 July 1959; Von Eschen, *Satchmo Blows Up the World*, p.95.
4 Hixson, *Parting the Curtain*, p.204.
5 Michel Abeßer, "Between Cultural Opening, Nostalgia and Isolation: Soviet Debates on Jazz between 1953 and 1964," in Pickhan and Ritter (eds.), *Jazz behind the Iron Curtain*, pp.108–16; Rüdiger Ritter, "Negotiated Spaces: Jazz in Moscow after the Thaw," in Pickhan and Ritter (eds.), *Meanings of Jazz in State Socialism*, pp.176–80; Irina Novikova, "Black Music, White Freedom: Times and Spaces of Jazz Countercultures in the USSR," in Heike Raphael-Hernandez (ed.), *Blackening Europe: The African American Presence* (London: Routledge, 2003), p.80.
6 NARA, RG 59, CDF 1955-59, Box 104, 032 Goodman, Benny, Goodman to Bohlen, 19 August 1955; Bohlen to Goodman, 29 August 1955; Goodman to Stoessel, 12 September 1955; McCardle to Goodman, 4 October 1955. For Goodman's early attempt to tour the Soviet Union, see also Ross Firestone, *Swing, Swing, Swing: The Life & Times of Benny Goodman* (New York: W. W. Norton and Company, 1994), pp.405, 407.
7 CU, Box 64-24, "Benny Goodman and His Band in the Soviet Union," 10 July 1962.
8 Ibid. For Goodman's Soviet tour in general, see also Von Eschen, *Satchmo Blows Up the World*, pp.92–120; Davenport, *Jazz Diplomacy*, pp.118–20; Cohen, *Duke Ellington's America*, pp.419–21.
9 CU, Box 64-24, "Benny Goodman and His Band in the Soviet Union," 10 July 1962.
10 Ibid.
11 CU, Box 64-24, *Pravda* (translated), 31 May 1962; "Benny Goodman and His Band in the Soviet Union," 10 July 1962.
12 CU, Box 64-24, "Benny Goodman and His Band in the Soviet Union," 10 July 1962.
13 Ibid.
14 Ibid.
15 CU, Box 64-24, "Goodman's Bandsmen Upset by Selections," *Vanity Star*, 1 July 1962; "Benny Goodman and His Band in the Soviet Union," 10 July 1962. See also Firestone, *Swing, Swing, Swing*, p.413; Von Eschen, *Satchmo Blows Up the World*, pp.102–3, 107, 111–13, 116; Davenport, *Jazz Diplomacy*, pp.119–20.
16 CU, Box 64-24, "Benny Goodman and His Band in the Soviet Union," 10 July 1962. See also Firestone, *Swing, Swing, Swing*, pp.413–14; Von Eschen, *Satchmo Blows Up the World*, pp.112–13.
17 US Department of State (ed.), *FRUS, 1961–63, Volume V, Soviet Union* (Washington, DC: Government Printing Office, 1987), p.441, "Telegram from the Embassy in the Soviet Union to the Department of State," 31 May 1962.
18 Leonard Feather, "Inside the Soviet Jazz," *Down Beat*, vol.29 no.22, 16 August 1962.
19 See Von Eschen, *Satchmo Blows Up the World*, p.100.
20 CU, Box 49-15, "Cultural Presentations Plan, FY 1966," undated.
21 Ritter, "Negotiated Spaces," pp.172–76. In the previous year, Utesov had publicly defended the value of jazz in *Sovetskaya Kultura*, declaring that jazz's roots was "not in the bankers' safes but in the poor Negro quarters." For Utesov, who was brought up in Odessa, "musicians always improvised at weddings" and in that sense "so-called Dixieland existed in Odessa before New Orleans." Firestone, *Swing, Swing, Swing*, p.407.
22 Caute, *The Dancer Defects*, p.462. See also Brown, *The Rise and Fall of Communism*, pp.410–11.

23 CU, Box 95-19, "Transcript of Proceedings. Advisory Committee on the Arts. Room 1406. Department of State. Monday, April 3, 1967," undated.
24 CU, Box 66-14, "Cultural Exchange: The Earl Hines Band in the USSR," 6 September 1966. For the Hines tour in general, see also Von Eschen, *Satchmo Blows Up the World*, pp.198–200; Davenport, *Jazz Diplomacy*, pp.130–31.
25 CU, Box 66-14, "Cultural Exchange: The Earl Hines Band in the USSR," 6 September 1966.
26 Ibid.
27 Ibid.
28 Ibid.
29 Ibid.
30 Ibid.
31 CU, Box 51-1, "List of Jazz Groups for Soviet Program," 4 May 1967.
32 CU, Box 95-16, "Advisory Committee on the Arts, Dinner Meeting, City Tavern Association, Washington, D.C., April 3, 1967," undated.
33 NARA, RG 59, CDF 1967–69, Box 370, EDX US - USSR, "Gerry Mulligan Performs in Moscow," 16 July 1967.
34 Ibid.
35 Ibid. See also Davenport, *Jazz Diplomacy*, pp.136–37.
36 NARA, RG 59, CDF 1967–69, Box 370, EDX US - USSR, "Gerry Mulligan Performs in Moscow," 16 July 1967. For more on the Komsomol's policy toward jazz and jazz cafes, see Gleb Tsipursky, *Pleasure, Power, and the Pursuit of Communism: Soviet Youth and State-Sponsored Popular Culture during the Early Cold War, 1945–1968* (PhD Thesis, University of North Carolina, 2011), pp.376–99.
37 Starr, *Red and Hot*, pp.282–84; Ritter, "Negotiated Spaces," pp.180–85.
38 Ira Gitler, "Charles Lloyd in Russia: Ovations and Frustrations," *Down Beat*, vol.34 no.14, 13 July 1967; Starr, *Red and Hot*, pp.286–8. See also Tiit Lauk, "Estonian Jazz before and behind the 'Iron Curtain'," in Pickhan and Ritter (eds.), *Jazz behind the Iron Curtain*, pp. 160–63; Davenport, *Jazz Diplomacy*, pp.135–36.
39 CU, Box 64-24, "Benny Goodman and His Band in the Soviet Union," 10 July 1962.
40 Ritter, "Negotiated Spaces," pp.186–88.
41 CU, Box 61-15, "The Duke Ellington Orchestra, Final Itinerary," undated.
42 CU, Box 61-15, "Duke Ellington Orchestra, USSR, September 10 – October 3, 1971, Recapitulation," undated; "Duke Ellington in the USSR," 10 December 1971; "Duke Ellington in the USSR, September – October 1971. Joseph A. Presel," undated; "Cultural Presentations, List of Attractions, Touring Fiscal Year 1972," undated; AmEmbassy Moscow to USINFO WashDC, 16 September 1971.
43 CU, Box 61-15, "Duke Ellington in the USSR, September – October 1971. Joseph A. Presel," undated.
44 See Von Eschen, *Satchmo Blows Up the World*, pp.204–6; Cohen, *Duke Ellington's America*, pp.542, 549.
45 CU, Box 61-15, "Duke Ellington in the USSR," 10 December 1971; AmEmbassy Moscow to USINFO WashDC, 14, 16 and 19 September 1971. For Ellington's Soviet tour in general, see also Von Eschen, *Satchmo Blows Up the World*, pp.204–15; Cohen, *Duke Ellington's America*, pp.541–55.
46 CU, Box 61-15, AmEmbassy Moscow to USINFO WashDC, 22 and 30 September 1971; AmEmbassy Moscow to USINFO WashDC, 6 October 1971; "Duke Ellington in the USSR, September – October 1971. Joseph A. Presel," undated. Ellington reminisced that although the audience continued requesting for "When the Saints Go Marching In," he refused to play this piece because "Now 'The Saints' is a legitimate hymn to play at the right time, in the right place." Instead he let Johnson play "Hello Dolly." See Ellington, *Music Is My Mistress*, p.368.

47 CU, Box 61-15, AmEmbassy Moscow to USINFO WashDC, 10 and 12 October 1971; "Duke Ellington Orchestra, USSR, September 10 – October 3, 1971, Recapitulation," undated.
48 CU, Box 61-15, "Duke Ellington in the USSR," 10 December 1971. For Ellington's performance in Moscow, see also Von Eschen, *Satchmo Blows Up the World*, p.213; Cohen, *Duke Ellington's America*, pp.553–54.
49 CU, Box 61-15, AmEmbassy Moscow to USINFO WashDC, 9 October 1971; "Duke Ellington Orchestra, USSR, September 10 – October 3, 1971, Recapitulation," undated; "Jazz at the Znaniye Society," 20 October 1971.
50 CU, Box 61-15, AmEmbassy Moscow to USINFO WashDC, 20 September 1971; "Duke Ellington in the USSR," 10 December 1971; "Some Notes on the 1971 Leningrad Jazz Scene," 22 October 1971. See also Von Eschen, *Satchmo Blows Up the World*, pp.208, 210; Cohen, *Duke Ellington's America*, pp.547–48.
51 CU, Box 61-15, "Duke Ellington in the USSR," 10 December 1971.
52 CU, Box 61-15, "Duke Ellington Orchestra, USSR, September 10 – October 3, 1971, Recapitulation," undated.
53 CU, Box 61-15, Lewis to Richardson, 28 September 1971.
54 CU, Box 61-15, "Orchestra of Virtuosos, Translation, *Pravda*," 13 October 1971.
55 CU, Box 61-15, "'Caravan' Comes to Moscow, Translated, *Sovetskaya Kultura*," 9 October 1971; "Duke Ellington in the USSR," 10 December 1971. See also Von Eschen, *Satchmo Blows Up the World*, p.215; Cohen, *Duke Ellington's America*, pp.550–51.
56 CU, Box 61-13, "Duke to Play in Russia," *Evening Star*, 30 August 1971; Box 61-15, AmEmbassy Moscow to USINFO WashDC, 24 September 1971.
57 Box 61-15, AmEmbassy Moscow to USINFO WashDC, 30 September 1971; "Duke Ellington Orchestra, USSR, September 10 – October 3, 1971, Recapitulation," undated.
58 Box 61-17, AmEmbassy Moscow to SecState WashDC, 15 October 1971; "Music Helps Us Understand," *The Washington Post*, 22 September 1971.
59 Box 61-15, "'Caravan' Comes to Moscow, translated, Sovetshkaya Kultura," 9 October 1971.
60 Box 61-15, "Variations on the Theme 'I Love You Madly', translated, Nedelya," 4 October 1971.
61 Box 61-15, "Duke Ellington, the Duke of Jazz, translated, Vecherniy Minsk," 22 September 1971.
62 Novikova, "Black Music, White Freedom," pp.74–75.
63 CU, Box 61-15, "Duke Ellington in the USSR, September – October 1971. Joseph A. Presel," undated.
64 Cohen, *Duke Ellington's America*, pp.544–50.
65 Richard M. Nixon, *Public Papers of the Presidents of the United States: Richard M. Nixon, 1974* (Washington, DC: Government Printing Office, 1975), p.451.

7 Contesting discourses in East European jazz scenes

After the death of Stalin, the Soviet leadership began to modify its relationship with the satellite countries across Eastern Europe. Maintaining stability in these Communist regimes remained a top priority for Moscow, but to this end promoting de-Stalinization was first required.

In the midst of this de-Stalinization process, Poland was the most open country to the West, and anti-Russian emotion and opposition to the postwar domestic Sovietization was strong among its people. Unsurprisingly, in Poland cultural Stalinism experienced a rapid demise. After the workers' protest at Poznan in June 1956, Władysław Gomułka was reinstated to the Polish United Workers' Party, and soon initiated a set of domestic changes as First Secretary of the party. While upholding Poland's responsibilities to the Warsaw Pact, he allowed a certain degree of liberalization to occur through improving relations with the Catholic Church and relaxing ideological controls in various cultural fields. As a result, although intellectual freedom was not necessarily enjoyed to the fullest extent, the local arts scene was soon reinvigorated, resulting in innovative cultural productions in such fields as film, theater, literature and music.[1] However, the domestic jazz scene had been a harbinger of change even before the first mass protests against the Communist rule had begun. The first jazz journal, *Jazz*, had in fact been launched in February 1956, as the only jazz journal in the Eastern bloc countries at the time. Introducing domestic jazz clubs and jazz events, as well as disseminating information from various Western jazz scenes, was the staple output of *Jazz*. Printing 40,000 copies at its peak, the journal boasted a large readership. Importantly, even cross-border exchanges with fans among satellite countries was encouraged through *Jazz*. East German critic Reginald Rudorf, for example, introduced his country's jazz scene to readers through the article titled "A Letter from the GDR: Leipzig – The Centre of All Things Jazz in the GDR."[2]

Jazz festivals served as another venue for cross-border communication among Eastern bloc jazz fans and musicians. At the fifth World Festival of Youth and Students organized in Warsaw in August 1955, a Polish jazz band performed, eliciting an enthusiastically warm response from the audience.[3] According to RFE's field report, a musician from Denmark told a reporter from the Danish Communist daily, *Land of Folk*, that both the musicians' and the audience's mood lifted as the consumption of vodka continued and the music became louder.[4] In addition, a festival held in Sopot on the Baltic Sea in August 1956 attracted 25,000 people, becoming a major turning point in the development of the East European jazz scene in the postwar period. It was six months after Khrushchev's secret speech that resulted in the fall of "little Stalin" in some of the satellite countries. At this festival, held under the slogan of "the green light for jazz," there was a parade commemorating New Orleans jazz. Just like jazz was played in New Orleans during funerals, the parade took place symbolizing sending Stalinism and "little Stalin" to the grave. Many musicians both from inside and outside Poland participated in this event. However, it was the polish doctor Krzysztof Komeda – a future symbol of modern Polish jazz – who received the most enthusiastic audience response with his performance of Bach's Invention No. 14 to cool jazz.[5] The following year, jazz critic Joachim Berendt and the Frankfurt All Stars, with Joki Freund and Albert Mangelsdorff, visited the same festival from West Germany, collaborating with Komeda.[6] Moreover, as the largest international jazz festival in Eastern Europe, the Jazz Jamboree started in 1958, turning Poland into the country where the latest jazz from the East could be heard.

However, as the recent historiography of jazz in Communist countries shows, the expansion of the Polish jazz scene was not autonomous, nor was it free from official interventions.[7] In this regard, this series of new developments surrounding jazz in Poland in fact reflected the jazz control policy the authorities had implemented. While fans and musicians started to openly appreciate and play jazz, they nonetheless remained acutely aware of the limits local authorities would tolerate. Keeping these limitations in mind, the following sections examine prominent American jazz figures' tours to East European countries, examining the context in which locals – including fans, authorities and media – reacted to this music. Local Communist authorities accepted visits by these high-profile Americans but they did not necessarily acquiesce to the "American music" discourse – this perspective will foreground the politics behind depoliticizing jazz. Following which, the politics of jazz at the local level is further investigated by focusing on the official policy of repression of a specific Czechoslovakian jazz group, and the ensuing global backlash against these actions that occurred in the final phase of the Cold War.

Brubeck and Conover in a changing jazz scene

In considering jazz's social standing in Poland in the late 1950s, visits by American jazz figures Dave Brubeck and Willis Conover provide telling examples.[8] Brubeck was Secretary of State Dulles's favorite musician, who described him as being nothing short of a "brilliant pianist."[9]

Starting from Szczecin, a city near the East German border, the Brubeck quartet toured seven cities – including the port city of Gdańsk, Poznan where the memory of the 1956 riots was still fresh, as well as the capital city of Warsaw. During each performance, according to Frank J. Lewand, the cultural attaché from the US embassy, young Polish fans focused on the quartet's musical techniques, while elder fans, albeit being somewhat perplexed and confused with the quartet's improvisation, kept an open mind and did not show an outwardly negative reaction to this music. In Szczecin, Brubeck's two sons, Darius and Michael, played "Take the A Train" on the piano and drums respectively, causing much excitement among the fans in attendance.[10] As the local paper *Życie Warszawy* reported, the atmosphere was "similar to that at symphony concerts which take place in the same concert hall."[11] Brubeck himself composed a piece, named "Dziękuję (Thank You)," dedicated to Chopin and the Polish people. According to his own recollection, when the piece was played as a part of the encore repertoire, the concert hall was in complete and solemn silence. At that moment, Brubeck later recalled, he regretted playing that piece, thinking "now I've ruined all 12 concerts." But the next moment, the concert hall echoed in enthusiastic applause and loud cheers. It turned out that the audience had been stunned by Brubeck's jazz rendition of Chopin's repertoire.[12] The State Department, which had aimed to sell jazz as a "serious" culture by distinguishing it from rock music, was pleased to hear distinctive elements of classical music in Brubeck's modern jazz performances. In Warsaw, Lewand commented that modern jazz had "gained respectability and is no longer linked with hooliganism as an undesirable form of entertainment." Even after Brubeck had left Poland, the local paper *Przekroy* featured photos of his tour which were provided by the US embassy – while local newspapers published a series of articles about the tour, recalling the quartet as "one of the best in the world," with such titles as "Dave Brubeck – Non Plus Ultra" and "The Success of Dave Brubeck and the Satisfied Public."[13]

For the US embassy, Brubeck's tour confirmed "the fact that modern jazz performances by recognized American groups represent a worthy cultural export." In this sense, what the embassy saw in Polish fans' enthusiastic reactions strengthened their impression that jazz embodied America. But for Brubeck, it was Poland's recent past that he saw as substantially enhancing the value of jazz. On one day partway through the visit, Brubeck visited the Chopin statue, built in Łazienkowski Park in 1926 but later destroyed by the Nazis when Poland came under German occupation during the Second World War. The Chopin statue had been rebuilt in 1958 just before Brubeck's visit, which somewhat aligned with Brubeck's view that Poland was at a political turning point – a viewpoint he hinted at during one of his Polish performances when he remarked that "No dictatorship can tolerate jazz. It is the first sign of a return to freedom." His remark saw the audience erupt in rapturous applause. After returning home to America, Iola Brubeck, clearly impressed with the jazz culture in Poland, pointed out in her *Down Beat* article that jazz was a "symbol of protest to the Poles." In Iola's eyes, the presence of African American bassist Eugene Wright had a special meaning. When introduced during the performances, Wright was greeted with the loudest applause, as if they were protesting the Little Rock crisis the previous year.[14]

Iola's emphasis on racial factors is important when put into the context of the Polish authorities' reaction to the tour. The authorities saw the tour differently from the US embassy. That is, they had a special interest in associating jazz with American racial problems, portraying them as America's Achilles heel. As detailed by music historian Keith Hatschek, the official program book, created with the approval of authorities prior to the Brubeck tour, took pains to highlight the difference between capitalism and socialism. In addition, the white pianist Brubeck, who was born into a wealthy family and had received a privileged first-rate education with the finest musical teachers in America, was disingenuously contrasted with trumpeter Charlie Parker, who they pointedly noted was raised as a "poor black boy."[15] Therefore, although the authorities accepted the Brubeck tour, they harbored concerns that Americanism – as it was associated with jazz – would take root in Poland through Brubeck, resulting in the Polish authorities taking every opportunity to remind local jazz fans about the reality of race problems in American society at this time.

In that sense, the expansion of the Polish jazz scene was the result of a policy of controlled deregulation in a specific cultural field, carefully overseen by the Polish authorities. The institutionalization of jazz, which started in 1958 when the Polish Jazz Clubs Federation was founded, should also be understood in this context. Roman Waschko, local jazz critic who accompanied Brubeck in Warsaw, was inaugurated as its first president. It was later found that Waschko was an informer for the Polish secret police. This indicates that he was probably well aware of the still precarious position of the Polish jazz scene, which was under strict party supervision at this time.[16]

Still, the Polish authorities' acceptance of Willis Conover in 1959 was a clear indication that Poland was by far the most open place for jazz among the Soviet satellite countries. The initial plan outlining sending Conover to the region was firmly supported by Dulles, who assessed him as "quiet, sincere and personable." After examining what a possible tour by Conover would look like – it was proposed that he should give a series of public talks on the history of jazz and perform recordings with local musicians for radio programs, as well as participate in other cultural exchange events – Dulles ordered the Eastern European diplomatic missions to ascertain the feasibility of such a plan.[17] To this request, the US embassy in Prague was "not at all certain that the Czechoslovak Government would cooperate by issuing a visa to Mr. Conover."[18] The US legation in Budapest also harbored some reservations, in noting "it would not be feasible at this time, or in the near future, to have him visit Hungary." According to the legation, jazz musicians would be more acceptable to the authorities. However, because Conover was a well-known figure working for the VOA, and the Hungarian government was "attacking VOA broadcasts in general as slanderous, inciting, and the usual epithets," legation officials saw it as "extremely doubtful" that he would be able to obtain the necessary visa for such a visit.[19] Eventually, it was Poland that was selected as the target country. The fact the Polish government agreed to this visit, despite the air of caution expressed by American officials in the region, somewhat suggested that the Polish jazz scene was a relatively open environment in Eastern Europe.

The local reaction to Conover's visit proved beyond doubt his popularity. On 6 June 1959, when Conover landed at the airport in Warsaw, a number of journalists, fans and a welcome performance by local jazz musicians awaited him. Some fans came all the way from regional cities such as Kraków. They were clearly overjoyed at receiving Conover's autograph and shaking hands with him, seeing the face up close that they had only ever imagined on radio. In a special event at the Warsaw Philharmonic Hall, where local musicians performed and Conover evaluated their playing, Waschko introduced Conover to 700 ardent young fans. On another day, Conover busily edited the locally recorded tapes for the future broadcasts over the VOA in its Warsaw series, while also giving press interviews. According to Frank G. Siscoe, the counselor at the US embassy in Warsaw, Conover's visit provided Polish jazz fans with an "unprecedented experience."[20]

Importantly, a week after he left Poland, the local weekly magazine *Kulisy* carried an article about a specific comment Conover had made about jazz. Asked about the relationship between jazz and rock music, Conover replied that although both were the same in essence, "whereas from a diamond one may obtain a gem, coal will only give some warmth when it is burned. Jazz is diamond."[21] The publication of this article seems to have reflected an aspect of the Polish jazz scene of the day. With the rise of rock music, which was increasingly seen as a symbol of noise and decadence in place of jazz, the social standing of jazz was clearly changing and steadily improving. Subsequently, jazz became more institutionalized, and jazz festivals became increasingly commonplace, frequently supported by public subsidies throughout the 1960s.[22] Moreover, during this decade, jazz became incrementally de-Americanized. In May 1962, when the possibility of "Polish jazz" was being discussed – and when Benny Goodman was in the midst of his Soviet tour – Waschko accompanied the Polish modern jazz band the Wreckers to America for a six-week tour. Upon accepting an invitation from the American Council on Education, the band appeared at the Newport Jazz Festival, following an introduction by Conover himself.[23] In addition, the state-owned record company began releasing records under the series title "Polish jazz" from 1964. Of the 76 albums produced up to 1989, Krzysztof Komeda's *Astigmatic* (1966) became an iconic work illustrating the rich history of Polish jazz. Unfortunately, he was killed in a traffic accident in Los Angeles three years later, but talented young Polish musicians such as Adam Makowicz, Urszula Dudziak and Michal Urbaniak successfully debuted in America during the 1970s.[24]

A search for a national jazz style was not a phenomenon uniquely seen in Poland. In Hungary, Kádár János had commenced a relatively moderate policy of control under the so-called "Goulash Communism" idea, following Khrushchev's repeated criticisms of Stalin at the Twenty-Second Congress of the Communist Party of the Soviet Union in 1961. Although Kádár would not countenance political opposition – and free elections were never considered – literary and other cultural activities became freer. Symbolizing this shift, the number of people who traveled to Western countries reached 70,000 in 1963.[25] As for jazz, the authorities tried to win people's hearts and minds by placing the jazz scene under party control. In 1962, the jazz cafe Dália opened in Budapest with the support of the Hungarian Young Communist League, having the aim of propagating the party's cultural and ideological policies among youth circles.

While jazz in general was seen as a lesser evil than rock music, "sophisticated" jazz with less improvisation became the officially sanctioned model for jazz. As long as the color of Americanism was not publicly emphasized – nor social issues raised – the authorities permitted the broadcasting of jazz programs. At the same time, record production by state-supported record labels, as well as jazz education at music schools, also started. In addition, any musician assessed as unlikely to apply for refugee status abroad – nor was in the business of criticizing government cultural policies – generally had little difficulty receiving official permission to travel to international jazz festivals and perform in foreign countries. All of these official policy changes were in part attempts to make it compatible to be a good Communist and a jazz fan.[26]

Taming and institutionalizing jazz

In May 1964, Lyndon B. Johnson announced a policy of "bridge building" with East Europe, urging expansion of trade and cultural exchange with the aim of bringing long-term change to the people of Eastern Europe. The policy's main aim was stressed again in Johnson's October 1966 speech.[27] Although the ongoing war in Vietnam limited the prospect of a comprehensive easing of tensions between the two competing ideological blocs, the US government maintained high expectations around its jazz musicians and their roles performing in the Warsaw Pact countries.

In Romania, Nicolae Ceaușescu had strengthened his power base since 1965. Although belonging to the Warsaw Pact, the Ceaușescu regime interacted with the West to some extent. At the same time, Romania was developing friendly relations with China and Albania, both of which were experiencing deteriorating relations with the Soviet Union.[28] Thus, the US government kept close watch on this maverick East European country. There was also a certain domestic demand for jazz, as exemplified by Louis Armstrong's commercial tour to Romania in 1965. Furthermore, Woody Herman's performances in Bucharest occurred under this particular socio-political environment. However, Richard H. Davis, the US ambassador to Romania at the time, reported that Herman was not necessarily received with much enthusiasm. Davis usefully pointed out the local background that jazz had become acceptable only in recent years.[29]

The Charles Lloyd quartet, recognized as avant-garde within the State Department, was sent to Romania in October 1967 as part of the jazz diplomacy program. This is a curious example because, according to embassy reporting, "Bucharest is not Warsaw or Prague as far as acceptance of jazz is concerned." Moreover, the US embassy had even felt there was a risk in asking permission for a jazz quartet to perform in a city where "no built-in audience for avant-garde jazz" could be found. In reality, the performance itself "ended with the hall only sixty to seventy percent full" as the audience was not accustomed to the quartet's style of jazz. Without "tuneful or clearly recognizable jazz compositions" improvised jazz was not well understood, and even those who had regarded themselves as jazz enthusiasts seemed unable to "adjust to the non-traditional jazz program." Nonetheless, the State Department found there had been meaning in sending the Lloyd quartet to Bucharest. Lloyd's jazz might have been a "huge step away from what a Bucharest audience is used to," yet the embassy concluded that the risk in sending the quartet was justifiable. Together with other American musicians who had performed in Bucharest in previous months, including Isaac Stern, Van Cliburn and the Los Angeles Philharmonic, Lloyd's performance introduced "something of the range of musical activity in the United States."[30] When recalling the State Department's reluctance to send free jazz to Africa and the Soviet Union, the Department's stance with regard to avant-garde jazz for Eastern Europe stood in stark contrast.

Having established the non-aligned movement in the years leading up to 1955, Yugoslavia, while not a member of the Warsaw Pact but still a socialist country, normalized relations with the Soviet Union in 1955, just one year before fans warmly welcomed Dizzy Gillespie as the first American jazz ambassador. The commercial tours of Louis Armstrong (in 1959) and Ella Fitzgerald (in 1961) excited fans, while the first jazz festival was held in Bled in 1960. These events demonstrate that jazz had become somewhat a safe bet for the authorities, supported by the fact that jazz had increasingly become perceived as elitist with the rise of rock music – a phenomenon also observed in the Soviet bloc countries. Importantly, at jazz festivals musicians were requested to play at least two Yugoslav compositions, indicating that authorities viewed it as important that a sample of domestic music featured in these jazz performances.[31]

When Woody Herman visited Belgrade, Ljubljana and Zagreb as a jazz ambassador in April 1966, there was an element of "Yugoslav jazz" in his program. During the tour, Herman's theme song "Blue Flame," as well as "Woodchoppers Ball," "Early Autumn," "Four Brothers" and "Apple Honey" invited older fans on a trip down memory lane. But more than 80 percent of the audience were young fans, who were attracted by relatively new numbers such as "The Preacher," "Watermelon Man" and "Sister Sadie."[32] However, trumpeter Duško Gojković was the musician who grabbed more of the spotlight than Herman. Born in the town of Jajce in Yugoslavia, he had spent some years working with Herman in America. Understandably, his triumphant return home was enthusiastically welcomed by local jazz fans. The local paper *Večernje Novosti* celebrated the return of "our Duško Gojković," some ten years after Gillespie's first performance.[33] According to the Zagreb weekly paper *Studio*, Gojković was "received with ovations by our public after nearly 11 years of absence, which is quite in order because of all Yugoslav jazz-musicians he has achieved the most success in that field."[34]

Eastern Europe of the 1970s saw no Poznan (1956), Budapest (1956) or Prague (1968)-style uprisings or disturbances. In that sense, the Soviet-East European political relationship appeared stable on the surface. Under the gradual easing of Cold War tensions, East-West negotiations started to produce fruit. In February 1970, Poland signed a bilateral treaty with West Germany. The treaty officially recognized the Oder–Neisse line, which had been devised by the Allied powers at the end of the Second World War but long disputed as it had not been agreed to by any West German Chancellor since Konrad Adenauer. This diplomatic victory for Poland, however, was not accompanied by its domestic economic reform. Instead, after the Polish government announced a substantial increase in food prices, rolling strikes occurred at the shipyards in Gdansk and Gdynia in December 1970, which later developed into large-scale national demonstrations. This event saw Gomułka replaced with Edward Gierek as First Secretary of the ruling party. Gierek, on the one hand, launched a series of innovative policies such as liberalizing state control of writers and intellectuals. On the other, in order to solve a raft of economic problems and to comply with the people's demand for a consumerist society, Gierek deepened the country's financial dependence on Western banks – flush with a large influx of petrodollars – which led to Poland rapidly running up a large external debt with these external financiers. As a condition of the finance it received, the Polish government was required to relax the hitherto policy of state control and oversight of its internal political dissidents. As a result, the domestic cultural sphere flourished, and literature that had been banned from being translated previously, like the works of George Orwell, began to be translated and published for the public.[35]

During this period, the institutionalization of jazz further advanced in Poland. For example, the faculty of jazz and popular music was established at the Katowice Academy of Music. From housing to vouchers for purchasing musical instruments, the authorities provided jazz musicians with many new opportunities to further their art. It also became easier for musicians to travel abroad, and to receive public subsidies for holding jazz festivals and concerts, while earning money by playing jazz in the West also received official approval. In this way, jazz in Poland became increasingly "tamed."[36] The taming of jazz was more or less a common phenomenon across Eastern Europe. Being no longer a "forbidden fruit," jazz's symbolic power of resistance was seen as weakened. Accordingly, jazz festivals in Eastern Europe witnessed more American jazz musicians than before. In this context, it has been argued that during the 1970s there was a "convergence of interest" among the US State Department, jazz musicians and fans in Eastern Europe. However, this must be read against a broader backdrop of the official "taming" of local jazz scenes by Communist regimes in the region.[37]

At the vanguard of this wave of frequent appearances by American jazz musicians in the East European jazz scene were Dave Brubeck and Gerry Mulligan, who visited Poland and Romania in November 1970, as part of a broader European tour under the banner of George Wein's Newport Jazz Festival. Together with bassist Jack Six and drummer Alan Dawson, they appeared at the Jazz Jamboree in Warsaw on 4 November. Brubeck, who had visited Warsaw for the first time during his legendary 1958 concert tour, had clearly left an indelible impression on the Polish audience with his impressive performance at that time. This time, most of the audience were young fans who had not seen Brubeck's previous performances, but their applause started even before the first notes of his modern pieces were played, showing his unchanging popularity in Poland. Numbers such as "Lady Is a Tramp" and "St. Louis Woman" were played with long solos, inviting rhythmic applause from the audience. The US ambassador to

Poland Walter J. Stoessel proudly reported that "there were no groups and no musicians capable of coming close to the level of Brubeck and Mulligan." The members of the quartet also enjoyed positive interactions with local fans, while they happily agreed to interviews with local newspapers. People were attracted by the quartet members' suave personalities and their intellectualism.[38]

Then, the quartet headed for Romania, the country where American officials held high expectations for positive results. The US government, now trying to improve relations with China, had prioritized improving diplomatic relations with Romania because of its good relations with Beijing – hence the summit meeting with Ceauşescu only seven months after Nixon had assumed the presidency. In Bucharest, the quartet appeared at the Jazz Week festival, scheduled for the beginning of November 1970. Among the two standing-room-only performances held at the Palace of Culture, young fans and workers gathered eagerly for the daytime performance. According to Leonard C. Meeker, the US ambassador to Romania, they initially responded with modest applause, but Brubeck's rhythmical and powerful piano performance soon inspired them to sway, stomp their feet and offer enthusiastic applause. The night performance saw the entire audience applauding thunderously after each number, with the performance closing with "Take Five."[39] The local paper *Romania Libera* introduced Brubeck as an "excellent thinker, constructor and improvisator," while another newspaper, *Informatia Bucurestiului*, saw the influence of the symphonism behind his musical technique – Brubeck himself had studied under the tutelage of Arnold Schoenberg and Darius Milhaud.[40] The closeness of jazz and intelligence was stressed when *Romania Libera* reported: "Each rhythmic formula was logically elaborated, each musical period was attentively thought. He introduces waltz and rumba rhythm into jazz, transforms the most complex harmonic features by spontaneous improvisations, of an unusual savour."[41] In the same vein, an article in *Romania Literara*, an organ of the Romanian Writers' Union, depicted Brubeck as having "intellectual, [and] a reflective spirit" and reviewed his performance also in a highly constructive light: "the smoothly conducted tension of every fragment was endowed not only with the agitated, almost shocking color of jazz but also with an expressionistic flavour."[42] For the local authorities, the growing distance between jazz and rock music served to lower the hurdle for accepting jazz ambassadors from America.

Originally, the Bill Evans Trio was also scheduled to participate in the Jazz Week festival. However, Evans was caught at New York's JFK Airport the day before the performance carrying a suitcase containing 220 packs of heroin, leading to Earl Hines being called up. Hines's band included baritone saxophonist Haywood Henry, bassist Larry Richardson, drummer Richie Goldberg and vocalist Marva Josie, who all led the concert to a successful conclusion through their advanced musical techniques and dynamic rhythms. Josie was a vocalist hurriedly recruited by Wein after the cancellation of the Evans Trio. The audience was varied, ranging from young to elderly people, reflecting the growing diversity of jazz fans in Bucharest. Meeker reported that when Hines played a solo, they listened carefully, leaning forward so as not to miss a single melody, and applauding loudly at the end of each piece.[43] *Romania Libera* praised Hines for taking the audience "on a journey into the wonderful world of classical jazz," whose style was "devoid of the impurities which are characteristic to newer trends in jazz." The same paper's description of Hines's style was accurate when it was noted in some detail that "his right hand has taken over something of Armstrong's way of playing the trumpet."[44] Although Bucharest had been often depicted as having only a short jazz history, by this time the first Romanian jazz club was born in Bucharest, and the first jazz festival was also organized in this city.[45] For American officials in the State Department, this suggested that the city held a deep understanding of jazz.

As jazz was understood as an art genre throughout Eastern Europe, the influx of jazz ambassadors from America had become more tolerable for the Communist authorities. It is noteworthy that Meeker himself was conscious of this dynamic. While he mentioned the existence of local musicians who attempted to "emulate the sounds and rhythms of American jazz" on the one hand, he also stressed on the other that "since jazz is considered a form of art, recognized, serious composers of contemporary music use the polyrhythmic and polytonal base of jazz in many of their compositions as well as to integrate it into conceptions of their own folk music."[46] The reinterpretation of the music in a local context – and its association with traditional music – prompted local authorities to become more tolerant of jazz. It seems this enabled American musicians to interact more openly with local fans and musicians compared with those jazz ambassadors who had visited the Soviet Union earlier. Reportedly, American musicians were "so open and available to Romanians that the number of contacts they made were almost infinite." Still, it should be also noted that reporting from the US embassies tended to stress the American-ness of the music rather than commenting on how jazz had taken on – and adapted to – local contexts and developed a local meaning for East European audiences. Meeker congratulated the organizers on the success of the tours by Brubeck and Hines that ended in "reinforcing America's image as a culturally productive and vigorous nation."[47]

Later, when Willis Conover revisited Warsaw in 1977 – Conover had been a frequent visitor to Eastern Europe since he first visited Poland in 1959 – the Polish Ministry of Culture awarded him a medal for his contribution to not only jazz but also Polish culture. Significantly, this Polish medal was also awarded to West German critic Joachim Berendt and Russian jazz critic Alexei Batashev.[48] Two days after the presentation ceremony, the Duke Ellington Big Band, now led by Mercer Ellington, took part in a concert to commemorate the twentieth anniversary of the Jazz Jamboree, co-starring with the Warsaw Philharmonic Orchestra and the Polish jazz star Adam Makowicz.[49] By this time, Conover had built solid ties with radio stations operating in the region, and his jazz programs were broadcast by several radio stations in Poland, Hungary and Czechoslovakia. These programs were first recorded at his studio in Washington DC – taking into account each country's distinctive jazz scene – and were then broadcast by these individual East European radio stations. The authorities saw merit in diverting jazz fans' attention away from the VOA broadcasts and promoting their own interests, which came via developing their recently nationalized jazz scenes.[50]

Competing assessments of controversial jazz musicians

Placing the Communist authorities' reinterpretation of jazz aside, there was also a persistent gap among American officials in their own interpretations and appraisal of specific jazz styles, which is another area that has been under-researched in the existing work. While jazz ambassadors represented various styles of jazz developed in America, and in that sense they were thought to be representing America itself, a specific style of jazz, most notably free jazz, or a particular musician, was often a source of friction among officials – as was shown in the process of selecting musicians for Africa. Two more cases examined below seek to examine the reactions of American officials to some of the most controversial musicians.

The first case is shown by the contrasting reactions to the performances of Lionel Hampton and Ornette Coleman by American officials. Of the two, Hampton – a vibraphonist and leading figure in the swing era but open-minded with other styles such as bebop, rhythm and blues, as well as rock music – was the next target of the joint project by the State Department and George Wein. In March 1971, Hampton visited Poland, Hungary and Romania during his commercial tour through Western Europe and Yugoslavia. Prior to his departure, Lionel Hampton and His All Star Jazz Inner Circle, composed of 14 musicians including saxophonist Illinois Jacquet and organist Milt Buckner, met with President Nixon. Having once played the piano at Duke Ellington's birthday event, Nixon jokingly pleaded with Hampton to include him as a pianist.[51]

Hampton's tour through three countries in Eastern Europe was seen as "highly successful," according to American diplomatic reporting. In Warsaw, the first stop of the tour, 3,000 excited fans – most of whom were young people – reacted enthusiastically with thunderous applause, which only became more heated when Hampton led the brass section along the aisles. When Hampton reappeared on the stage, following raucous applause and an encore performance, fans began singing the local celebration song "Sto Lat (One Hundred Years)" for him. The repertoire consisted of both nostalgic traditional jazz that "delighted those who grew up during the forties and fifties," and the latest numbers that entertained "younger people musically reared on the Beatles and acid rock." Two days later, 3,000 fans attended his Budapest performance, where Hampton co-starred with several local musicians on stage. When the brass section walked along the aisle, playing "When the Saints Go Marching In," fans exploded with loud cheers, with some of them even joining in the march. After the performance ended at midnight, Hampton joined a reception hosted by the US ambassador, where he interacted with local musicians and music critics.[52] The last stop on his tour was Bucharest. Attracting 8,000 fans, the standing-room-only performance began with "A Taste of Honey" and "On the Sunny Side of the Street," followed by "Shortnin' Bread," "Ring Dem Bells," "Avalon" and "Flying Home." After the curtain closed with "When the Saints Go Marching In" the audience refused to leave the concert hall, while solo performances of "Tenderly" and "Summertime" by Jacquet and Buckner further excited fans at this performance. When Hampton changed instruments from vibraphone to piano, he then took off his jacket and belted out a rhythm on the drums – concluding the session by throwing the drumsticks into the air – which thrilled the audience to such an extent they excitedly rushed the stage. Unsurprisingly, the performance ended much later than the originally scheduled time. State Department officials placed high value on the fact that Hampton had received an enthusiastic reaction from the Bucharest fans, much the same way as Brubeck, Mulligan and Hines had excited audiences in the previous year. For one State Department official, growing local press reactions to Hampton's performance was another testimony that jazz had been accepted as "a serious musical art form."[53]

Local media reporting is important in showing the degree of local acceptance of Hampton's showmanship. In this regard, the Romanian Writers' Union magazine *Luceafărul*, praised his style when it asserted: "the great vibe player is not today the walking fossil of the forties. It is the quality of an authentic musician that brings to life old styles and remakes the long forgotten hits unforgettable."[54] Whereas the Polish youth newspaper *Sztandar Młodych* praised Hampton's skill in managing his entire performance by stressing that "A concert like a theatrical play calls for stage management which consists in good selection of musical pieces, culminational moments, and relaxation moments." According to the paper, "because Hampton can combine [drumstick] juggling with dynamic drum solos it changes into its contrast – a real culmination, and in this form it is accepted by the audience." Hampton's sensational parading around the aisles of the venues with the brass section was acclaimed as an attempt to create the "closest possible contact with the audience."[55]

In analyzing the treatment of a specific style of jazz in the jazz ambassadors program, it is equally important to understand how free jazz was interpreted by American government officials. Just after the Hampton performances, one Polish jazz critic published a comment in the local paper *Życie Warszawy*, suggesting why Hampton was popular among Polish people: "Hampton's big band plays the jazz of the thirties, but they do it in a truly masterful way. There are no traces of any influence of the contemporary avant-garde in their play, nor of any earlier trends; it is purely recreational music, easy in reception, and thanks to the highest skill of the instrumentalists – extremely attractive."[56] In addition, according to a review by a local radio program, "Hampton's concert signals the end of free jazz in Poland."[57] Notably, the US ambassador Stoessel strongly concurred with these local reviews of Hampton's performance. For Stoessel, his performance was "a masterful combination of showmanship with controlled, but vital jazz." Hampton's jazz, he continued, seemed all spontaneous at first glance, but it was well rehearsed. Likewise, he and his band members' ability to control the performance was seen as "both aurally and visually obvious." Accordingly, Stoessel declared that "The result was a revelation to the audience, lately used to the convolutions of occasionally incomprehensible free jazz concerts."[58]

This assessment of free jazz contrasted with Ornette Coleman's performance in Warsaw. Coleman, together with Duke Ellington – who had just finished his Soviet tour – vibraphonist Gary Burton, the Preservation Hall Jazz Band and the Giants of Jazz, toured through Eastern Europe in October 1971. Formed under Wein's direction, the Giants of Jazz – consisting of trumpeter Dizzy Gillespie, tenor saxophonist Sonny Stitt, trombonist Kai Winding, pianist Thelonious Monk, bassist Al McKibbon and drummer Art Blakey – were touring Japan and Europe at this time. Among the performances they conducted in various parts of Eastern Europe, the Jazz Jamboree had been seen by the State Department as the most important event in the region, where 25 groups from such countries as Britain, France, West Germany, Denmark, Hungary and Romania attended this time. Ellington's performance, with a focus on the history of jazz over the past 50 years, invited cheers from the audience, while they also showed their enthusiasm for the Preservation Hall Jazz Band – pleasing the US embassy in Warsaw, which believed that "the roots of American jazz" had been proudly introduced at this event. After the Giants of Jazz appeared on stage the next day, the Jazz Jamboree concluded with a performance by Ornette Coleman, a leading figure in free jazz.[59]

Unlike Stoessel's comment about free jazz, US embassy reporting did not show disapproval nor any particular wariness around Coleman's "brilliant performance" that had been well received by the audience. Apparently, the US government's perceptions around free jazz were not yet unanimous or settled. A music advisor for the USIA greatly appreciated Coleman, pointing out that young Poles had understood that "woven deeply into the texture of jazz are the qualities of spirit, courage, optimism, hope and freedom." This advisor celebrated the fact that at the end of Coleman's performance "the audience stormed the stage applauding and demanding further music from this great American master of free jazz."[60] At least, judging from the reaction of the Warsaw jazz fans, they saw no element of disorder or confusion in free jazz, somewhat easing concerns by the US government around this particular style of jazz.

The second case examined here is Charles Mingus. If Coleman's jazz was believed to embody the idea of freedom, Mingus represented the idea of resistance when he visited Romania as part of the Newport Jazz Festival' program in October 1975. Romania had just been granted Most-Favored Nation (MFN) treatment by the US government, and President Ford had visited the country two months before Mingus's performance. From a purely artistic point of view, his performance was successful, but the US embassy had trouble in handling Mingus while in country. Deputy chief of mission Richard N. Viets proffered the comment that other diplomatic posts "should be forewarned that Mingus projects his political views into song titles in a way which could prove to be embarrassing."[61] As one American official commented to George Wein, Mingus was a "difficult man to deal with and he had some rather unkind things to say to me when I made a request concerning the program." Mingus sought to play some pieces that "involved references to American political figures and incidents that we simply could not allow in a government-operated cultural center."[62] Although the title of the concerning number was not specified, presumably it was

"Remember Rockefeller at Attica" as his performance mirrored the track list of the album Mingus had released that same month. "Remember Rockefeller at Attica" was dedicated to the riot that occurred in Attica prison, New York, in 1971, when prisoners demanding better treatment clashed violently with prison guards. Nelson Rockefeller, then Governor of New York, ordered state troopers to quell this riot and retake the facility using armed force, which eventually resulted in many casualties. Although 16 years had passed since he composed "Fables of Faubus," Mingus was again protesting racial discrimination in American society in his own way.

Mingus's attack on his own government was not an event exclusively seen in Romania. When Mingus visited Portugal, joining the three-day Cascais jazz festival with Earl Hines and Benny Carter the following month, he witnessed Portugal in the midst of democratization after the Carnation Revolution of the previous year, which had led to the collapse of the far-right regime the Estado Novo. The festival was co-sponsored by the Portuguese Ministry of Mass Communications, Cascais Department of Tourism and the USIS. The "Mingus problem" clearly also arose here when he again played "Remember Rockefeller at Attica." Further, while criticizing the Watergate scandal, Mingus also "chanted critical, sometimes profane commentary of former President Nixon," the US ambassador to Portugal Frank Carlucci reported despondently. However, the more important fact for Carlucci was arguably that the audience who could understand English was "stunned by the fact that a U.S. musician whose attendance at the Festival was made possible through U.S. government support would feel free to criticize his country's political leaders."[63] For Carlucci, therefore, the idea of resistance seen in Mingus's jazz, supported by the fact that he was raised in the Watts area in Los Angeles, paradoxically symbolized American freedom in an unmistakable way to his audiences.

In this sense, even if jazz became tamed, elitist or institutionalized, this did not mean that the critical ideas of freedom and resistance that had been associated with jazz lost any political meaning. Even when it seemed so on the surface, the politics of jazz never completely disappeared. Just like the Swingjugend, the zazou and the stilyagi – or any counter-culture groups of Eastern Europe – jazz aficionados had little interest in going out onto the streets to publicly demand political reform. Still, as the case of Czechoslovakia examined below shows, East European jazz scenes during the 1970s had still kept their political meaning at the grass-roots level.

Jazz as a driver of détente from below

Jazz could not but co-exist in a tense relationship with politics. After the momentum of détente further increased during the mid-1970s, the politics of jazz came to the fore once again in Czechoslovakia, soon gathering global attention. As in other countries of the region, Czechoslovakia had experienced an expansion of its jazz scene during the 1960s through a set of regularly held jazz festivals (in Karlovy Vary since 1962 and Prague since 1964). However, when the so-called Prague Spring – a liberal movement directed by Alexander Dubček under the slogan of "socialism with a human face" – collapsed under the Soviet military intervention in 1968, the local jazz scene entered a new and difficult phase. With the introduction of the conservative-led process of "normalization," jazz musicians started to search for an autonomous space for musical activities. For instance, they asked the Ministry of the Interior for permission to set up their own professional union. Although this request was rejected, they were urged to join the Czechoslovak Musicians' Union that had been established earlier under the jurisdiction of the Ministry of the Interior. This course of events resulted in the creation of the Jazz Section within the Union in October 1971. Born in a legal organization, however, the Jazz Section soon came under criticism by the authorities. This showed the existence of a temporal and translucent space in the Czechoslovak jazz scene, which has been called a gray zone – not entirely independent nor comprehensively suppressed by officialdom.[64]

On living in this gray zone, Czech novelist Josef Škvorecký describes it as such: "They hang portraits of the Big Brothers over their desks, but right under their eyes they read Orwell and listen to Charlie Parker."[65] Škvorecký was a leading figure in the Czechoslovak literary world together with Milan Kundera, but was exiled to Canada after the Czech crisis, because "the steel chariots of the Soviets swung low." In Toronto, he established Sixty Eight Publishers to distribute books that were difficult to publish in his home country, while continuing to make critical remarks about the Czechoslovak situation. In the introductory essay titled "Red Music" that sets the scene in his novella *The Bass Saxophone*, Škvorecký recollects how jazz was regulated during the Nazi period, by listing the commands issued by a Gauleiter, a regional leader of the Nazis. These included bans on the saxophone, prohibition of improvisation and the use of the wah-wah mute, and a preference in major key. When he published the essay "I Won't Take Back One Word" in the first Czechoslovak almanac, the authorities confiscated all the published copies. Understanding deeper than others why "dictators don't swing," Škvorecký, in his two novellas in *The Bass Saxophone*, compared the dictatorship under the Nazi regime with that of the Soviet ruling system, with jazz serving as an analytical tool for revealing the similarities of the two.[66]

The activities of the Jazz Section were extensive, from planning jazz concerts and screening movies to publishing the newsletter *Jazz*. The number of members was restricted to 3,000 by the authorities, but its influence was much larger than membership numbers suggest. When the Jazz Section organized the first Prague Jazz Days festival in 1974, favorable reviews were published in the monthly magazine *Melodie*. The festival continued and eventually grew into a large jazz festival, also taking up then-popular jazz rock. Sometimes the Jazz Section's activities extended to the avant-garde field, as seen in their inviting the American experimental theater company the Living Theater to perform *Antigone*, as well as screening the experimental film *Easy Rider*. In 1979, publishing of the *Situace* and *Jazzpetit* series started. *Jazzpetit* dealt with art in general, including such themes as Dada and Surrealism, Boris Vian, the music of the Terezín ghetto, and rock music. In the same year, the Jazz Section joined the International Jazz Federation, a member of UNESCO.[67]

The expansion of its activities, which contrasted with the doctrine of socialist realism, gradually evoked strong criticism from various official quarters. The Musicians' Union, for instance, tried to dismantle the Jazz Section, while the Jazz Section's request seeking confirmation of its autonomy was flatly rejected by the Ministry of the Interior. However, it was not long before these incidents attracted foreign media attention, such as from the VOA and RFE. Karel Srp, the leader of the Jazz Section, was reluctant to establish a formal connection with political organizations, but developments surrounding his group unavoidably gave rise to political implications. Soon, its bank account was closed, members were monitored and their phones were tapped. In 1980, the authorities decided to legally dismantle the Jazz Section. However, they continued their activities as best as possible, despite having a somewhat precarious legal status. The Jazz Section managed to continue the Prague Jazz Days, and to publish Czech novelist Bohumil Hrabal's *I Served the King of England* from the *Jazz Petit* series. Nevertheless, in 1983, the Prague branch of the Musicians' Union in which the Jazz Section belonged finally closed, on the basis of a decision by the Central Committee of the Communist Party. Soon Srp was dismissed from his job in the Union's publishing division. Gradually his group was forced to limit its activities, but it still somehow published Jaroslav Seifert's speech when he won the Nobel Prize for Literature in 1984. However, Srp's house was repeatedly raided by security officials and he personally came under pressure by authorities. And at last he was arrested in September 1986 with six other members for alleged "illegal commercial activities." Following a brief trial that began the following year, he was sentenced to 16 months' imprisonment.[68]

The suppression of the Jazz Section triggered far-reaching global repercussions, which was related to the politics of détente in 1970s Europe. In August 1975, heads of the 35 countries in Europe, both from the East and the West, signed the Helsinki Final Act at the summit of the Conference on Security and Cooperation in Europe (CSCE). The CSCE was first proposed by the Soviet Union as a mechanism by which it could demand the recognition of the status quo of postwar Europe by the West. In response to the Soviet proposal, the West demanded thorough discussions to be held on respect for human rights and the promotion of East-West exchanges. As a result, the provisions in the Final Act reflected the interests of both the East and the West. To review the implementation of the Final Act, follow-up meetings were held every two or three years. After the two meetings in Belgrade (1977–78) and Madrid (1980–83), the third follow-up meeting was scheduled for Vienna in November 1986. Seminars, forums and expert meetings around various themes from human rights to the protection of the environment were also organized. They were all part of the so-called Helsinki process. When the CSCE cultural forum was held in Budapest in 1985, Srp was in Hungary to monitor the discussions. At the forum, British representatives protested the Czechoslovak authorities' repression of the Jazz Section, criticizing the police raids targeting musicians.[69] Srp was arrested the next year, just two months before the Vienna follow-up meeting. As RFE's situation report argued, this left the impression that the Czechoslovakian government was seeking to avoid further opprobrium from the West in Vienna.[70]

Inside the Communist countries that signed the Final Act, several so-called Helsinki Watch groups were formed to monitor the implementation of the Act by their own governments. Charter 77 was one such group in Czechoslovakia, whose formation was motivated by events surrounding the rock band, the Plastic People of the Universe. Formed in Prague in the "normalization" period, the band was named after Frank Zappa's first track "Plastic People" from the album *Absolutely Free*. When all its members were arrested and imprisoned in 1976 for instigating a public disturbance, Charter 77 was formed around the writer and dissident Václav Havel to protest against the authorities' repressive actions. The Jazz Section used a manual written by Charter 77 to criticize the authorities on the grounds of the Final Act. When Srp was arrested, the Jazz Section argued their action was a clear violation of the Final Act.[71]

Shortly thereafter, a petition was sent by American citizens to the Czechoslovak government, defending the Jazz Section and its work in partnership with UNESCO, while also calling out the conduct of the authorities as an egregious violation of the Final Act. Signatories to the petition included musicians such as Dave Brubeck, Gerry Mulligan, Gil Evans, Sonny Rollins, Tommy Flanagan, Billy Taylor and Wynton Marsalis; writers such as Arthur Miller, John Updike, Kurt Vonnegut and Susan Sontag; as well as jazz critics such as Nat Hentoff and Dan Morgenstern. Among them, Updike and Vonnegut had once planted trees in a garden in front of the Jazz Section's office in 1985. "Can't Prague Leave Even Jazz Alone?" was the unambiguously critical title given to the protest by Vonnegut. From Britain, musicians such as Paul McCartney and Elton John lent their support to a similar petition.[72] Whereas in France, a campaign in support of the Jazz Section received signatures from more than 300 writers, artists and journalists. Notably, the French Communist Party was among those who criticized Czechoslovak authorities for their treatment of the issue.[73]

The transnational voices defending the Jazz Section soon began to resonate with the various anti-nuclear movements of the 1980s. At that time, the European Nuclear Disarmament (END) had mobilized activist groups to protest against the recent deployment of nuclear weapons in Central Europe by both sides. As the CND had once had a close relationship with jazz, END's criticism also targeted the arrest of members of the Jazz Section. In a letter addressed to the END, the Jazz Section expressed its appreciation for the support the END provided, while in full agreement that its activities should be guaranteed under the Final Act. Notably in the same letter, the Jazz Section positioned the importance of its work in promoting the ideologically unbiased comprehension of their own as well as others' culture.[74]

Some governments also voiced protests over the arrests in Czechoslovakia. In addition to the US government that accused the Czechoslovak government of violating the Final Act, a statement was issued in London by the British

Minister of State Timothy Renton, articulating the British government's hope that the sentence be judged "in the light of the commitments Czechoslovakia has undertaken under the Helsinki Final Act."[75] According to an situation report of RFE, at the CSCE Vienna follow-up meeting, the chief of the British delegation Laurence O'Keeffe complained about the attendance of the Czechoslovak representative in discussions on cultural issues.[76]

The Czechoslovak government legitimized the arrests by stressing that members of the Jazz Section had violated domestic laws, while denying jazz had had any influence during the sentencing. At the trial, Srp and the other members were sentenced to up to 16 months in prison, as described above. Contrary to many expectations, however, this judgment was surprisingly light, compared with the Havel case, whose arrest in 1979 had resulted in a prison term of four years.[77] Global as well as domestic pressures on the authorities arguably had a certain effect on the sentencing. After being released in January 1988, Srp became one of the most popular dissidents in Czechoslovakia. He worked with Charter 77 and founded a new organization Art Forum, while also engaging in activities related to the Civic Forum – an opposition group established in November 1989. Reflecting his newfound transnational fame, Srp was invited, together with Havel, to a breakfast meeting with the French President François Mitterrand. Two years after the Velvet Revolution, the Jazz Section was finally rehabilitated through the Supreme Court decision to annul the sentence of 1987.[78]

The history of the Jazz Section was evidence that jazz still played a social role. Srp had not publicly pursued political objectives, nor had he any intention of confronting the authorities from the beginning. However, as the Jazz Section expanded its activities in the gray zone, it presented a socio-political message of protest against the colorless everyday life of unfree Czechoslovak society. In this sense, the authorities had plenty of reasons to repress the Jazz Section. This repression backfired, however. Generating transnational protests and grass-roots support, the life of the Jazz Section and its repression by the authorities became a final fitting reminder of the notion that "dictators don't swing" in the Cold War period. Jazz, born in America, was able to build an extensive transnational relationship because this music transcended American exceptionalism. Curiously, however, jazz was "rediscovered" in 1980s America and people started to celebrate the American-ness of the music more often than they had during the previous decade. The next chapter examines how the new discourse celebrating "American music" developed toward the turn of the century, and explores the music's possibility of transcending American borders in the new century.

Notes

1 Jerzy Lukowski and Hubert Zawadzki, *A Concise History of Poland* (Cambridge: Cambridge UP, 2001), pp.262–63; Andrzej Antoszek and Kate Delaney, "Poland: Transmissions and Translations," in Alexander Stephan (ed.), *The Americanization of Europe: Culture, Diplomacy, and Anti-Americanism after 1945* (New York: Berghahn Books, 2006), p.221.

2 Marta Domurat, "The Jazz Press in the People's Republic of Poland: The Role of Jazz and Jazz Forum in the Past and Today," in Pickhan and Ritter (eds.), *Jazz behind the Iron Curtain*, pp.119–21, 127; Schmidt-Rost, "1956," p.69.
3 Pietraszewski, *Jazz in Poland*, pp.58–59.
4 Open Society Archives, HU OSA 300-1-2-61683, "Interest for Jazz and American Customs," 2 September 1955.
5 Pietraszewski, *Jazz in Poland*, p.65; Schmidt-Rost, "1956," pp.62–67; Marta Domurat-Linde, "From 'Jazz in Poland' to 'Polish Jazz'," in Pickhan and Ritter (eds.), *Meanings of Jazz in State Socialism*, pp.88–90.
6 Christian Schmidt-Rost, "Freedom within Limitations: Getting Access to Jazz in the GDR and PRP between 1945 and 1961," in Pickhan and Ritter (eds.), *Jazz behind the Iron Curtain*, p.237.
7 See for example, Pietraszewski, *Jazz in Poland*, pp.69–70; Rüdiger Ritter, "Jazz in State Socialism: A Playground of Refusal?," in Pickhan and Ritter (eds.), *Meanings of Jazz in State Socialism*, pp.25–26.
8 Brubeck was the second jazz ambassador after the Glenn Miller Orchestra, which had been led by Ray McKinley after the film hit of *The Glenn Miller Story* in 1954. The orchestra was sent to Poland in April 1957. Many fans attended performances at the Palace of Culture, and the "sardine-packed textile mill hall" at Lodz, as well as the "steel mill recreational halls" at Katowice. According to US embassy reporting, the media's treatment of the orchestra was "highly complimentary," stressing that they played "sweet swing" numbers which were different from the "extreme type of modern jazz with its bizarre improvisations." It was also reported that evening jam sessions often continued until the next morning. NARA, RG 59, CDF 1955–59, Box 104, 032 Glenn Miller, Band, "Glenn Miller – Ray McKinley Orchestra in Poland," 24 April 1957; "Educational Exchange: President's Fund – ANTA Tour – Glenn Miller Orchestra," 6 June 1957.
9 NARA, RG 59, CDF 1955–59, Box 96, 032 Brubeck, Dave Jazz Quartet, Dulles to Warsaw and Bucharest, 18 October 1957; Dulles to Prague, 5 November 1957; Lightner, Jr. to Flemming, 12 February 1958.
10 NARA, RG 59, CDF 1955–59, Box 96, 032 Brubeck, Dave Jazz Quartet, "Report on Dave Brubeck Jazz Quartet Concerts in Poland," 24 March 1958; Ralph J. Gleason, "Mrs. Dave Brubeck Discusses Jazz Abroad," *Down Beat*, vol.25 no.14, 10 July 1958.
11 CU, Box 93-21, "President's Special International Program, Fourth Semi-Annual Report," undated.
12 Dave Brubeck with Dana Gioia, "Cool Jazz and Cold War," *The American Interest*, vol.1 no.3, 2006.
13 NARA, RG 59, CDF 1955–59, Box 96, 032 Brubeck, Dave Jazz Quartet, "Report on Dave Brubeck Jazz Quartet Concerts in Poland," 24 March 1958. For the Brubeck tour in Poland, see also Von Eschen, *Satchmo Blows Up the World*, pp.50–51; Davenport, *Jazz Diplomacy*, p.75.
14 NARA, RG 59, CDF 1955–59, Box 96, 032 Brubeck, Dave Jazz Quartet, "Report on Dave Brubeck Jazz Quartet Concerts in Poland," 24 March 1958; Ralph J. Gleason, "Mrs. Dave Brubeck Discusses Jazz Abroad," *Down Beat*, vol.25 no.14, 10 July 1958.
15 Hatschek, "The Impact of American Jazz Diplomacy in Poland During the Cold War Era," p.282.
16 Pietraszewski, *Jazz in Poland*, pp.64, 68–70; Rüdiger Ritter, "Jazz in State Socialism: A Playground of Refusal?," in Pickhan and Ritter (eds.), *Meanings of Jazz in State Socialism*, pp.25–26.
17 NARA, RG 59, CDF 1955–59, Box 99, 032 Conover, Willis, "Proposed Visit of Willis Conover," 26 May 1958.

18 NARA, RG 59, CDF 1955–59, Box 99, 032 Conover, Willis, "Visit of Willis Conover," 16 June.
19 NARA, RG 59, CDF 1955–59, Box 99, 032 Conover, Willis, "Visit of Willis Conover," 19 September 1958.
20 NARA, RG 59, CDF 1955–59, Box 99, 032 Conover, Willis, "Visit in Warsaw of Willis Conover, Narrator of Music U.S.A. Program, VOA, June 6–13, 1959," 24 June 1959.
21 NARA, RG 59, CDF 1955–59, Box 99, 032 Conover, Willis, "Polish Magazine Reports on Willis Conover Visit," 1 July 1959. Conover repeatedly stressed the importance of sending jazz musicians to Eastern Europe in the jazz subcommittee of the Musical Advisory Panel. CU, Box 47-27, "Summary of Minutes of Meeting Held in New York, N.Y., December 12, 1966," undated.
22 Domurat-Linde, "From 'Jazz in Poland' to 'Polish Jazz'," p.92.
23 CU, Box 47-21, "Special Cases," undated. Davenport mentioned the Wreckers' visit to America. See Davenport, *Jazz Diplomacy*, pp.116–17.
24 Pietraszewski, *Jazz in Poland*, pp.73–75; Domurat-Linde, "From 'Jazz in Poland' to 'Polish Jazz'," pp.80, 92–94.
25 Joseph Rothschild, *Return to Diversity: A Political History of East Central Europe since World War II* (Oxford: Oxford UP, 1989), pp.203–5; Toshitaka Yada, *Hungary Czechoslovakia Gendaishi* (Tokyo: Yamakawa, 1978), p.255.
26 Gergő Havadi, "Individualists, Traditionalists, Revolutionaries, or Opportunists?," in Pickhan and Ritter (eds.), *Meanings of Jazz in State Socialism*, pp.138–49.
27 Kovrig, *Of Walls and Bridges*, pp.108–9; Thomas Alan Schwartz, *Lyndon Johnson and Europe: In the Shadow of Vietnam* (Cambridge: Harvard UP, 2003), pp.134–36.
28 Elena Dragomir, *Cold War Perceptions: Romania's Policy Change towards the Soviet Union 1960–1964* (Cambridge: Cambridge Scholars Publishing, 2015), pp.178–236.
29 CU, Box 66-10, American Embassy Bucharest to Department of State, 29 August 1966.
30 CU, Box 97-1, "Charles Lloyd Jazz Quartet, Poland, Romania, Czechoslovakia, October 11 – October 23, 1967," undated; Box 49-3, "Annual Report of the Cultural Presentations Program, Department of State for the Year July 1, 1967 to June 30, 1968," January 1969; Box 47-27, Thomas D. Huff to Ralph T. Backlund, 2 November 1967.
31 Joachim E. Berendt, "Jazz in Yugoslavia," *Down Beat*, vol.30 no.31, 5 December 1963; Radina Vucetic, *Coca-Cola Socialism: Americanization of Yugoslav Culture in the Sixties* (Budapest: Central European UP, 2018), pp.87–105.
32 CU, Box 66-10, "Cultural and Educational Exchange: Cultural Presentations Program: Woody Herman Band/Phoenix Singers," 19 July 1966.
33 CU, Box 66-10, "A 'Randez Vous' with Swing," *Večernje Novosti*, translated, 20 May 1966.
34 CU, Box 66-10, "Jazz – Rhythm, 'Phoenix Singers' and Woody Herman," *Zabreb Weekly Studio*, translated, 4 June 1966.
35 Rothschild, *Return to Diversity*, pp.194–97; Lukowski and Zawadzki, *A Concise History of Poland*, pp.266–71.
36 Pietraszewski, *Jazz in Poland*, pp.76–77; Igor Pietraszewski, "Jazz Musicians in Post-War Poland," in Pickhan and Ritter (eds.), *Meanings of Jazz in State Socialism*, pp.104–5.
37 For the "convergence of interest," see Von Eschen, *Satchmo Blows Up the World*, pp.189–91.
38 CU, Box 57-20, "Brubeck – Mulligan Concert in Warsaw," 2 November 1970; "Concert by Dave Brubeck and Trio with Gerry Mulligan at 1970 Warsaw Jazz Jamboree," 4 November 1970. For Brubeck's performances in Warsaw and the

State Department's relationship with George Wein, see also Von Eschen, *Satchmo Blows Up the World*, pp.187–90.
39 CU, Box 57-20, "Educational and Cultural Exchanges: Cultural Presentations, The Earl 'Fatha' Hines Quartet Featuring Marva Josie and the Dave Brubeck Trio plus Gerry Mulligan," 28 December 1970.
40 CU, Box 57-20, "Taken from the Cultural Calendar of Informatia Bucurestiului," 9 November 1970.
41 CU, Box 57-20, "The Jazz Concerts, translated, Romania Libera," 11 November 1970.
42 CU, Box 57-20, "Jazz, Reality and Premonition, an Article Published in the Romanian Weekly 'Romania Literara'," 12 November 1970.
43 CU, Box 57-20, "Educational and Cultural Exchanges: Cultural Presentations, The Earl 'Fatha' Hines Quartet Featuring Marva Josie and the Dave Brubeck Trio plus Gerry Mulligan," 28 December 1970; "Dave Brubeck – Gerry Mulligan and Trio, Earl 'Fatha' Hines, Eastern Europe, Recapitulation," undated.
44 CU, Box 57-20, "The Jazz Concerts, translated, Romania Libera," 11 November 1970. For the performances of Brubeck and Hines in Bucharest, see also Von Eschen, *Satchmo Blows Up the World*, pp.192–95.
45 Adrian Popan, "Jazz Revival in Romania 1964–1971," in Pickhan and Ritter (eds.), *Jazz behind the Iron Curtain*, p.210.
46 CU, Box 57-20, Educational and Cultural Exchanges: Cultural Presentations, The Earl 'Fatha' Hines Quartet Featuring Marva Josie and the Dave Brubeck Trio plus Gerry Mulligan," 28 December 1970.
47 Ibid.
48 In 1978, Benny Carter, Archie Shepp and Dexter Gordon participated in the Jazz Jamboree. CU, Box 84-6, "Cultural Presentations, List of Attractions, Touring Fiscal Year 1979," undated.
49 CU, Box 66-9, P&C AmEmbassy Warsaw to USIA Washington, 27 October 1977.
50 Ritter, "Jazz in State Socialism," pp.21–22; Rüdiger Ritter, "Broadcasting Jazz into the Eastern Bloc: Cold War Weapon or Cultural Exchange? The Example of Willis Conover," in Yvetta Kajanová, Gertrud Pickhan and Rüdiger Ritter (eds.), *Jazz from Socialist Realism to Postmodernism* (Bern: Peter Lang, 2016), pp.37–38.
51 CU, Box 66-6, "Hampton Visit," *The Washington Post*, 20 February 1971.
52 CU, Box 66-6, Memorandum for the President," 12 April 1971; "Lionel Hampton Orchestra, EE (Romania, Poland, Hungary), March 24, 26, 29, 1971," undated; Stoessel to Department of State, 5 April 1971. For Hampton's performances in Eastern Europe in general, see also Von Eschen, *Satchmo Blows Up the World*, pp.196–97.
53 CU, Box 66-6, AmEmbassy Bucharest to Secstate WashDC, 30 March 1971; Lewis to Lewis, 17 May 1971.
54 CU, Box 66-6, "A Force of Nature," *Luceafărul*, translated, 3 April 1971.
55 CU, Box 66-6, "Hampton in Warsaw," *Sztandar Młodych*, translated, 27–28 March 1971.
56 CU, Box 66-6, "Hampton & Co.," *Życie Warszawy*, translated, 1 April 1971.
57 CU, Box 66-6, Stoessel to Department of State, 5 April 1971.
58 Ibid.
59 CU, Box 61-15, "Performing Arts and Athletics – Weekly Activities Report, October 21 – November 3, 1971," 3 November 1971.
60 Ibid.
61 CU, Box 73-2, "1975 American Music Festival in American Library," 9 December 1975.
62 CU, Box 73-2, Chaplin to Wein, 26 November 1975.
63 CU, Box 58-10, AmEmbassy to SecState WashDC, 26 November 1975. See also Fosler-Lussier, *Music in America's Cold War Diplomacy*, p.94.

64 Peter Bugge, "Normalization and the Limits of the Law: The Case of the Czech Jazz Section," *East European Politics and Societies*, vol.22 no.2, 2008, pp.285–86; Wakagi Akatsuka, "'Grey Zone' ni Ikiru Geijutsu: 'Seijouka' Jidai niokeru Jazz Section no Katsudo ni tsuite," *Shisou*, vol.4, 2012, pp.243–44.
65 Josef Škvorecký, "Hipness at Noon: Communism's Crusade against Jazz and Rock in Czechoslovakia," *New Republic*, vol.191, 1984, p.28; Akatsuka, "'Grey Zone' ni Ikiru Geijutsu," p.244.
66 Josef Škvorecký, "Red Music," and "The Bass Saxophone," in Josef Škvorecký, *The Bass Saxophone: Two Novellas* (New York: Ecco Press, 1994), pp.1–28, 115–209.
67 Bugge, "Normalization and the Limits of the Law," pp.285–87; Yvetta Kajanová, "Slovak and Czech Jazz Emigrants after 1948," *Jazzforschung / Jazz Research*, vol.41, 2009, p.58; Peter Motyčka, "The Jazz Section: Disintegration through Jazz," in Pickhan and Ritter (eds.), *Meanings of Jazz in State Socialism*, pp.159–67; Akatsuka, "'Grey Zone' ni Ikiru Geijutsu," pp.245–51.
68 Bugge, "Normalization and the Limits of the Law," pp.290–93; Kajanová, "Slovak and Czech Jazz Emigrants after 1948," p.58; Akatsuka, "'Grey Zone' ni Ikiru Geijutsu," pp.255–58.
69 Josef Škvorecký, "Hipness at Dusk," *Cross Currents*, vol.6, 1987, p.56; Akatsuka, "'Grey Zone' ni Ikiru Geijutsu," pp.256–57.
70 Open Society Archives, HU OSA 300-8-47-81-13, "Situation Report: Czechoslovakia, 23 September 1986," 23 September 1986.
71 Barbara Day, *The Velvet Philosophers* (London: Claridge Press, 2000), p.202; Bugge, "Normalization and the Limits of the Law," p.297.
72 Kurt Vonnegut Jr., "Can't Prague Leave Even Jazz Alone?," *Cross Currents*, vol.6, 1987; Akatsuka, "'Grey Zone' ni Ikiru Geijutsu," pp.237–41.
73 Open Society Archives, HU OSA 300-8-47-84-1, "Situation Report: Czechoslovakia, 22 January 1988," 22 January 1988.
74 LSE Library, London, UK, Papers of European Nuclear Disarmament, END/10/8, Jazz Section to END, 20 October 1986.
75 "U.S. Denounces Trial of Czech Jazz Section," *The New York Times*, 13 March 1987; Day, *The Velvet Philosophers*, p.211.
76 Open Society Archives, HU OSA 300-8-47-84-1, "Situation Report: Czechoslovakia, 22 January 1988," 22 January 1988.
77 Bugge, "Normalization and the Limits of the Law," pp.293, 306. Akatsuka, "'Grey Zone' ni Ikiru Geijutsu," p.258.
78 Bugge, "Normalization and the Limits of the Law," p.311, fn.58; Kajanová, "Slovak and Czech Jazz Emigrants after 1948," p.59.

8 Making jazz great again

Détente, which defined the US-Soviet relationship during the early to mid-1970s, had found itself in irrevocable decline by the late 1970s. Mutual boycotts of two Olympic Games in Moscow and Los Angeles in the early 1980s, as well as the enforcement of martial law in Poland in 1981 had caused cultural exchanges to stagnate between the two countries. Once committed to anti-Communist activities as president of Hollywood's Screen Actors Guild, Ronald Reagan, upon becoming President of the US, set out to fulfill the public's expectations of rebuilding a strong America – a nation that was still reeling from the Vietnam War. Under renewed international tension, dubbed the New Cold War, a massive military build-up was initiated, while Reagan frequently ordered interventions in leftist regimes in Latin America.

It was no coincidence that under the Reagan administration, new momentum was given to the popular discourse equating jazz with "American music." Jazz critics and musicians started to re-discover American values in jazz. For example, this idea was unequivocally portrayed in critic Grover Sales's book *Jazz: America's Classical Music* (1984), and pianist Billy Taylor's article "Jazz: America's Classical Music" (1986).[1] In contrast to the widely spread jazz discourse of the 1960s emphasizing its black origins, jazz had now returned to the spotlight as "American music." This chapter traces how a re-emergence of the "American music" discourse shaped the hegemonic interpretation of the music, promoting jazz diplomacy from the 1980s onwards. It then explores how jazz transcended American sovereign borders in attempts at peace building in the global arena.

The politics of memory

Congress was one powerful body that recognized the significance of the shift behind the revitalized jazz discourse. The concurrent resolution adopted by both chambers of Congress on 23 September 1987 was one typical example illustrating the rediscovery of jazz. The resolution was initiated by the then Representative for Michigan, John Conyers Jr., who had been supported by Rosa Parks for over 20 years – since she had first become a political staffer – and was someone who had a deep understanding of the civil rights movement in America. While referring to its black origins, this "jazz resolution" found in jazz a centripetal force for bridging cultural and religious differences. Jazz as "an indigenous American music and art form" was, the resolution declared, "designated as a rare and valuable national American treasure." The resolution referred to jazz as an "outstanding artistic model of individual expression and democratic cooperation," thus realizing the "highest ideals and aspirations of our republic." Focusing on jazz's function of integrating society, the resolution also stressed the ideal of a racially integrated America.[2] Coincidentally, it was on John Coltrane's birthday that the resolution was passed in Congress.

The power of the narrative recognizing the end of the Cold War as a victory of freedom, or a victory of America, boosted the post-Cold War popularity of the "American music" discourse. It was not long before jazz received widespread attention again as an embodiment of Americanism in political circles. A proposal to award Willis Conover the Presidential Medal of Freedom was repeatedly made during the George H.W. Bush administration. Although this proposal did not materialize, the US Congress did adopt a resolution in 1993 to honor Conover's career, celebrating his many achievements as follows.

> Whereas since 1955, Willis Conover of Voice of America has been broadcasting the best of American jazz to millions around the world;
> Whereas during that time, the music of Duke Ellington, Charlie Parker, Ella Fitzgerald, Benny Goodman, Dizzy Gillespie, and other great American artists, broadcast by Mr. Conover, have come to symbolize the freedom and creativity of democracy for those denied freedom.[3]

Three years later, when Conover died at the age of 75, the *New York Times* praised him in a well-cited obituary as winning the hearts and minds of people in the Communist bloc countries. In the battle against Communism, it was recalled, Conover was "more effective than a fleet of B-29s."[4] Furthermore, in 1997, voices calling for awarding the Presidential Medal of Freedom to Norman Granz grew around Oscar Peterson, who was an active member of the JATP troupe. Granz himself appealed to President Bill Clinton to award Benny Carter the National Medal of Arts, and while precise causation remains unclear, it was finally realized in 2000. Although Peterson's pleas were unmet, partly because of speculation Granz would refuse this award, he received a Lifetime Achievement Award from the Jazz at Lincoln Center (JALC) in 1999, largely as a result of Peterson's strenuous persuasion.[5]

The age of honor continued well into the new century. The concurrent resolution, adopted in September 2004 by Congress, praised the life of Duke Ellington, who had toured various countries under the banner of the jazz ambassadors program. During the same month, to celebrate the 100th anniversary of the birth of Count Basie, his achievement of fusing jazz and blues was publicly commended in Congress. In addition, the achievements of the Jazz/Blues singer Dinah Washington were also honored the same year. In the same way, Lionel Hampton, who had once played in the Benny Goodman Orchestra and performed at President Harry Truman's inauguration in 1949 for the first time as an

African American musician, was formally honored as a figure embodying "acceptance, tolerance, and the celebration of racial and cultural diversity." In 2005, when jazz singer and pianist Shirley Horn died, another concurrent resolution was adopted paying tribute to her "achievements and contributions to the world of jazz and American culture."[6] Those celebrated were not limited to musicians. When the Smithsonian National Museum of American History hosted a ceremony in March 2004 to celebrate the 50th anniversary of the recording of John Coltrane's *A Love Supreme*, his son Ravi donated his father's favorite saxophone to this iconic institution.[7] In addition, in July of the same year, the Senate blessed the 60th anniversary of the first opening of the Newport Jazz Festival.[8] And finally, in 2009, to commemorate the 50th anniversary of the release of Miles Davis's *Kind of Blue*, the House of Representatives adopted a resolution reaffirming "the status of jazz as a national treasure."[9]

As the age of honor shed light on the history of jazz, the music became increasingly recognized as integral to America's cultural heritage – and a product to be protected. For instance, a bill to protect jazz through the Smithsonian museum was introduced by Conyers Jr. The bill stipulated a variety of means such as establishing archives relating to the documentation of jazz, the use of jazz in education, and formally designating April each year as Jazz Appreciation Month (introduced earlier by the Smithsonian museum in 2001).[10]

Paralleling the age of honor was an attempt at reconstructing the history of jazz. This exercise produced a set of new polemic issues. Here it is enough to take two examples as representative of this predicament – with both relating to how jazz should be remembered. The first occurred when controversy arose over the ownership of jazz. This concern centered on the question of whether to remember jazz as a symbol of racial integration or as black culture. An earlier incarnation of this controversy was seen during the era of the civil rights movement in the 1960s. Even after the discourse of "American music" had become broadly accepted after the 1980s, this issue had not been completely resolved. At the center of the controversy was Wynton Marsalis, a trumpeter and JALC music director. Marsalis's *Blood on the Fields* was awarded the Pulitzer Prize for Music in 1997, the first time a jazz musician had received this prestigious award. Recalling that Duke Ellington was not awarded a special citation 32 years earlier, with Marsalis receiving this award, it seemingly brought jazz's color-blind idealism and reality closer than ever before – only in 1999 did the Pulitzer committee award Ellington a special citation to commemorate the 100th anniversary of his birth.

However, Marsalis and the other so-called neoclassicists' view of jazz was not necessarily completely color-blind. This could be seen in the film *Jazz*, one of the leading attempts to reconstruct the history of jazz by neoclassicists. In this 19 hour-long film, directed by documentary filmmaker Ken Burns and broadcast on PBS in 2001, Burns tried to represent what he believed was part of American history, together with the Constitution and baseball. Marsalis frequently appears and responds to interviews in the film. *Jazz* soon triggered a controversy, for Burns placed the main focus of this work on the golden age of swing – while the period after the 1960s occupied only one-tenth of the story, thus unduly reducing the importance of subsequent musical styles that came after free jazz. Moreover, Burns's portrayal of the role of African American musicians – the film's focus is mainly on achievements of legends like Louis Armstrong and Duke Ellington – triggered an outburst of alleged bias regarding who to value in the history of jazz. In other words, *Jazz* had the effect of portraying African American musicians as the creators of various jazz styles, much more than emphasizing the notion of jazz as "American music."[11]

Still, what should be stressed here is that Marsalis, Burns, and even others who regarded such neoclassicists as akin to the "Ronald Reagan of jazz" dismissing avant-garde styles, all share the same narrow perspective.[12] They are to a large extent inward-looking, and tend to discount the notion that certain genres and elements of jazz have developed outside America. Therefore, the diversity that characterizes the origins of jazz has been overlooked for the most part, and as a result, the construction of an alternative history of jazz that examines the various routes jazz has taken outside America has been largely unexamined.

The second contentious issue is related to the notion that jazz represents the idea of resistance. From the 1990s, the US government developed infrastructure to institutionalize the memory of jazz. One example is the New Orleans Jazz National Historical Park, founded in Louis Armstrong Park close to the French Quarter in New Orleans.[13] Here, it is expected that New Orleans functions as a place to symbolize Americanism. But New Orleans has another memory – being that jazz has long been played in this city as funeral music. This enables the music to function as a eulogy of sorts to an incumbent government. For instance, in January 2005, when the second inauguration ceremony of the George W. Bush administration was being held in Washington DC, people gathered in New Orleans from all over America to organize an anti-government rally. There were those who had opposed the Iraq war, calling President Bush and Vice President Dick Cheney war criminals. On the day of the rally, there was a jazz march to "bury" ongoing wars and the USA Patriot Act that was enacted shortly after the September 11, 2001 terrorist attacks. Those who participated in the march, which started from Louis Armstrong Park, wore decorative pins marked with a rallying cry: "Jazz Funeral for Democracy: A Wake for Peace." Anti-war organizations such as Vietnam Veterans against the War, Veterans for Peace, and Code Pink also participated.[14] The carnivalesque scenery jazz produced at its roots was a reminder that the memory of jazz is not uniform, and is instead open to numerous distinct interpretations.

Jazz diplomacy revitalized

While jazz was being historicized, governmental efforts were being made again to globally disseminate jazz for cultural diplomacy purposes. Although the State Department's jazz ambassadors program officially ended in 1978, jazz nonetheless continued to be an important diplomatic tool for the US government afterwards. To take just one example, Dave Brubeck performed in the Soviet Union in March 1987. The trigger was the Geneva summit meeting in 1985 between Ronald Reagan and the new Soviet leader Mikhail Gorbachev. At a concert hall owned by the Rossiya Hotel near the Kremlin, Brubeck received a warm welcome from an audience of around 2,500 fans. Starting with "St. Louis Blues," which had been played with various titles under totalitarian regimes, his repertoire also notably included "Dziękuję" – the piece composed during his Polish tour in 1958. The audience enjoyed not only Brubeck's rendition of Gershwin's "Summertime" and Strayhorn's "Take the A Train," but also his son Chris's performance on the bass and the trombone, with the biggest audience response coming at the conclusion with "Take Five." However, showing an unchanging aspect of Soviet society, the police closed the road leading to the concert hall to prevent fans from spontaneously gathering. Nonetheless, Brubeck also conducted a performance for members of the Union of Soviet Composers, once a guardian of socialist realism, indicating at least a small change of the times. After this event, he visited Tallinn and Leningrad where he carried out additional performances.[15]

The relationship between Brubeck and the White House has a long history. In the early 1960s, President John F. Kennedy invited Brubeck to a concert at the Ellipse located south of the White House. During the Johnson administration, Brubeck participated at a dinner party welcoming King Hussein of Jordan. While at the Moscow summit meeting in May 1988, he accompanied President Reagan to entertain Gorbachev. At a concert held at the US embassy where a number of senior Soviet officials were in attendance, he quickly vanquished the air of fatigue that had set in over the drawn-out talks with his performance of "Take the A Train," pleasing the Soviet officials greatly. Also during the Reagan administration, Brubeck played before Bill Clinton, then Governor of Arkansas and himself a saxophonist, in a meeting of the National Governors Association. Having honed his saxophone skills through listening to "Take Five," Clinton was naturally fascinated with Brubeck's magic. Brubeck's musical contributions were officially recognized in 1994 under the Clinton administration when he was awarded the National Medal of Arts.[16]

While it is well known that Clinton is a jazz aficionado, Madeleine Albright, the first female Secretary of State, is rarely mentioned as a high-profile figure deeply involved in jazz diplomacy – both before and during the Clinton administration. Born in Czechoslovakia and later emigrating to America, Albright came close to jazz when Charter 77 and the Jazz Section were being repressed in Prague. Around this time, she was teaching International Politics at Georgetown University in Washington DC, when she had an opportunity in 1986 to visit Prague as a member of the USIA educational delegation. There she had a chance to clandestinely meet with officials of Charter 77. With another opportunity arising to visit Prague again the next year, Albright took a bolder approach, which, using her own words, was "all very cloak-and-dagger."[17] According to her autobiography, following arrangements being made by the US embassy, she was told to wait for a man with a raincoat at a predetermined place and time, and soon began to walk with an unknown man who suddenly appeared beside her. Advised not to ask where she was going, she sought to appear as if they were a couple so as not to raise any suspicions. After getting on the metro, "I then received a nice kiss on the lips from a man I didn't know en route to a destination about which I could only guess." Eventually they arrived at a basement where copies of *Rolling Stone* were strewn on shelves, and members of the Jazz Section were waiting for her. They discussed their problems, hopes, and the strategies dissidents used against the authorities for many hours.[18]

After the Velvet Revolution of 1989 that led Czechoslovakia to commence a process of democratization, the socialist republic collapsed. Václav Havel assumed office as the first President of the Federal Republic, but in 1993 the Czech and the Slovak republics dissolved the federal system and became independent entities of each other. About this time, a number of East European countries requested to join the North Atlantic Treaty Organization (NATO) as a result of the changes in the security environment after the end of the Cold War. On its part, the Clinton administration advocated the Partnership for Peace program to institutionalize cooperation with these countries as an alternative to the Eastward expansion of NATO, which was approved at the NATO summit in January 1994. Just after the summit meeting, Clinton traveled to Prague where Havel awaited him. Havel welcomed Clinton at the old jazz club Reduta and gifted him a Czech-made saxophone. Albright, then the US ambassador to the United Nations, was also present at this iconic example of jazz diplomacy where Clinton played "My Funny Valentine" and "Summertime," which undoubtedly entertained Havel.[19]

In this way, the relationship between Albright and jazz is far from fleeting. In 2012, she was recognized for her close affiliation with jazz by the Thelonious Monk Institute of Jazz. At the music festival entitled "Women, Music and Diplomacy," which celebrated the contributions of female jazz musicians such as Ella Fitzgerald and Anita O'Day, Albright was presented a Maria Fisher Founder's Award, named after one of the co-founders of the Institute. At the ceremony hall, she appeared alongside trumpeter Chris Botti, exciting the audience by playing "None Shall Sleep" as the guest drummer.[20] Albright, knowing in some detail how the Jazz Section was once repressed in Czechoslovakia, saw the role of jazz as follows:

> They started literally as a group of musicians playing jazz because that was a way to oppose the system, and then they actually became a political force. I visibly saw the role of American music, jazz specifically, in terms of revolting against the regime. It was a way of expressing support and wanting to be part of the West without going out there and marching.[21]

She continued to deepen her relationship with jazz through the course of her stellar career, even playing host to the Monk Institute's major international jazz competition. Notably, former US President Bill Clinton won the same Maria Fisher Founder's Award in 2014.

The jazz ambassadors program, although in a downsized way, saw somewhat of a revival in 1997 under the support of the State Department (initially driven by the USIA), and later in partnership with the Kennedy Center. Targeting strategically important areas such as the Middle East, Africa, South Asia and Southern Europe, seven duos were initially sent to 33 places for four to six weeks. In 2000 and 2001, special programs celebrating the 100th anniversary of the births of Duke Ellington and Louis Armstrong were implemented.[22] Since then, five to ten groups had been dispatched every year to more than 100 countries in those same regions. The State Department noted in the final report of the new jazz ambassadors program that jazz was a "metaphor for many of the values we hold dear as Americans," with the conclusion noting that its objectives were achieved in such fields as fostering mutual understanding, promoting policy dialogue, and reaching out to youth and Muslims. While the report categorized policy goals into eight fields such as targeting key audiences and fostering awareness of American culture, most weight was accorded to the importance behind improving the image of the US government and its policies, rather than interacting with local people around the world per se.[23] Whereas in 2005, the State Department started a new program called Rhythm Road with the JALC as a new partner. Not limiting itself to jazz but including music born in America like hip hop, blues and gospel, this program had dispatched 118 musicians to 97 countries by 2010.[24] In 2011, it was succeeded by the American Music Abroad program.

The State Department's other program, initiated in cooperation with the Monk Institute, had a similar remit to the original program in actively sending jazz stars abroad. Launched during the Clinton administration, musicians such as pianist Herbie Hancock, drummer T. S. Monk – the son of pianist Thelonious Monk – saxophonist Wayne Shorter, and singer Dee Dee Bridgewater were sent to various countries under the auspices of American jazz diplomacy. In 1996, Monk, Hancock and Shorter visited Thailand to attend the 50th anniversary celebration of King Bhumibol's ascension to the throne. When the Americas summit was held in Chile in 1998, Hancock and Shorter played jazz in front of numerous heads of state. They also performed in Hanoi and Ho Chi Minh City in 2005 in commemoration of the tenth anniversary of normalizing relations between America and Vietnam. In addition, Hancock visited Shanghai and Beijing in 2010, and Moscow and St. Petersburg in 2012 to further a program of music education for young musicians.[25]

In these ways, jazz diplomacy is still alive today. In 2006, Secretary of State Condoleezza Rice praised the interplay between American diplomacy and "that uniquely American form of music ... jazz" at an event commemorating the 50th anniversary of Dizzy Gillespie's first State Department tour. In 2008, to commemorate half a century since Dave Brubeck's historic performance in Poland, the State Department awarded him the Benjamin Franklin Award, in recognition of his "outstanding leadership in advancing America's ideals through public diplomacy." Brubeck was celebrated as exemplifying "the best of America's cultural diplomacy," and was officially honored for his role in "offering a positive vision of hope, opportunity and freedom through a musical language that is truly American."[26]

Jazz for peace

In 2011, UNESCO designated 30 April as International Jazz Day. The initial idea was first proposed by the US government. The US representative to UNESCO submitted a joint proposal for the establishment of International Jazz Day to the Executive Board at the end of July 2011. Since the UN General Assembly had proclaimed the previous year as the International Year for the Rapprochement of Cultures, it was expected that jazz, with its origins in New Orleans where various cultures intermingle, should serve as a symbol of cross-cultural dialogue. The proposal was premised on the notion that UNESCO could harness the power of jazz to disseminate universal values such as furthering mutual understanding between peoples, as well as respect for human rights and diversity.[27] The proclamation document, on which the establishment of International Jazz Day is based, emphasizes jazz's function of embracing people by giving them opportunities for freedom of expression. Therefore, although jazz was born in America, as a unique musical genre it is expected to encourage intercultural ties and understanding in a global context.[28]

Behind the initial proposal was Herbie Hancock. Serving as the chairman of the Monk Institute – from January 2019 it was renamed the Herbie Hancock Institute of Jazz – Hancock was concurrently a UNESCO goodwill ambassador from July 2011. He criticized the US government for freezing its financial contributions to UNESCO after it approved Palestine becoming a member in October 2011, strongly demanding the continuation of its commitment.[29] For Hancock, the role of UNESCO was self-explanatory. He had once been impressed by the way heads of states relaxingly listened to his performance at the 1998 Americas summit meeting, where he came to the personal conclusion that the origin of jazz was not America but humanity itself.[30]

While Hancock believed in the universality of jazz, the General Secretary of UNESCO Irina Bokova spoke about jazz as if the music was a diaspora:

> Jazz is music of boundless creativity. Mixing composition and improvisation, the formal and informal, it renews itself every time it is played. Born in the United States, jazz is owned by the world. Rooted in African traditions and drawing on European musical forms, it has taken on new shapes in cultures across the globe. Jazz makes the most of the world's diversity, effortlessly crossing borders and bringing people together.[31]

At the first International Jazz Day in April 2012, UNESCO in coordination with several US embassies organized numerous special events, while cultural institutions around the world also held concerts, photo exhibitions and film screenings. The Monk Institute undertook a special initiative by holding jazz-related events at the UNESCO Headquarters in Paris, Louis Armstrong Park in New Orleans, and the UN General Conference Hall in New York, where many musicians including Hancock and Wynton Marsalis participated. Susan Rice, the US ambassador to the United Nations, also took the opportunity to emphasize jazz's American origins in her speech, although she also noted that jazz "became the world's music long ago" by mentioning pianist Toshiko Akiyoshi and other non-American jazz musicians.[32] This was the point Bokova stressed at an International Jazz Day event hosted in Istanbul the following year – that is, jazz has traveled far and beyond American diplomatic strategies. While jazz was born and nurtured in America, "it is now woven into the fabric of every society, played across the world, enjoyed everywhere." This music's diversity creates a powerbase for "dialogue and understanding." Once providing the "soundtrack for past struggles for dignity and civil rights," jazz continues to be a power for "social transformation" by disseminating a "story of freedom." In an era of change and uncertainty, she asserts, we need jazz more than ever before.[33]

The host city for International Jazz Day in 2014 was Osaka, Japan's "jazz Mecca" according to Bokova. A variety of events characterized this project – in Osaka there were lectures to discuss the value of music for supporting peace, with Hancock himself leading these discussions, and UNESCO peace artist Marcus Miller was also in attendance. Other activities included a public seminar to explore the relationship between *rakugo* (the traditional Japanese form of storytelling) and jazz, and a lecture on philosophy by Wayne Shorter. The lecture titled "Women in Jazz" was hosted by Toshiko Akiyoshi and bassist Esperanza Spalding, while the "Tohoku Earthquake/Hurricane Katrina" panel discussed the healing power of music. The "Jazz and Human Rights" lecture was organized by Dee Dee Bridgewater, which looked back on the lives of those who had engaged in the civil rights movement, such as Billie Holiday, Nina Simone and Abbey Lincoln.[34] Jazz represents what we need most in the world today. In Paris, the host city of International Jazz Day in 2015, Bokova underscored this point, stating that jazz means freedom, diversity, dialogue, courage, understanding others, respecting human rights and dignity, letting others speak, listening with respect, and standing up for freedom in the spirit of solidarity. "All of this is the power of jazz," she enthusiastically proclaimed.[35] In 2016, Washington DC became the host of International Jazz Day, thereby seeing jazz return home.

In the case of Japan, the Japan Foundation promotes cultural exchanges via jazz. Although there is no defined jazz ambassadors program, the Foundation has been sending Japanese jazz musicians abroad since the late 1980s. The music is often played for anniversary projects. For instance, the Creative Jazz Ensemble Japan led by pianist Makoto Kuriya visited Brazil in August 2015 to celebrate the 120th anniversary of the establishment of diplomatic relations between the two countries. In addition to six performances in five cities, a successful collaboration with local musicians was also held. Various music across styles and genres was played on this occasion, ranging from widely known jazz numbers, to samba and Japanese children's songs such as "Kutsu-ga-Naru" with jazz-like arrangements.[36]

Introducing Japanese culture through jazz is also a part of the Foundation's activities. Just like attempts to blend musical instruments of different genres were practiced by American jazz ambassadors, Japanese musical instruments such as the *koto* and *shakuhachi* have also been frequently used in jazz performances. When the event Japan Music Now was organized in Africa (Senegal, Nigeria, Zaire, Kenya, Tanzania and Zambia) in 1989, introducing the "essence of Japanese music" to African audiences, Yosuke Yamashita and the Japanese *taiko* (a large vertical drum) musician Eitetsu Hayashi participated in this cultural diplomacy event. While the first and second parts of the overall performance saw distinct Japanese *taiko* and jazz performances, the event reached a climax in the third part when an exciting mixture of piano, saxophone and Japanese *taiko* generated a dynamic-sounding festival atmosphere.[37]

This event provided a vital platform for important issues relating to universality and the particularity of jazz. First, the musical commonality between Japanese and African music was among the main topics keenly reported by the local press. The huge Japanese *taiko* naturally surprised locals, but one local journalist put a focus on musical commonality when they reported that Japanese musical instruments "reminded us of the sound of a drum and whistles that occupy an important part in many village festivals in Nigeria, which evoked a sense of *déjà vu* among many in the audience." Another report opined that the sound of the *shakuhachi* "was almost indistinguishable from the Ibo flute," which was a reminder that jazz serves as a functional medium for promoting ties among different cultures. At this African event, Yamashita and the other musicians also enjoyed interesting exchanges with local musicians by visiting local jazz clubs. In an interview with a local magazine, Yamashita interpreted the meaning of Japanese jazz in Africa as follows:

> Jazz, born when Europe and Africa met on the New American Continent, crossed the Pacific Ocean to Japan, yet this time we as jazzmen come to Africa. In this way, the music has gone around the earth.[38]

Secondly, local African critics also pointed out the particularity of Japanese musicians. The herald of a particular "Japanese jazz" was celebrated when it was reported that their performance did not "fit into the concept of classical jazz." Importantly, instead of setting the American understanding of jazz as the only standard, it was recognized here that these musicians were "leading jazz in a new direction" just as pioneers Louis Armstrong and Charlie Parker had once done.[39]

In any case, transnational cultural exchanges have long been promoted through jazz as a component of Japan's cultural diplomacy. In the 2000s, the Japan Foundation supported the multinational group Unit Asia with the aim of "creating new music by excellent jazz musicians active in Asia." The group conducted concerts in Southeast Asia, the Middle East and Europe. One of the Japanese musicians opined that a feeling of swing was born when listening to another musician's performance with respect, and at that moment they were fully able to understand each other – "music will easily cross borders and grow bigger and stronger," they felt.[40] If so, the Asian Youth Jazz Orchestra was a good example of promoting cross-border understandings and ties with different cultures. Composed of 28 young adults from Japan and

Southeast Asia, the Orchestra conducted tours both in Southeast Asia (Indonesia, Philippines, Singapore, Thailand and Malaysia) and Japan (Tokyo, and the prefectures of Fukushima and Miyagi) in 2015.[41]

At the same time, the role of jazz in promoting peacebuilding and reconstruction after natural disasters is also increasing. In March 2016, Sato Masahiko & NoModismo conducted performances in Nepal in support of local reconstruction efforts following a major earthquake, as seen by a collaboration with local musicians and a series of workshops.[42] Similar efforts were also made in Sri Lanka following the devastating civil war that concluded in 2009. Local jam sessions were organized with the purpose of promoting cross-cultural dialogues, and thereby encouraging reconciliation between the Sinhalese and the Tamil groups.[43] Not that only jazz is used in these programs, but it is true that many jazz musicians are supportive and receptive to participating in such projects. Highly mobile, they can perform in small units, and have a high degree of musical versatility that enables them to play with local musicians who come from various musical genres. Jazz musicians also have an advantage in being able to gain local empathy by playing folk songs with traditional musical instruments. In short, jazz that encourages such empathy between peoples and cultures is very much needed in today's world.

Notes

1 Grover Sales, *Jazz: America's Classical Music* (New York: Da Capo Press, 1984); William "Billy" Taylor, "Jazz: America's Classical Music," *The Black Perspective in Music*, vol. 14 no.1, 1986. See also Anderson, *This Is Our Music*, pp.182–83.
2 H. Con. Res. 57 (100th), 4 December 1987.
3 H. Res. 189 (103th), 14 June 1993.
4 Thomas Jr. "Willis Conover, 75, Voice of America Disc Jockey."
5 Hershorn, *Norman Granz*, pp.377–78.
6 See the following resolutions. H.Con.Res.363 (107th), 20 March 2002; H.Con.Res.467 (107th), 10 October 2002; H.Con.Res.144 (108th), 9 April 2003; H. Con. Res.63 (108th), 14 June 2004; H.Res.778 (108th), 17 September 2004; H.Con.Res.501 (108th), 28 September 2004; and H.Con.Res.300 (109th), 6 February 2006. Hampton also played at the inauguration ceremonies of Eisenhower, Nixon and Reagan, and was seen as close to the Republican Party. See Burton W. Peretti, "Republican Jazz? Music and Conservative Ideology since 1969," in Jeffrey Jackson (ed.), *Music and History: Bridging the Disciplines* (Jackson: UP of Mississippi, 2005), pp.101–2.
7 National Museum of American History, News Release, "Smithsonian Celebrates 50th Anniversary of John Coltrane's A Love Supreme," 26 March 2014. www.si.edu/newsdesk/releases/smithsonian-celebrates-50th-anniversary-john-coltrane-s-love-supreme-0 [accessed 8 January 2017].
8 S.Res.510 (113th), 22 July 2014.
9 H.Res.894 (111th), 15 December 2009.
10 H.R.4280 (113th), 21 March 2014.
11 For more on the controversy and neoclassicists' view of jazz, see Porter, *What Is This Thing Called Jazz?*, pp.287–334; Gennari, *Blowin' Hot and Cool*, pp.339–71; Anderson, *This Is Our Music*, pp.182–90; Yusuke Torii, "'American Classical

Music' Jazz no Seidoka to Bannen no Amiri Baraka," *Setsunan Jimbun Kagaku*, vol.23, 2016.
12 Peretti, "Republican Jazz?," p.103.
13 S.1586 (103th), 12 April 1994.
14 Adrienne Schwisow, "Democrat Urging Anti-Bush Boycott on Inauguration Day," *The Associated Press*, 11 January 2005; Ward Reilly, "Jazz Funeral for Democracy." www.vvaw.org/veteran/article/?id=525 [accessed 12 January 2017].
15 Fred Hall, *It's About Time: The Dave Brubeck Story* (Fayetteville: University of Arkansas Press, 1996), pp.78, 150–52; Thom Shanker, "Jazz Menu Has Soviets Cookin' With Brubeck," *Chicago Tribune*, 27 March 1987.
16 Hall, *It's About Time*, p.150. In 1982, pianist Chick Corea and vibraphonist Gary Burton visited the Soviet Union as guests of the US ambassador, and conducted performances at the US embassy in Moscow as well as the US consulate in Leningrad. See Gary Burton, *Learning to Listen: The Jazz Journey of Gary Burton* (Boston: Berklee Press, 2013), chap.23.
17 Madeleine Albright, *Madam Secretary: A Memoir* (New York: Miramax, 2003), pp.111–13.
18 Ibid., p.113.
19 Ibid., pp.168–71.
20 Thelonious Monk Institute of Jazz, Press Release, 25 September 2012. http://monkinstitute.org/media/TMIJ_Competition_wrap-up_20120925.pdf [accessed 26 June 2015].
21 John F. Kennedy Center for the Performing Arts, *2012 Thelonious Monk International Jazz Drums Competition Program*, 2012, p.24.
22 The Kennedy Center, Press Release, 30 July 1998, 13 March 2000 and 16 March 2001. www.kennedy-center.org/programs/jazz/ambassadors/pressrelease.html, www.kennedy-center.org/programs/jazz/ambassadors/pressrelease_spring00.html, www.kennedy-center.org/programs/jazz/ambassadors/pressrelease01.html [all accessed 26 June 2012].
23 US Department of State, Bureau of Educational and Cultural Affairs Office of Policy and Evaluation, "Evaluation of the Jazz Ambassadors Program, Final Report, Volume 1," March 2006. https://eca.state.gov/files/bureau/jazz-amb-program-vol.-i-final-report-march-2006.pdf [accessed 28 February 2019].
24 Department of State, "The Rhythm Road: American Music Abroad Program Fact Sheet," undated. https://photos.state.gov/libraries/shenyang/173680/Everyday%20Diplomat/1_%20The%20Rhythm%20Road%20Fact%20Sheet_2010.doc [accessed 15 September 2016].
25 Thelonious Monk Institute of Jazz, "Education – International." http://monkinstitute.org/education/international [accessed 26 June 2016].
26 Condoleezza Rice, "Jazz, Public Diplomacy and Dizzy Gillespie," at USC Center on Public Diplomacy, 12 October 2006. https://uscpublicdiplomacy.org/sites/uscpublicdiplomacy.org/files/legacy/pdfs/rice_speech.pdf [accessed 15 September 2016]; Department of State, Office of the Spokesman, Media Note, 8 April 2008. http://2001-2009.state.gov/r/pa/prs/ps/2008/apr/103121.htm [accessed 26 June 2016].
27 UNESCO, Executive Board, 187EX/46, 26 August 2011. https://unesdoc.unesco.org/ark:/48223/pf0000211275 [accessed 8 February 2019].
28 UNESCO, General Conference, 36C/65, 21 October 2011. https://unesdoc.unesco.org/ark:/48223/pf0000213361 [accessed 8 February 2019].
29 Herbie Hancock, "Without the U.S., UNESCO Would Be Greatly Diminished," *The Washington Post*, 2 December 2011.
30 "Interview with Herbie Hancock: The Roots of Jazz Are in Humanity," *The UNESCO Courier*, 27 April 2012. https://en.unesco.org/courier/news-views-online/herbie-hancock-roots-jazz-are-humanity [accessed 26 June 2016].

164 *Making jazz great again*

31 Message from Ms Irina Bokova, Director-General of UNESCO on the Occasion of the International Jazz Day, 30 April 2012. https://unesdoc.unesco.org/ark:/48223/pf0000216082 [accessed 12 January 2019].
32 Susan E. Rice, "Remarks by Ambassador Susan E. Rice, U.S. Permanent Representative to the United Nations, at the International Jazz Day Sunset Concert at the United Nations," 30 April 2012. http://usun.state.gov/remarks/5422 [accessed 26 June 2016].
33 Message from Ms Irina Bokova, Director-General of UNESCO, on the Occasion of International Jazz Day, 30 April 2013. https://unesdoc.unesco.org/ark:/48223/pf0000220551 [accessed 12 January 2019].
34 International Jazz Day, Daytime Educational Program, 30 April 2014. www.unesco.org/new/fileadmin/MULTIMEDIA/HQ/ERI/pdf/IJD_DaytimeEdProgramG.pdf [accessed 12 January 2019].
35 Message from Ms Irina Bokova, Director-General of UNESCO, on the Occasion of International Jazz Day, 30 April 2015. https://unesdoc.unesco.org/ark:/48223/pf0000232248 [accessed 12 January 2019].
36 "Seikyo no Kuriya Makoto Koen, Hatsu no Brazil Koen ni Tegotae," *São Paulo Shimbun*, 28 August 2015.
37 Ritsuko Takahata, "Kokusai Koryu Kikin no Katsudo kara, Atarashii Deai wo Motomete: Jazz + Wadaiko Africa wo Yuku," *Kokusai Koryu*, vol.50, 1989, pp.71–73.
38 Ibid.
39 Ibid.
40 The Japan Foundation, "'UNIT ASIA' Chuto, India Junkai Koen, 2010." www.jpf.go.jp/j/project/culture/archive/information/1011/11-02.html [accessed 12 June 2016]; Isao "3 Kichi" Miyoshi, "Otagai no Oto wo Mitomeau. Sore ga Jazz no Inochi da," *Wochikochi*, vol.27, 2009, pp.66–67.
41 Japan Foundation, "Asian Youth Jazz Orchestra Nihon Koen," 28 January 2016. https://jfac.jp/culture/events/ayjo-program-2 [accessed 10 June 2016].
42 Japan Foundation, "Sato Mitsuhiko & NoModismo Jazz Nepal India Koen," undated. www.jpf.go.jp/j/project/culture/perform/oversea/2016/03-01.html [accessed 10 June 2016].
43 Japan Foundation, "Sri Lanka niokeru Bunka wo Tsujita Heiwa Kochiku Jigyo, 'Seika Hokoku Symposium – Randooga in Sri Lanka'," undated. www.jpf.go.jp/j/project/intel/archive/information/1311/11-02.html [accessed 10 June 2016].

Conclusion

There was no preordained – or *a priori* – specific meaning in jazz before its interaction with society. As time passed, places shifted and its musical styles changed, we found signs of hope, fear, decadence and modernity in jazz. Similarly, its representative functions have been tightly intertwined with the political environment around it – such as war, the Cold War, the peace movement, détente, decolonization, race, and the cross-cultural dialogues reflective of the postwar world. In this sense, this book's focus is on jazz as a symbol, rather than as a music. Jazz is a site for discursive politics and is open to multiple interpretations. It is not only a symbol of freedom, but also an impulse behind an unfulfilled struggle for democracy. In an unfree society, it is the subject of repression, but it also serves as a medium to encourage resistance and solidarity. At one time it was seen as close to Communism, while at other times it took on the function of anti-Communism. It embodies Americanism, but it could be also become the basis for anti-Americanism.

There is no doubt jazz was born in and still remains a symbol of America. Nonetheless, jazz goes beyond Americanism. Taking the argument of Paul Gilroy, the numerous routes jazz has followed in the process of spreading outside America's sovereign borders obscure its roots, yet enrich the color of jazz.[1] What we may call the "diaspora-ness" of jazz makes this music culturally hybrid and color-affluent.

This book took a position of challenging the hegemonic interpretation of jazz that equates the music exclusively with "American music." This discourse first emerged during the interwar period, maintaining a close relationship with the ideology of the popular front, and was officially sanctioned in the mid-1950s when jazz became a tool for winning the hearts and minds of people outside America as a cultural diplomacy tool. Subsequently, jazz's power of representing free and democratic America was appreciated by the Cold War liberals in the State Department. Secretary of State Dulles was among those who understood the power of culture, believing that the strength of American culture did not stem from its materialistic affluence. At the first meeting of the Advisory Committee on the Arts in January 1958, Dulles stressed "cultural things – things of beauty" would enhance America's external influence and respect. According to Dulles, "even the poorest people cultivate beauty." Therefore, even if international friendship with other countries could be achieved through harnessing America's substantial material production capacity, "there will always be a flaw in our friendship if we don't also win the respect of people who to a very great extent value beauty and art in its various forms very highly." Accordingly, he thought America could not effectively beguile the world if it only showed the world how many automobiles, washing machines and radios it could produce. For Dulles, America possessed "culture and art which should command the respect of other peoples of the world." While conscious of the Soviet cultural offensive that saw Moscow send its refined ballet troupes around the world, he nonetheless believed this was "one of the few remnants of the old Czarist society."[2] In this context, jazz became understood as America's most quintessential and effective weapon for winning the respect of the developing world.

This book has traced how jazz has been interpreted differently by various groups during different periods of world history – and has thereby examined the genealogy of the "American music" discourse. It has also elaborated on the people who sought to construct jazz scenes autonomous from that found in America. First of all, early examples of those who denied the equation of jazz with "American music" appeared in the interwar period. The Quintette du Hot Club de France and DTU in Germany both encouraged the development of distinctive national jazz styles. Whereas in Japan, jazz-arranged folk songs exemplified the search for a version of Japanese jazz.

Secondly, after the Second World War, similar projects were institutionalized extensively in the Communist bloc countries to de-Americanize the music. After the death of Stalin, Communist authorities sought to contain the musical effects of jazz in society by creating officially sanctioned jazz scenes. Accordingly, new jazz festivals were established, while jazz magazines were launched and jazz cafes were opened. These were also tactical responses to the rise of rock music that boasted a higher popularity but was seen as a genre with distinctly negative social connotations. Starting in the 1960s, live recordings of jazz festivals were released to the public, and musicians were able to make a living by playing jazz. As a result, being a jazz fan and a Communist at the same time was no longer contradictory. In the process, jazz became tamed – it ceased to be a "forbidden fruit." Whereas an institutionalized, tamed and de-Americanized jazz scene created the right set of domestic conditions for more American jazz ambassadors to visit Communist countries. Furthermore, this wave of jazz localization produced many non-American jazz musicians who also traveled all over the world, such as Krzysztof Komeda and Adam Makowicz of Poland. Soviet jazz musicians, on their part, began releasing unique albums around the same period. A good example is the Ganelin Trio, who combined jazz with folk and theatrical performance, attracting keen attention abroad.[3] Its new style of jazz, dubbed "new jazz," soon gained attention abroad through the new label Leo Records founded in 1979. The Ganelin Trio were invited to the Berliner Jazztage in 1980, conducted concerts in the UK in 1984, and appeared at the New York

Jazz Festival in 1986. According to Leo Feigin, the founder of the label, jazz in the Soviet Union was once just "aping the American," but this changed with the advent of new jazz. During the 1980s, "Soviet jazz" pioneered its own path in the jazz world, even carrying out an American tour.[4]

Thirdly, what was unforeseen by Communist authorities was that jazz was gradually able to promote diverse sets of transnational ties. Jazz festivals in Eastern Europe, as represented by the Jazz Jamboree, became venues for musicians and fans from all over the world to exchange ideas, and learn new musical techniques. Transnationalism via jazz was certainly seen in the protesting voices against the oppression of the Jazz Section in Czechoslovakia. When an autonomous space granted to the Czechoslovak jazz scene came under threat from authorities, musicians, critics and novelists across the world began to explicitly link the Czechoslovak Jazz Section to the central tenets underpinning the Helsinki Final Act. Establishing a transnational relationship was possible because jazz, born in America, had traveled well beyond American exceptionalism.

Fourthly, there were those who positioned jazz as a strategy to protest against America as the sole hegemonic power. In the postwar era when the homogeneity of America and Western Europe was emphasized with such political terms as the "Atlantic Community," leftist intellectuals became critical of their countries becoming American allies in the Cold War struggle, and thus sought to differentiate themselves from things American.[5] Against this backdrop, jazz was accepted as a music for expressing dissatisfaction with the present, and treated not so much as "American music," but as having deep roots in the concept of the repressed. This enabled jazz fans in France and Britain to indulge in illusions of guiding America from their own moral and cultural heights, just when the influence of their colonial empires was experiencing terminal and irreversible decline. If the tone of leftist criticism against the hegemon was in harmony with the popularity of jazz among intellectuals in both countries, it was based on a sense of obligation as a "parent" to nurture the music on behalf of the "big child" who seemed to have no appreciation for jazz. This was reflected in the "Athenian complex" – the conviction that the Greeks could guide the Romans. In this context, jazz could not be "American music." In the same vein, jazz had to transcend Americanism in West Germany and Japan in order to overcome the historical past. And when transnational exchanges were possible in both countries, be it through the Berliner Jazztage or through the Osaka Expo, the music's roots became increasingly obscured.

What should the role of jazz be in the twenty-first century? For many decades, jazz has been an important tool for strategic cultural diplomacy and will continue to be so. Having said this, the success of jazz diplomacy is often beholden to the whim of global politics. JALC's world tour provides a good example. During preparation for their Venezuela tour, originally scheduled for 2015, a joint performance by Wynton Marsalis and the Simon Bolivar Youth Orchestra was planned in collaboration with El Sistema, a Venezuelan national program for youth musical education. However, as the relationship between the two countries worsened, characterized by mutual expulsion of diplomats, the tour was unsurprisingly canceled.[6]

Still, at the end of his career, the former jazz ambassador Dave Brubeck evaluated the role of cultural diplomacy in glowing terms, asserting that at no time did we need it more. In an interview conducted in 2006 with the chair of the National Endowment for the Arts, Brubeck referred to a speech made by Martin Luther King: "We must live together as brothers or die together as fools." In this context, Brubeck emphasized the importance of promoting mutual understanding through any form of cultural exchange available. It is obvious that in Brubeck's mind was the increasingly intolerant world defined by such problems as terrorism, racism and xenophobia. In the same interview, he stressed: "if you dig deep enough, you're going to find a oneness of man."[7] His remark is quite suggestive of the problem we are facing in the current world – the need for respecting diversity while also bridging cultural divides. There is no role American exceptionalism can realistically play here. In retrospect, it was Brubeck himself who relativized American exceptionalism through promoting interactions between jazz and Indian classical music, thus signifying that long-held ties between jazz and Americanism have been irreversibly deconstructed. We can observe in the twenty-first century, jazz is becoming increasingly dynamic and hybrid in nature, while still serving to successfully connect people of the world.

Notes

1 Paul Gilroy, *The Black Atlantic: Modernity and Double-Consciousness* (Cambridge: Harvard UP, 1993).
2 CU, Box 95-4, "Agencies of Government Concerned with the Role of the Arts in International Relations," undated, "Remarks by the Secretary at the First Meeting of the Advisory Committee on the Arts," undated.
3 Vladimir Tarasov (trans. Masami Suzuki), *Trio* (Tokyo: Hosei UP, 2016); Masami Suzuki, *Russian Jazz: Samui Kuni no Atsui Ongaku* (Tokyo: Toyo Shoten, 2006), pp.43–46.
4 Leo Feigin, "Introduction," in Leo Feigin (ed.), *Russian Jazz: New Identity* (London: Quartet Books, 1985), p.1; S. Frederick Starr, "Soviet Jazz: The Third Wave," in Feigin (ed.), *Russian Jazz*, pp.7–10; Efim Barban, "Soviet Jazz: New Identity," in Feigin (ed.), *Russian Jazz*, pp.15–22; Leo Feigin, "Notes of a Record Producer," in Feigin (ed.), *Russian Jazz*, p.183.
5 For more on the discourse of the "Atlantic Community," see Valérie Aubourg, Gérard Bossuat and Giles Scott-Smith (eds.), *European Community, Atlantic Community?* (Paris: Soleb, 2008).
6 Official Statement Re: Jazz at Lincoln Center's Jazz across the Americas Tour in Caracas, Venezuela, 10 March 2015. www.jazz.org/press/official-statement-re-jazz-at-lincoln-centers-jazz-across-the-americas-tour-in-caracas-venezuela [accessed 19 January 2017].
7 Gioia with Brubeck, "Cool Jazz and the Cold War."

Bibliography

Primary sources

Archival documents

London School of Economics and Political Science (LSE) Library, London, UK
　Papers of European Nuclear Disarmament
The National Archives, Kew, London, UK
　FCO 13, Foreign and Commonwealth Office and Predecessors: Cultural Relations Departments
　KV 2, The Security Service: Personal Files
National Archives and Records Administration, College Park, Maryland, US
　Record Group 59, General Records of the Department of State
　Record Group 306, General Records of the United States Information Agency
Open Society Archives at Central European University, Budapest, Hungary (Online)
　Records of Radio Free Europe/Radio Liberty Research Institute
Richard Nixon Presidential Library, Yorba Linda, California, US (Online)
　WHCF: SMOF: Office of Presidential Papers and Archives
University of Arkansas Library, Fayetteville, Arkansas, US
　Special Collections Division, Bureau of Educational and Cultural Affairs (CU) Historical Collection

Published documents

Committee on Un-American Activities. *Investigation of Un-American Propaganda Activities in the U.S. (Regarding Leon Josephson and Samuel Liptzen): Hearings before the United States House Committee on Un-American Activities, Eightieth Congress, First Session, on Mar. 5, 21, 1947* (Washington, DC: Government Printing Office, 1947).
Eisenhower, Dwight D. *Public Papers of the Presidents of the United States: Dwight D. Eisenhower, 1958* (Washington, DC: Government Printing Office, 1959).
Nixon, Richard M. *Public Papers of the Presidents of the United States: Richard M. Nixon, 1969* (Washington, DC: Government Printing Office, 1971).
Nixon, Richard M. *Public Papers of the Presidents of the United States: Richard M. Nixon, 1974* (Washington, DC: Government Printing Office, 1975).
United States Department of State. *Foreign Relations of the United States, 1955–1957, vol.IX, Foreign Economic Policy; Foreign Information Program* (Washington, DC: Government Printing Office, 1987).

170 *Bibliography*

United States Department of State. *Foreign Relations of the United States, 1964–1968, vol. XVII, Eastern Europe* (Washington, DC: Government Printing Office, 1996).
United States Department of State. *Foreign Relations of the United States, 1961–1963, vol. V, Soviet Union* (Washington, DC: Government Printing Office, 1998).
United States Department of State. *Foreign Relations of the United States, 1964–1968, vol. XIV, Soviet Union* (Washington, DC: Government Printing Office, 2001).

Newspapers and magazines

Cross Currents
Down Beat
Esquire
Jazz Hihyo
Jazz Times
Kokusai Koryu
The Nation
New Republic
The New York Times
The New York Times Magazine
São Paulo Shimbun
Swing Journal
The UNESCO Courier
The Washington Post
Wochikochi

Websites

The American Presidency Project
The Associated Press
GovTrack
The Japan Foundation
Jazz at Lincoln Center
The John F. Kennedy Center for the Performing Arts
Thelonious Monk Institute of Jazz/Herbie Hancock Institute of Jazz
UNESCO
US Department of State
US House of Representatives
US Senate
Vietnam Veterans Against the War

Secondary sources

Abeßer, Michel. "Between Cultural Opening, Nostalgia and Isolation: Soviet Debates on Jazz between 1953 and 1964," in Gertrud Pickhan and Rüdiger Ritter (eds.), *Jazz behind the Iron Curtain* (Bern: Peter Lang, 2010).
Akatsuka, Wakagi. "'Grey Zone' ni Ikiru Geijutsu: 'Seijouka' Jidai niokeru Jazz Section no Katsudo ni tsuite," *Shisou*, vol.4, 2012.
Akio, Satoko. *Swing Japan: Nikkei Beigunhei Jimmy Araki to Senryo no Kioku* (Tokyo: Shinchosha, 2012).

Akiyama, Tatsuhide. *Nihon no Yogaku Hyakunen-shi* (Tokyo: Daiichi Hoki Shuppan, 1966).

Albright, Madeleine. *Madam Secretary: A Memoir* (New York: Miramax, 2003).

Anderson, Iain. *This Is Our Music: Free Jazz, the Sixties, and American Culture* (Philadelphia: University of Pennsylvania Press, 2012).

Ansari, Emily Abrams. "Shaping the Policies of Cold War Musical Diplomacy: An Epistemic Community of American Composers," *Diplomatic History*, vol.36 no.1, 2012.

Ansari, Emily Abrams. *The Sound of a Superpower: Musical Americanism and the Cold War* (Oxford: Oxford UP, 2018).

Ansell, Gwen. *Soweto Blues: Jazz, Popular Music, and Politics in South Africa* (London: Bloomsbury Academic, 2004).

Antoszek, Andrzej and Kate Delaney. "Poland: Transmissions and Translations," in Alexander Stephan (ed.), *The Americanization of Europe: Culture, Diplomacy, and Anti-Americanism after 1945* (New York: Berghahn Books, 2006).

Arndt, Richard T. *The First Resort of Kings: American Cultural Diplomacy in The Twentieth Century* (Washington, DC: Potomac Books, 2005).

Ashton, N. *Kennedy, Macmillan and the Cold War: The Irony of Interdependence* (London: Palgrave Macmillan, 2002).

Atkins, E. Taylor. *Blue Nippon: Authenticating Jazz in Japan* (Durham: Duke UP, 2001).

Atkins, E. Taylor. *Jazz Planet* (Jackson: UP of Mississippi, 2003).

Aubourg, Valérie, Gérard Bossuat and Giles Scott-Smith (eds.). *European Community, Atlantic Community?* (Paris: Soreb, 2008).

Baade, Christina L. *Victory through Harmony: The BBC and Popular Music in World War II* (Oxford: Oxford UP, 2011).

Baarsen, G. H. Joost. "'Sucking on [America's] Tit': Metaphorical Dimensions of the Family in Conservative American Discourses on Europe," *Traversea*, vol.3, 2013.

Bakan, Jonathon. "Jazz and the 'Popular Front': 'Swing' Musicians and the Left Wing Movement of the 1930s-1940s," *Jazz Perspectives*, vol.3 no.1, 2009.

Barban, Efim. "Soviet Jazz: New Identity," in Leo Feigin (ed.), *Russian Jazz: New Identity* (London: Quartet Books, 1985).

Barghoorn, Frederick Charles. *The Soviet Cultural Offensive: The Role of Cultural Diplomacy in Soviet Foreign Policy* (Princeton: Princeton UP, 1960).

Barnhisel, Greg. *Cold War Modernists: Art, Literature, and American Cultural Diplomacy* (New York: Columbia UP, 2015).

Bartlett, Djurdja. "Socialist Dandies International: East Europe, 1946–1959," *Fashion Theory: The Journal of Dress, Body and Culture*, vol.17 no.3, 2013.

Békés, Csaba. "East Central Europe, 1953–1956," in Melvyn P. Leffler and Odd Arne Westad (eds.), *The Cambridge History of the Cold War Volume 1: Origins* (Cambridge: Cambridge UP, 2010).

Belmonte, Laura A. *Selling the American Way: U.S. Propaganda and the Cold War* (Philadelphia: University of Pennsylvania Press, 2008).

Bender, Otto. *Swing unterm Hakenkreuz in Hamburg 1933–1945* (Hamburg: Christians, 1993).

Berghahn, Volker R. *America and the Intellectual Cold Wars in Europe: Shepard Stone Between Philanthropy, Academy, and Diplomacy* (Princeton: Princeton UP, 2001).

Bergmeier, Horst J. P. and Rainer E. Lotz. *Hitler's Airwaves: The Inside Story of Nazi Radio Broadcasting and Propaganda Swing* (New Haven: Yale UP, 1997).

Berliner, Brett A. *Ambivalent Desire: The Exotic Black Other in Jazz Age France* (Amherst: University of Massachusetts Press, 2002).

Berliner, Paul F. *Thinking in Jazz: The Infinite Art of Improvisation* (Chicago: University of Chicago Press, 1994).

Beyer, Wolfgang and Monica Ladurner. *Im Swing gegen den Gleichschritt: Die Jugend, der Jazz und die Nazis* (St. Pölten: Residenz, 2011).

Blake, Jody. *Le Tumulte Noir: Modernist Art and Popular Entertainment in Jazz-Age Paris, 1900–1930* (University Park: Pennsylvania State Press, 2003).

Borstelmann, Thomas. *The Cold War and the Color Line: American Race Relations in the Global Arena* (Cambridge: Harvard UP, 2003).

Bounds, Philip. "From Folk to Jazz: Eric Hobsbawm, British Communism and Cultural Studies," *Critique: Journal of Socialist Theory*, vol.40 no.4, 2012.

Braggs, Rashida Kamilah. *"American" Jazz: Traversing Race and Nation in Postwar France* (PhD Thesis, Northwestern University, 2006).

Braggs, Rashida Kamilah. *Jazz Diasporas: Race, Music, and Migration in Post-World War II Paris* (Oakland: University of California Press, 2016).

Breckenridge, Mark. *"Sounds for Adventurous Listeners": Willis Conover, the Voice of America, and the International Reception of Avant-garde Jazz in the 1960s* (PhD Thesis, University of North Texas, 2012).

Brown, Archie. *The Rise and Fall of Communism* (London: Bodley Head, 2009).

Brown, Karl. "Dance Hall Days. Jazz and Hooliganism in Communist Hungary, 1948–1956," in Gertrud Pickhan and Rüdiger Ritter (eds.), *Jazz behind the Iron Curtain* (Bern: Peter Lang, 2010).

Brubeck, Dave with Dana Gioia. "Cool Jazz and Cold War," *The American Interest*, vol.1 no.3, 2006.

Bugge, Peter. "Normalization and the Limits of the Law: The Case of the Czech Jazz Section," *East European Politics and Societies*, vol.22 no.2, 2008.

Burton, Gary. *Learning to Listen: The Jazz Journey of Gary Burton* (Boston: Berklee Press, 2013).

Carletta, David M. "'Those White Guys Are Working for Me': Dizzy Gillespie, Jazz, and the Cultural Politics of the Cold War during the Eisenhower Administration," *International Social Science Review*, vol.82, 2007.

Carr, Graham. "Diplomatic Notes: American Musicians and Cold War Politics in the Near and Middle East, 1954–1960," *Popular Music History*, vol.1 no.1, 2004.

Caute, David. *The Dancer Defects: The Struggle for Cultural Supremacy during the Cold War* (Oxford: Oxford UP, 2003).

Clark, Gregory. *Civic Jazz: American Music and Kenneth Burke on the Art of Getting Along* (Chicago: University of Chicago Press, 2015).

Cliff, Nigel. *Moscow Nights: The Van Cliburn Story-How One Man and His Piano Transformed the Cold War* (New York: Harper, 2016).

Cohen, Harvey G. *Duke Ellington's America* (Chicago: University of Chicago Press, 2011).

Corke, Sarah-Jane. *US Covert Operations and Cold War Strategy: Truman, Secret Warfare and the CIA, 1945–53* (London: Routledge, 2007).

Costigliola, Frank. *Awkward Dominion: American Political, Economic, and Cultural Relations with Europe, 1919–1933* (Ithaca: Cornell UP, 1988).

Cox, Annette. *Art as Politics: The Abstract Expressionist Avant-Garde and Society* (Ann Arbor: UMI Research Press, 1982).

Cull, Nicholas J. *The Cold War and the United States Information Agency: American Propaganda and Public Diplomacy, 1945–1989* (Cambridge: Cambridge UP, 2008).

D'Almeida, Fabrice. *High Society in the Third Reich* (Cambridge: Politi, 2008).

Dalton, Karen C. C. and Henry LouisGates, Jr. "Josephine Baker and Paul Colin: African American Dance Seen Through Parisian Eyes," *Critical Inquiry*, vol.24 no.4, 1998.

Davenport, Lisa. "Jazz and the Cold War," in Darlene Clark Hine and Jacqueline McLeod (eds.), *Crossing Boundaries: Comparative History of Black People in Diaspora* (Bloomington: Indiana UP, 2001).

Davenport, Lisa. *Jazz Diplomacy: Promoting America in the Cold War Era* (Jackson: UP of Mississippi, 2013).

Day, Barbara. *The Velvet Philosophers* (London: Claridge Press, 2000).

De Beauvoir, Simone (trans. Carol Cosman). *America Day by Day* (Berkeley: University of California Press, 2000).

Denning, Michael. *The Cultural Front: The Laboring of American Culture in the Twentieth Century* (Brooklyn: Verso, 2011).

Deveaux, Scott. *The Birth of Bebop: A Social and Musical History* (Berkeley: University of California Press, 1999).

Domurat, Marta. "The Jazz Press in the People's Republic of Poland: The Role of Jazz and Jazz Forum in the Past and Today," in Gertrud Pickhan and Rüdiger Ritter (eds.), *Jazz behind the Iron Curtain* (Bern: Peter Lang, 2010).

Domurat, Marta. "From 'Jazz in Poland' to 'Polish Jazz'," in Gertrud Pickhan and Rüdiger Ritter (eds.), *Meanings of Jazz in State Socialism* (Bern: Peter Lang, 2015).

Dragomir, Elena. *Cold War Perceptions: Romania's Policy Change Towards the Soviet Union 1960–1964* (Cambridge: Cambridge Scholars Publishing, 2015).

Dregni, Michael. *Django: The Life and Music of a Gypsy Legend* (Oxford: Oxford UP, 2006).

Drott, Eric. "Free Jazz and the French Critic," *Journal of the American Musicological Society*, vol.61 no.3, 2008.

Dudziak, Mary L. *Cold War Civil Rights: Race and the Image of American Democracy* (Princeton: Princeton UP, 2000).

Dunkel, Mario. "Marshall Winslow Stearns and the Politics of Jazz Historiography," *American Music*, vol.30 no.4, 2012.

Dunkel, Mario. "Jazz Made in Germany and the Transatlantic Beginnings of Jazz Diplomacy," in Rebekah Ahrendt, Mark Ferraguto and Damien Mahiet (eds.), *Music and Diplomacy from the Early Modern Era to the Present* (London: Palgrave Macmillan, 2014).

Duus, Masayo. *Tokyo Rose* (Tokyo: Bungeishunju, 1990).

Eames, Anthony. "The Maturation of Anglo-American Protest Music in the Antinuclear Environment from 1957–1969," *Journal of Studies in History & Culture*, vol.1 no. 1, 2014.

Ellington, Edward Kennedy. *Music Is My Mistress* (New York: Da Capo, 1976).

Ellwood, David. *The Shock of America: Europe and the Challenge of the Century* (Oxford: Oxford UP, 2012).

English, Robert E. *Russia and the Idea of the West: Gorbachev, Intellectuals and the End of the Cold War* (New York: Columbia UP, 2000).

Erenberg, Lewis A. *Swingin' the Dream: Big Band Jazz and the Rebirth of American Culture* (Chicago: University of Chicago Press, 1998).

Evans, Nicholas M. *Writing Jazz: Race, Nationalism, and Modern Culture in the 1920s* (London: Routledge, 2000).
Faine, Edward Allan. *Ellington at the White House 1969* (Takoma Park: IM Press, 2013).
Faine, Edward Allan. *The Best Gig in Town: Jazz Artists at the White House, 1969–1974* (Takoma Park: IM Press, 2015).
Falk, Andrew J. *Upstaging the Cold War: American Dissent and Cultural Diplomacy, 1940–1960* (Amherst: University of Massachusetts Press, 2009).
Fanon, Frantz (trans. Constance Farrington). *The Wretched of the Earth* (New York: Grove Press, 1963).
Fay, Jennifer. "That's Jazz Made in Germany!": "Hallo, Fräulein!" and the Limits of Democratic Pedagogy," *Cinema Journal*, vol.44 no.1, 2004.
Feather, Leonard. *Jazz Years: Earwitness to an Era* (New York: Da Capo Press, 1987).
Feigin, Leo. "Introduction," in Leo Feigin (ed.), *Russian Jazz: New Identity* (London: Quartet Books, 1985a).
Feigin, Leo. "Notes of a Record Producer," in Leo Feigin (ed.), *Russian Jazz: New Identity* (London: Quartet Books, 1985b).
Feigin, Leo. *Russian Jazz: New Identity* (London: Quartet Books, 1986).
Fejtö, François (trans. Toru Kumada). *Stalin Jidai no Touo* (Tokyo: Iwanami Shoten, 1979).
Fenemore, Mark. *Sex, Thugs and Rock 'n' Roll: Teenage Rebels in Cold-War East Germany* (New York: Berghahn, 2007).
Finn, Peter and Petra Couvee. *The Zhivago Affair: The Kremlin, the CIA, and the Battle over a Forbidden Book* (London: Harvill Secker, 2014).
Firestone, Ross. *Swing, Swing, Swing: The Life & Times of Benny Goodman* (New York: W. W. Norton and Company, 1994).
Fosler-Lussier, Danielle. "Cultural Diplomacy as Cultural Globalization: The University of Michigan Jazz Band in Latin America," *Journal of the Society for American Music*, vol.4 no. 1, 2010.
Fosler-Lussier, Danielle. *Music in America's Cold War Diplomacy* (Berkeley: University of California Press, 2015).
Franklin, Benjamin. *Jazz & Blues Musicians of South Carolina: Interviews with Jabbo, Dizzy, Drink, and Others* (Columbia: University of South Carolina Press, 2008).
Frascina, Francis (ed.). *Pollock and After: The Critical Debate* (New York: Harper and Row, 1985).
Fujita, Fumiko. *America Bunka Gaiko to Nihon: Reisenki no Bunka to Hito no Koryu* (Tokyo: University of Tokyo Press, 2015).
Furuya, Jun. *Americanism: Fuhen Kokka no Nationalism* (Tokyo: University of Tokyo Press, 2002).
Gabbard, Krin. *Jazz among the Discourses* (Durham: Duke UP, 1995a).
Gabbard, Krin. *Representing Jazz* (Durham: Duke UP, 1995b).
Gac, Scott. "Jazz Strategy: Dizzy, Foreign Policy, and Government in 1956," *Americana*, vol.4 no. 1, 2005.
Garment, Leonard. *Crazy Rhythm: From Brooklyn and Jazz to Nixon's White House, Watergate, and Beyond* (Cambridge: Da Capo Press, 2001).
Gennari, John. *Blowin' Hot and Cool: Jazz and Its Critics* (Chicago: University of Chicago Press, 2006).

Gienow-Hecht, Jessica C. E. "'How Good Are We?': Culture and the Cold War," in Giles Scott-Smith and Hans Krabbendam (eds.), *The Cultural Cold War in Western Europe, 1945–1960* (London: Frank Cass, 2003).

Gienow-Hecht, Jessica C. *Music and International History in the Twentieth Century* (New York: Berghahn, 2015).

Gillespie, Dizzy and Al Fraser. *To Be or Not to Bop: Memoirs of Dizzy Gillespie* (New York: Da Capo, 1985).

Gilroy, Paul. *The Black Atlantic: Modernity and Double-Consciousness* (Cambridge: Harvard UP, 1993).

Godbolt, Jim. *A History of Jazz in Britain 1919–50* (London: Northway Publications, 2006).

Gondola, Ch. Didier. "'But I Ain't African, I'm American!': Black American Exiles and the Construction of Racial Identities in Twentieth-Century France," in Heike Raphael-Hernandez (ed.), *Blackening Europe: The African American Presence* (London: Routledge, 2003).

Gould-Davies, Nigel. "The Logic of Soviet Cultural Diplomacy," *Diplomatic History*, vol.27 no.3, 2003.

Guilbaut, Serge. *How New York Stole the Idea of Modern Art: Abstract Expressionism, Freedom, and the Cold War* (Chicago: University of Chicago Press, 1985).

Hall, Fred. *It's about Time: The Dave Brubeck Story* (Fayetteville: University of Arkansas Press, 1996).

Hall, James C. *Mercy, Mercy Me: African-American Culture and the American Sixties: African American Culture and the American Sixties* (Oxford: Oxford UP, 2001).

Harris, Sarah Miller. *The CIA and the Congress for Cultural Freedom in the Early Cold War: The Limits of Making Common Cause* (London: Routledge, 2016).

Hatschek, Keith. "The Impact of American Jazz Diplomacy in Poland During the Cold War Era," *Jazz Perspectives*, vol.4 no.3, 2010.

Hattori, Ryoichi. *Boku no Ongaku Jinsei* (Tokyo: Nihon Bungeisha, 1993).

Havadi, Gergő. "An Individual Subculture Reflected in Domestic Spies' Reports. Hungarian Jazz in the Socialist Period," in Gertrud Pickhan and Rüdiger Ritter (eds.), *Jazz behind the Iron Curtain* (Bern: Peter Lang, 2010).

Havadi, Gergő. "Individualists, Traditionalists, Revolutionaries, or Opportunists?," in Gertrud Pickhan and Rüdiger Ritter (eds.), *Meanings of Jazz in State Socialism* (Bern: Peter Lang, 2015).

Heffley, Mike. *Northern Sun, Southern Moon: Europe's Reinvention of Jazz* (New Haven: Yale UP, 2005).

Hersch, Charles. "Poisoning Their Coffee: Louis Armstrong and Civil Rights," *Polity*, vol.34 no.3, 2002.

Hershorn, Tad. *Norman Granz: The Man Who Used Jazz for Justice* (Berkeley: University of California Press, 2011).

Hixson, Walter L. *Parting the Curtain: Propaganda, Culture, and the Cold War, 1945–1961* (New York: St. Martin's Griffin, 1997).

Hoshino, Akio. *Europe Jazz Ogon Jidai* (Tokyo: Seidosha, 2009).

Hurley, Andrew Wright. *The Return of Jazz: Joachim-Ernst Berendt and West German Cultural Change* (New York: Berghahn Books, 2009).

Ikezaki, Tadataka. *Sekai wo Kyoi Suru Americanism* (Tokyo: Tenjinsha, 1930).

Jachec, Nancy. *The Philosophy and Politics of Abstract Expressionism* (Cambridge: Cambridge UP, 2000).

Jackson, Jeffry. *Making Jazz French: Music and Modern Life in Interwar Paris* (Durham: Duke UP, 2003).

Janik, Elizabeth. *Recomposing German Music: Politics and Musical Tradition in Cold War Berlin* (Leiden: Brill, 2005).

Jarab, Josef. "The Story of the Jazz Section," in R. Kroes, Robert W. Rydell and D. F. J. Bosscher (eds.), *Cultural Transmissions and Receptions: American Mass Culture in Europe* (Amsterdam: VU UP, 1993).

John F. Kennedy Center for the Performing Arts. *2012 Thelonious Monk International Jazz Drums Competition Program*, 2012.

Johnston, Timothy. *Being Soviet: Identity, Rumour, and Everyday Life under Stalin, 1939–53* (Oxford: Oxford UP, 2011).

Jones, LeRoi. *Blues People: Negro Music in White America* (New York: William Morrow, 1963).

Jordan, Matthew F. *Le Jazz: Jazz and French Cultural Identity* (Urbana: University of Illinois Press, 2010).

Josephson, Barney and Terry Trilling-Josephson. *Cafe Society: The Wrong Place for the Right People* (Urbana: University of Illinois Press, 2009).

Judt, Tony. *Postwar: A History of Europe Since 1945* (London: Penguin Books, 2005).

Kajanová, Yvetta. "Slovak and Czech Jazz Emigrants after 1948," *Jazzforschung / Jazz Research*, vol.41, 2009.

Kajanová, Yvetta, GertrudPickhan and Rüdiger Ritter (eds.). *Jazz from Socialist Realism to Postmodernism* (Bern: Peter Lang, 2016).

Kane, John. "Schizophrenic Nationalism and Anti-Americanism," in Brendon O'Connor, *Anti-Americanism: History, Causes, Themes, Vol.2: Historical Perspectives* (Oxford: Greenwood World Publishing, 2007).

Kater, Michael. *Different Drummers: Jazz in the Culture of Nazi Germany* (Oxford: Oxford UP, 2003).

Kater, Michael. *Hitler Youth* (Cambridge: Harvard UP, 2004).

Kater, Michael. "New Democracy and Alternative Culture: Jazz in West Germany after the Second World War," *Australian Journal of Politics and History*, vol.52 no.2, 2006.

Kelley, Robin D. G. *Africa Speaks, America Answers: Modern Jazz in Revolutionary Times* (Cambridge: Harvard UP, 2012).

Kibata, Yoichi. *Shihai no Daisho: Eiteikoku Hokai to Teikoku Ishiki* (Tokyo: University of Tokyo Press, 1987).

Kishi, Toshihiko. *Higashi Asia Ryukoka Hour* (Tokyo: Iwanami Shoten, 2013).

Kobayashi, Jun. "Jazz Gohatto no Jidai ga Atta," in Mainichi Shimbunsha, *Nihon no Jazz* (Tokyo: Mainichi Shimbunsha, 1982).

Koch, Hans-Joerg. *Das Wunschkonzert im NS-Rundfunk* (Köln: Boehlau, 2003).

Kofsky, Frank. *Black Nationalism and the Revolution in Music* (New York: Pathfinder, 1970).

Kolleritsch, Elisabeth. "Jazz in Toralitalian Systems (Nazi Germany and Former USSR): The Life of the Trumpet Player Eddie Rosner," *European Scientific Journal*, vol.2, May2015.

Kovrig, Bennett. *Of Walls and Bridges: The United States and Eastern Europe* (New York: New York UP, 1991).

Krabbendam, Hans and Giles Scott-Smith (eds.). *The Cultural Cold War in Western Europe, 1945–60* (London: Routledge, 2004).

Krenn, Michael L. *Fall-Out Shelters for the Human Spirit: American Art and the Cold War* (Chapel Hill: University of North Carolina Press, 2005).

Kuisel, Richard F. *Seducing the French: The Dilemma of Americanization* (Berkeley: University of California Press, 1997).

LaFeber, Walter, Richard Polenberg and Nancy Woloch. *The American Century: A History of the United States Since the 1890s 7th Edition* (London: Routledge, 2013)

Lane, Jeremy F. *Jazz and Machine-Age Imperialism: Music, "Race," and Intellectuals in France, 1918–1945* (Ann Arbor: University of Michigan Press, 2013).

Lauk, Tiit. "Estonian Jazz Before and Behind the 'Iron Curtain'," in Gertrud Pickhan and Rüdiger Ritter (eds.), *Jazz behind the Iron Curtain* (Bern: Peter Lang, 2010).

Laville, Helen and Hugh Wilford (eds.). *The US Government, Citizen Groups and the Cold War: The State-Private Network* (London: Routledge, 2006).

Layton, Azza Salama. *International Politics and Civil Rights Policies in the United States, 1941–1960* (Cambridge: Cambridge UP, 2000).

Lester, James. "Willis of Oz: A Profile of Famed Voice of America broadcaster Willis Conover," *Central Europe Review*, vol.1 no.5, 1999.

Lucas, Scott. *Freedom's War: The American Crusade against the Soviet Union* (New York: New York UP, 1999).

Lücke, Martin. "The Postwar Campaign against Jazz in the USSR (1945–1953)," in Gertrud Pickhan and Rüdiger Ritter (eds.), *Jazz behind the Iron Curtain* (Bern: Peter Lang, 2010).

Lukowski, Jerzy and Hubert Zawadzki. *A Concise History of Poland* (Cambridge: Cambridge UP, 2001).

Lundestad, Geir. *The United States and Western Europe since 1945: From "Empire" by Invitation to Transatlantic Drift* (Oxford: Oxford UP, 2005).

Lusane, Clarence. *The Black History of the White House* (San Francisco: City Lights Books, 2011).

Mancosu, Paolo. *Inside the Zhivago Storm. The Editorial Adventures of Pasternak's Masterpiece* (Milan: Feltrinelli, 2013).

Margolick, David. *Strange Fruit: Billie Holiday, Cafe Society, and an Early Cry for Civil Rights* (Philadelphia: Running Press, 2004).

McDaniel, Cadra Peterson. *American–Soviet Cultural Diplomacy: The Bolshoi Ballet's American Premiere* (Lanham: Lexington Books, 2014).

McDonough, Frank. *Opposition and Resistance in Nazi Germany* (Cambridge: Cambridge UP, 2001).

McGraw, Andrew. "The Ambivalent Freedoms of Indonesian Jazz," *Jazz Perspectives*, vol.6 no.3, 2012.

McKay, George. *Circular Breathing: The Cultural Politics of Jazz in Britain* (Durham: Duke UP, 2005).

McKenzie, Brian A. *Remaking France: Americanization, Public Diplomacy, and the Marshall Plan* (New York: Berghahn Books, 2005).

Meyer, Gerald. "Frank Sinatra: The Popular Front and an American Icon," *Science & Society*, vol.66 no.3, 2002.

Mikkonen, Simo and Pekka Suutari. *Music, Art and Diplomacy: East-West Cultural Interactions and the Cold War* (London: Routledge, 2015).

Minganti, Franco. "Jukebox Boys: Postwar Italian Music and the Culture of Covering," in Heide Fehrenbach and Uta Poiger (eds), *Transactions, Transgressions and Transformations: American Culture in Western Europe and Japan* (New York: Berghahn Books, 2000).

178 Bibliography

Mitrovich, Gregory. *Undermining the Kremlin: America's Strategy to Subvert the Soviet Bloc, 1947–1956* (Ithaca: Cornell UP, 2000).

Miyawaki, Toshifumi, Shuhei Hosokawa and Mike Molasky. *New Jazz Studies: Jazz Kenkyu no Aratana Chihei he* (Tokyo: Artes Publishing, 2010).

Molasky, Mike. *Sengo Nihon no Jazz Bunka* (Tokyo: Seidosha, 2005).

Monson, Ingrid. *Saying Something: Jazz Improvisation and Interaction* (Chicago: University of Chicago Press, 1996).

Monson, Ingrid. *Freedom Sounds: Civil Rights Call Out to Jazz and Africa* (Oxford: Oxford UP, 2007).

Moore, Hilary. *Inside British Jazz: Crossing Borders of Race, Nation and Class* (London: Routledge, 2007).

Mori, Masato. *Nippon Swing Time* (Tokyo: Kodansha, 2010).

Motyčka, Peter. "The Jazz Section: A Platform of Freedom in Czechoslovakia," in Gertrud Pickhan and Rüdiger Ritter (eds.), *Jazz behind the Iron Curtain* (Bern: Peter Lang, 2010).

Motyčka, Peter. "The Jazz Section: Disintegration through Jazz," in Gertrud Pickhan and Rüdiger Ritter (eds.), *Meanings of Jazz in State Socialism* (Bern: Peter Lang, 2015).

Nettelbeck, Colin. *Dancing with De Beauvoir: Jazz and The French* (Melbourne: Melbourne, 2005).

Nettelbeck, Colin. "Jean-Paul Sartre, Simone de Beauvoir and the Paris Jazz Scene," *Modern & Contemporary France*, vol.9 no.2, 2010.

Newton, Francis. *The Jazz Scene* (New York: Da Capo, 1975).

Nicholson, Stuart. *Jazz and Culture in a Global Age* (Boston: Northeastern UP, 2014).

Nilsen, Sarah. *Projecting America, 1958: Film and Cultural Diplomacy at the Brussels World's Fair* (Jefferson: McFarland, 2011).

Nolan, Mary. "America in the German Imagination," in Heide Fehrenbach and Uta G. Poiger (eds.), *Transactions, Transgressions, Transformations: American Culture in Western Europe and Japan* (New York: Berghahn Books, 2000).

Novikova, Irina. "Black Music, White Freedom: Times and Spaces of Jazz Countercultures in the USSR," in Heike Raphael-Hernandez (ed.), *Blackening Europe: The African American Presence* (London: Routledge, 2003).

Osgood, Kenneth. *Total Cold War: Eisenhower's Secret Propaganda Battle at Home and Abroad* (Lawrence: UP of Kansas, 2008).

Ostendorf, Berndt. "Subversive Reeducation?: Jazz as a Liberating Force in Germany and Europe," *Revue Francaise d'Etudes Américaines*, vol.5, 2001.

Panish, Jon. *The Color of Jazz: Race and Representation in Postwar American Culture* (Jackson: UP of Mississippi, 1997).

Parsonage, Catherine. *The Evolution of Jazz in Britain, 1880–1935* (London: Routledge, 2005).

Pells, Richard. *Not Like Us: How Europeans Have Loved, Hated, and Transformed American Culture since World War II* (New York: Basic Books, 1998).

Perchard, Tom. *After Django: Making Jazz in Postwar France* (Ann Arbor: University of Michigan Press, 2015).

Peretti, Burton W. *Jazz in American culture* (Chicago: Ivan R. Dee, 1997).

Peretti, Burton W. "Republican Jazz? Music and Conservative Ideology since 1969," in Jeffrey Jackson (ed.), *Music and History: Bridging the Disciplines* (Jackson: UP of Mississippi, 2005).

Peukert, Detlev J. K. (trans. Richard Deveson). *Inside Nazi Germany: Conformity, Opposition, and Racism in Everyday Life* (New Haven: Yale UP, 1987).

Pickhan, Gertrud and Rüdiger Ritter (eds.). *Jazz behind the Iron Curtain* (Bern: Peter Lang, 2010).

Pickhan, Gertrud and Rüdiger Ritter (eds.). *Meanings of Jazz in State Socialism* (Bern: Peter Lang, 2015).

Pietraszewski, Igor. "Being a Jazz Musician in Poland," in Gertrud Pickhan and Rüdiger Ritter (eds.), *Jazz behind the Iron Curtain* (Bern: Peter Lang, 2010).

Pietraszewski, Igor. *Jazz in Poland: Improvised Freedom* (Bern: Peter Lang, 2014).

Pietraszewski, Igor. "Jazz Musicians in Post-War Poland," in Gertrud Pickhan and Rüdiger Ritter (eds.), *Meanings of Jazz in State Socialism* (Bern: Peter Lang, 2015).

Plummer, Brenda Gayle. *Rising Wind: Black Americans and U.S. Foreign Affairs, 1935–1960* (Chapel Hill: The University of North Carolina Press, 1996).

Plummer, Brenda Gayle (ed.). *Window on Freedom: Race, Civil Rights, and Foreign Affairs, 1945–1988* (Chapel Hill: University of North Carolina Press, 2003).

Poiger, Uta. *Jazz, Rock, and Rebels: Cold War Politics and American Culture in a Divided Germany* (Oakland: University of California Press, 2000).

Poiger, Uta. "Searching for Proper New Music: Jazz in Cold War Germany," in Agnes Mueller (ed.), *German Pop Culture-How American Is It?* (Ann Arbor: University of Michigan Press, 2004).

Popan, Adrian. "Jazz Revival in Romania 1964–1971," in Gertrud Pickhan and Rüdiger Ritter (eds.), *Jazz behind the Iron Curtain* (Bern: Peter Lang, 2010).

Porter, Eric. *What Is This Thing Called Jazz?: African American Musicians as Artists, Critics, and Activists* (Berkeley: University of California Press, 2002).

Porter, Lewis and Michael Ullman. "Sidney Bechet and His Long Song," *The Black Perspective in Music*, vol.16 no.2, 1988.

Prevots, Naima. *Dance for Export: Cultural Diplomacy and the Cold War* (Hanover: Wesleyan UP, 1998).

Richmond, Yale. *Cultural Exchange and the Cold War: Raising the Iron Curtain* (University Park: Pennsylvania State UP, 2003).

Risso, Linda. *Propaganda and Intelligence in the Cold War: The NATO Information Service* (London: Routledge, 2014).

Ritter, Rüdiger. "Between Cultural Alternative and Protest. On the Social Function of Jazz after 1945 in Central Europe (GDR, Poland, Hungary, CSSR)," *Musicologica*, vol.1, 2011.

Ritter, Rüdiger. "Jazz in State Socialism: A Playground of Refusal?," in Gertrud Pickhan and Rüdiger Ritter (eds.), *Meanings of Jazz in State Socialism* (Bern: Peter Lang, 2015a).

Ritter, Rüdiger. "Negotiated Spaces: Jazz in Moscow after the Thaw," in Gertrud Pickhan and Rüdiger Ritter (eds.), *Meanings of Jazz in State Socialism* (Bern: Peter Lang, 2015b).

Ritter, Rüdiger. "Broadcasting Jazz into the Eastern Bloc: Cold War Weapon or Cultural Exchange? The Example of Willis Conover," in Yvetta Kajanová, Gertrud Pickhan and Rüdiger Ritter (eds.), *Jazz from Socialist Realism to Postmodernism* (Bern: Peter Lang, 2016).

Rosenberg, Emily. *Spreading the American Dream: American Economic and Cultural Expansion, 1890–1945* (New York: Hill and Wang, 1982).

Rosenberg, Victor. *Soviet-American Relations, 1953–1960: Diplomacy and Cultural Exchange during the Eisenhower Presidency* (Jefferson: McFarland, 2005).

Ross, Larry. *African American Jazz Musicians in the Diaspora* (Lewiston: Edwin Mellen, 2003).

Ross, Larry. "Jazz Musicians in Europe: 1919 to 1945," in James L.ConyersJr. (ed.), *Engines of the Black Power Movement: Essays on the Influence of Civil Rights Actions, Arts, and Islam* (Jefferson: Mcfarland, 2006).

Rothschild, Joseph. *Return to Diversity: A Political History of East Central Europe since World War II* (Oxford: Oxford UP, 1989).

Ryback, Timothy W. *Rock around the Bloc: A History of Rock Music in Eastern Europe and the Soviet Union* (Oxford: Oxford UP, 1990).

Sales, Grover. *Jazz: America's Classical Music* (New York: Da Capo Press, 1984).

Sandbrook, Dominic. *Never Had It So Good: A History of Britain from Suez to the Beatles* (London: Little, Brown, 2005).

Sartre, Jean Paul (trans. Lloyd Alexander). *Nausea* (New York: New Directions, 2013).

Sasaki, Takuya. "The Eisenhower Administration's Containment Policy and East-West Exchanges, 1955–1960," *Rikkyo Hogaku*, vol.56 and 57, 2000 and 2001.

Saunders, Frances Stonor. *The Cultural Cold War: The CIA and the World of Arts and Letters* (New York: New Press, 2000).

Schmidt-Rost, Christian. "Freedom within Limitations: Getting Access to Jazz in the GDR and PRP between 1945 and 1961," in Gertrud Pickhan and Rüdiger Ritter (eds.), *Jazz behind the Iron Curtain* (Bern: Peter Lang, 2010).

Schmidt-Rost, Christian. *Jazz in der DDR und Polen: Geschichte eines transatlantischen Transfers* (Bern: Peter Lang, 2015a).

Schmidt-Rost, Christian. "1956: A Turning Point for the Jazz Scenes in the GDR and Poland," in Gertrud Pickhan and Rüdiger Ritter (eds.), *Meanings of Jazz in State Socialism* (Bern: Peter Lang, 2015b).

Schwartz, Thomas Alan. *Lyndon Johnson and Europe: In the Shadow of Vietnam* (Cambridge: Harvard UP, 2003).

Schweitzer, Julie Kathleen. *Irresponsibly Engage: Boris Vian and Uses of American Culture in France, 1940–1959* (MA Thesis, University of Maryland, 2005).

Scott-Smith, Giles. "The 'Masterpieces of the Twentieth Century' Festival and the Congress for Cultural Freedom: Origins and Consolidation 1947–1952," *Intelligence and National Security*, vol.15 no.1, 2000.

Scott-Smith, Giles. *Politics of Apolitical Culture* (London: Routledge, 2001).

Scott-Smith, Giles. *Networks of Empire: The US State Department's Foreign Leader Program in the Netherlands, France and Britain 1950–1970* (Brussels: Peter Lang, 2008).

Scott-Smith, Giles. *Western Anti-Communism and the Interdoc Network: Cold War Internationale* (London: Palgrave Macmillan, 2012).

Segawa, Masahisa. *Jazz de Odotte* (Tokyo: Seiryu Shuppan, 2005).

Segawa, Masahisa and Yoshio Otani. *Nihon Jazz no Tanjo* (Tokyo: Seidosha, 2008).

Sehgal, Kabir. *Jazzocracy: Jazz, Democracy, and the Creation of a New American Mythology* (Mishawaka: Better World Books, 2008).

Shack, William A. *Harlem in Montmartre: A Paris Jazz Story between the Great Wars* (Berkeley: University of California Press, 2001).

Shipton, Alyn. *Groovin' High: The Life of Dizzy Gillespie* (Oxford: Oxford UP, 2001).

Shull, Tad. "East Meets West at Jazz Hot: Maoism, Race, and Revolution in French Jazz Criticism," *Jazz Perspectives*, vol.8 no.1, 2014.

Škvorecký, Josef. *The Bass Saxophone: Two Novellas* (New York: Ecco Press, 1994).

Starr, S. Frederick. "Soviet Jazz: The Third Wave," in Leo Feigin (ed.), *Russian Jazz: New Identity* (London: Quartet Books, 1985).

Starr, S. *Red and Hot: The Fate of Jazz in the Soviet Union 1917–1991* (New York: Limelight Editions, 2004).

Stites, Richard. "The Ways of Russian Popular Music to 1953," in Neil Edmunds (ed.), *Soviet Music and Society under Lenin and Stalin* (London: Routledge, 2004).

Stowe, David W. *Swing Changes: Big-band Jazz in New Deal America* (Cambridge: Harvard UP, 1998).

Strait, Kevin Michael Angelo. *"A Tone Parallel": Jazz Music, Leftist Politics, and the Counter-Minstrel Narrative, 1930–1970* (PhD Thesis, George Washington University, 2010).

Suponitskaya, Irina. "The Americanization of Soviet Russia in the 1920s and 1930s," *Social Science*, vol.45 no.2, 2014.

Suzuki, Masami. *Russian Jazz: Samui Kuni no Atsui Ongaku* (Tokyo: Toyo Shoten, 2006).

Suzuki, Masami. "1960 Nendai no Jazz Festival to Choshu," *Slav Eurasia Kenkyu Hokokushu*, vol.1, 2008.

Tackley, Catherine. *The Evolution of Jazz in Britain, 1880–1935* (London: Routledge, 2005).

Tarasov, Vladimir (trans. Masami Suzuki). *Trio* (Tokyo: Hosei UP, 2016).

Taylor, William "Billy". "Jazz: America's Classical Music," *The Black Perspective in Music*, vol. 14 no.1, Winter1986.

Torii, Yusuke. "Democracy no Shonin," *America Kenkyu*, vol.39, 2005.

Torii, Yusuke. *Swing ideology and Its Cold War Discontents in United States-Japan Relations, 1944–1968* (PhD Thesis, George Washington University, 2007).

Torii, Yusuke. "Sengo Nihon niokeru Beikoku no Kohobunka Katsudo to Jazz: Osaka CIE Toshokan/America Bunka Center no Jirei wo Chushin ni," *Setsunan Journal of English Education*, vol.4, 2010.

Torii, Yusuke. "'American Classical Music' Jazz no Seidoka to Bannen no Amiri Baraka," *Setsunan Jimbun Kagaku*, vol.23, 2016.

Tournès, Ludovic. *New Orleans sur Seine: Histoire de Jazz en France, 1917–1992* (Paris: Fayard, 1999).

Tournès, Ludovic. "La réinterprétation du jazz: un phénomène de contreaméricanisation dans la France d'après-guerre (1945-1960)," *Revue française d'études américaines*, vol.5, 2001.

Toya, Mamoru. *Shinchugun Club kara Kayokyoku he: Sengo Nihon Popular Ongaku no Reimeiki* (Tokyo: Misuzu Shobo, 2005).

Toynbee, Jason and Catherine Tackley. *Black British Jazz: Routes, Ownership and Performance* (London: Routledge, 2014).

Tsipursky, Gleb. *Pleasure, Power, and the Pursuit of Communism: Soviet Youth and State-Sponsored Popular Culture during the Early Cold War, 1945–1968* (PhD Thesis, University of North Carolina, 2011).

Tucker, Mark (ed.). *The Duke Ellington Reader* (Oxford: Oxford UP, 1995).

Tudda, Chris. *The Truth Is Our Weapon: The Rhetorical Diplomacy of Dwight D. Eisenhower And John Foster Dulles* (Baton Rouge: Louisiana State UP, 2006).

Uchida, Koichi. *Nihon no Jazz-shi* (Tokyo: Swing Journal, 1976).

Uchikawa, Yoshimi (ed.). *Gendaishi Shiryo: Mass Media Tosei*, 2nd ed. (Tokyo: Misuzu Shobo, 1973).

Vian, Boris (trans. Boris Vian and Milton Rosenthal). *I Spit on Your Graves* (Los Angeles: TamTam Books, 2013).
Vihlen, Elizabeth. "Jammin' on the Champs-Elysées: Jazz, France, and the 1950s," in Reinhold Wagnleitner and Elaine Tyler May (eds.), *"Here, There and Everywhere": The Foreign Politics of American Popular Culture* (Hanover: UP of New England, 2000).
Vihlen, Elizabeth. *Jazz and Postwar French Identity: Improvising the Nation* (Lanham: Lexington Books, 2016).
Von Eschen, Penny. *Race Against Empire: Black Americans and Anti-colonialism, 1937–1957* (Ithaca: Cornell UP, 1997).
Von Eschen, Penny. "The Real Ambassadors," in Robert O'Meall, Brent Hayes Edwards and Farah Jasmine Griffin (eds.), *Uptown Conversation: The New Jazz Studies* (New York: Columbia UP, 2004).
Von Eschen, Penny. *Satchmo Blows Up the World: Jazz Ambassadors Play the Cold War* (Cambridge: Harvard UP, 2006).
Vucetic, Radina. *Coca-Cola Socialism: Americanization of Yugoslav Culture in the Sixties* (Budapest: Central European UP, 2018).
Wagnleitner, Reinhold. *Coca-Colonization and the Cold War: The Cultural Mission of the United States in Austria after the Second World War* (Chapel Hill: University of North Carolina Press, 1994).
Wagnleitner, Reinhold (ed.). *Satchmo Meets Amadeus* (Innsbruck: Studienverlag, 2006).
Walser, Robert. *Keeping Time: Readings in Jazz History* (Oxford: Oxford UP, 1998).
Ward, Deborah E. "Race, Nationalism and Anti-Americanism in America," in Brendon O'Connor, *Anti-Americanism: History, Causes, Themes, Vol.2: Historical Perspectives* (Oxford: Greenwood World Publishing, 2007).
Watanabe, Takashi. *Propaganda Radio* (Tokyo: Chikuma Shobo, 2014).
Wellens, Ian. *Music on the Frontline: Nicolas Nabokov's Struggle against Communism and Middlebrow Culture* (London: Routledge, 2002).
Weston, Randy. *African Rhythms: The Autobiography of Randy Weston* (Durham: Duke UP, 2010).
Wilford, Hugh. *The CIA, the British Left and the Cold War: Calling the Tune?* (London: Routledge, 2003).
Wilford, Hugh. "Britain: In Between," in Alexander Stephan (ed.), *Americanization of Europe: Culture, Diplomacy, and Anti-Americanism after 1945* (New York: Berghahn Books, 2007).
Wilford, Hugh. *The Mighty Wurlitzer: How the CIA Played America* (Cambridge: Harvard UP, 2008).
Willett, Ralph. "Hot Swing and the Dissolute Life: Youth, Style and Popular Music in Europe 1939–1949," *Popular Music*, vol.8 no. 2, May1989.
Wintz, Cary D. and Paul Finkelman (eds.). *Encyclopedia of the Harlem Renaissance: A-J* (London: Routledge, 2004).
Wolin, Richard. *The Wind from the East: French Intellectuals, the Cultural Revolution, and the Legacy of the 1960s* (Princeton: Princeton UP, 2010).
Woods, Jeff. *Black Struggle, Red Scare: Segregation and Anti-Communism in the South, 1948–1968* (Baton Rouge: Louisiana State UP, 2003).
Wynn, Neil A. *Cross the Water Blues: African American Music in Europe* (Jackson: UP of Mississippi, 2010).
Yada, Toshitaka. *Hungary Czechoslovakia Gendaishi* (Tokyo: Yamakawa, 1978).

Yokoi, Kazue. *Avant-Garde Jazz: Europe Free no Kiseki* (Tokyo: Michitani, 2011).
Yui, Shoichi (ed. Hitoshi Namekata). *Jazz Showa-shi* (Tokyo: DU Books, 2013).
Zubok, Vladislav M. *A Failed Empire: The Soviet Union in the Cold War from Stalin to Gorbachev* (Chapel Hill: University of North Carolina Press, 2009).
Zubok, Vladislav M. and Constantine Pleshakov. *Inside the Kremlin's Cold War: From Stalin to Khrushchev* (Cambridge: Harvard UP, 1996).
Zwerin, Mike. *Swing under Nazis: Jazz as a Metaphor for Freedom* (New York: Cooper Square Press, 2000).

Index

Abraham Lincoln brigades 13
Absolutely Free 146
acid rock 140
Action Française 15
Adderley, Cannonball 73, 112, 117
Adenauer, Konrad 92, 137
"Admass" 89
Adolf Hitler Gives the Jews a City 24
Adorno, Theodor 17, 92
Advisory Committee on the Arts 68–9, 81n15, 113, 117, 165
Africa 4, 60, 65–6, 158; and Adam Clayton Powell Jr. 48; audiences 69, 74–6, 161; Central 81n11; countries 3, 52–3, 63n39, 67–8, 97; cultural ties between America and 7; decolonization process in 95; drum 49, 77; Duke Ellington's tour in 70–1; French musicians in 97, 99; Japanese musicians in 161; in the jazz ambassador selection process 68–70, 74–5, 117, 136, 140; Louis Armstrong's tour in 67–8, 81n11; music 77, 161; presence of 46; Randy Weston's tour in 77–9, 83n57; solidarity with 96; South 65, 82n31; sub-Saharan 75; traditions 75, 159; West 68, 77, 97; Wilbur De Paris's tour in 52, 63n39; Woody Herman's tour in 75–7
African American musicians 5, 51, 68, 132, 154–5; in the Benny Goodman band 11–2; Duke Ellington as one of 71; in the Harlem Hellfighters 13; and hot jazz 10; musical assets of 66; in postwar France 87–8; in the Randy Weston band 77; in the Southern Syncopated Orchestra; in the war period 23

African Cookbook 77–8
Agnew, Spiro 71
Aikura, Hisato 96
Akiyoshi, Toshiko 94, 96, 100–1, 160
Albania 135
Albright, Madeleine 156–7
Aldermaston March 89
Alexandra, Princess (Britain) 71
Allen, Red 73
Allied Forces Headquarters (AFHQ) 90
Althusser, Louis 95
America Day by Day 90
American Ballet Theater 111
American exceptionalism 59–60, 147, 167–8
American Expeditionary Forces 14
American Forces Network (AFN) 91–2
Americanism: of 1950s 32; anti 40, 91, 165; and the civil rights movement 4; color-blind 47, 50, 53, 66, 69, 77, 80, 87, 100, 126; and Communism 12; in Europe 5; and JATP 30; and jazz 2–4, 8–9, 11–12, 47, 98, 120, 125–6, 133, 135, 153, 165, 167–8; of the late 1940s 33; of New Deal era 12; and New Orleans 155; wartime 25, 34
Americanization 15, 40–1, 84
American Music Abroad program 158
American National Exhibition 106–7
American National Theatre and Academy (ANTA) 48, 72, 81n15, 117
Amerika Haus 91
Amis, Kingsley 89
Angry Young Men 89
An Nasr 79
anti-Communism: and Congress for Cultural Freedom 84; and Duke Ellington 125; and jazz 42, 46, 72, 87,

165; propaganda 97; and Ronald Reagan 152
Antigone 144
Araki, Jimmy 103n33
Argentina 67
Armstrong, Louis 3, 29, 51; 100th anniversary of the birth of 158; and American National Exhibition 107; and concentration camp 24; and Duke Ellington 121–2, 124; and Earl Hines 113, 139; in Europe 46; in France 16; in Italy 27n27; and Jack Teagarden 59; in the jazz ambassador selection process 48; as a legend 155, 161; and Little Rock crisis 66–7, 87, 108; as the quintessential official jazz ambassador 66; tour in Africa 67–8, 81n11; tour in Japan 94; tour in Romania 135; tour in South America 67; tour in Yugoslavia 136; in the war period 23; and Willis Conover 47
Art Forum 147
Ascenseur pour l'échafaud 95
Asia: and Adam Clayton Powell Jr. 48; Benny Goodman's tour in 53, 63n39; countries 3, 53, 99; East 82n33; Jack Teagarden's tour in 57, 63n39; and Japan 21; Japanese musicians in 161; presence of 46; solidarity with 96; South 49, 55, 63n39, 71, 158; Southeast 24, 53, 70, 161–2; Soviet cultural offensive in 61n4; transnational communication between Europe and 101; West German musicians in 98–9
Asian-African (Bandung) Conference 46, 48, 53, 61n4
Asian Youth Jazz Orchestra 161
Associated Press 76
Astigmatic 134
"Athenian complex" 90, 96, 167
Atkins, E. Taylor 6, 20, 104n34
Auschwitz 24, 91
avant-garde jazz: and Earl Hines 113; in Eastern Europe 135–6, 141; and neoclassicists 155; and Randy Weston 78; in Soviet Union 117–8, 121

Bach 131
Baker, Josephine 14, 17, 51, 70, 73
Balachander, Sundaram 56
Baltic Fleet Jazz Orchestra 34
Bane, David M. 78
Baraka, Amiri 75, 95

Barthes, Roland 95
Basie, Count 12, 48, 73, 153; Orchestra 23
Bass Saxophone, The 144
Batashev, Alexei 123, 139
Bauer, Robert 69
Beatles 140
bebop 2, 23, 29, 49; association with drugs and alcohol 46; and Earl Hines 113; in Eastern Europe 38; in France 102n11; heyday of 41; in Japan 103n33; and Lionel Hampton 140; resistance symbolized by 30–1, 36; revolution 45; rise of 33, 89; in West Germany 92
Bechet, Sidney 14, 17, 33, 87, 124
Beethoven, Ludwig van 40
Belarus State Jazz Orchestra 34
Belgium 17, 24, 85
Bellson, Louie 1, 73
Benjamin Franklin Award 158
Bennett, Max 86
Benny Goodman in Moscow 112
Berendt, Joachim 91–4, 98, 139; and Berliner Jazztage 93; and essentialism 94, 100; visit to Japan 93, 101; and West German jazz musicians' foreign tour 98–9, 131
Berlin All Stars 91
Berliner Jazztage 93, 100, 166–7
Berlin Philharmonic 18, 99
Berlin Wall 93
Berry, Bill 1
Bey, Chief 77
Bhumibol, King (Thailand) 53, 71, 98, 158
"bikiniarze" 38
Bill Evans Trio 138
Black Power: ideology of 95; movement 8, 28, 66, 71; rise of 72, 75, 94; struggle 79
Blackwell, Ed 77
Blakey, Art 79, 117, 142; and the Jazz Messengers 73
Blood on the Fields 154
blues 10, 75, 123, 125, 153, 158; culture 12
Blues People 95
Bohlen, Charles 36, 107
Bokova, Irina 159–60
Boland, Francy 101
Bolshoi Ballet 45, 48, 127
Bolshoi Theatre Orchestra 110
boogie-woogie 21, 36

Bossa Nova 93
Botti, Chris 157
Bourdieu, Pierre 95
Bradford, Clea 114–15
Brandt, Willy 93
Brazil 160
Brecht, Bertolt 17
Brezhnev, Leonid 35, 113
Bridgewater, Dee Dee 160
Britain 24, 52, 146, 167; as empire 8; Geneva Summit (1955) 45; imperial nostalgia in 88–90
British Council 76
Broadway 36, 114
Brocksieper, Fritz 91
Brookmeyer, Bob 73
Brookshire, Nell 123
Browder, Earl 12
Brown, Les 39–40
Brown, Ray 86
Brubeck, Darius 132
Brubeck, Dave 1, 7, 63n39, 146; and Bill Clinton 156; and cultural diplomacy 168; in the jazz ambassador selection process 117; and Johnson administration 71; quartet in America 87; tour in India 55–7; tour in Poland 131–3, 137–8, 141, 158; tour in Romania 138–9; visit to the Soviet Union 155–6
Brubeck, Iola 132
Brubeck, Michael 132
Brussels World's Fair 85
Bryant, Ray 73
Buckner, Milt 140–1
Budapest Jazz Festival 100
Bulgaria 38
Burma: Benny Goodman tour in 53–4; Jack Teagarden tour in 58
Burns, Ken 154–5
Burton, Gary 142, 163n16
Bush, George H. W. 153
Bush, George W. 155
Byeliye Nochi 123
Byrd, Charlie 71

Cafe Society 13, 31–2
Calloway, Cab 12, 42n6
Cambodia: Benny Goodman tour in 53
Cameroon 97
Campaign for Nuclear Disarmament (CND) 89–90, 146
Canada 99, 144
Carlucci, Frank 143

Carnation Revolution 143
Carnegie Hall 10, 12
Carter, Benny 94, 143, 153
Cascais jazz festival 143
Catherman, Terrence F. 108–10
Catholic Church 130
Ceaușescu, Nicolae 135, 138
Central Intelligence Agency (CIA) 38, 84, 93, 126n2,
Chambers, Paul 95
Charles Lloyd in the Soviet Union 120
Charleston dance 14
Charlie and His Orchestra 23, 91
Charter 77 146–7, 156
Cheney, Dick 155
Chile 158
China 135, 138
Chocolate Kiddies 17, 33
Chopin 132
Chou, En-Lai 53
Churchill, Winston 24
Civic Forum 147
Civil Air Transport Agreement 113
civil rights 33, 160; activists 4, 65; era 88; movement 4–5, 8, 29, 60, 65, 87, 95, 126, 152, 154, 160
Civil Rights Act 30
Civil War 10
Clarke, Kenny 87, 97
classical music 2, 10, 17, 57, 99; as an alternative to jazz 69; Bengali 57; and CCF 84; closeness with jazz 116, 132; as European culture 3, 66, 71; in Germany 92; Indian 57, 168; in Japan 95, 104n36
Cliburn, Van 85, 136
Clinton, Bill 153, 156–8
Coca-Cola 87
"Coca-Colonization" 4, 87
Cocteau, Jean 14
Cœuroy, André 20
Cohen, Harvey G. 72, 125
Cole, Cozy 69
Coleman, Ornette 8, 73–5, 140, 142
Cole, Nat "King" 42n6
Coles, Johnny 123
Colpix Records 112
Coltrane, John 73–4, 117–18, 153; "Alabama" 65; "My Favorite Things" 99
Coltrane, Ravi 154
Columbia records 13
Columbia Jazz Band 25
Commodore Records 13

Commonwealth 91
Communism 29, 38, 106–7, 153, 165; and Americanism 12; anti 165; in France 87; "Goulash" 134; and HUAC 31; infiltration of 7, 53; and jazz circles 72
Communist countries 1, 3, 5, 8, 33, 93, 131, 146; and Little Rock crisis 67
Communist International (Comintern) 12
Communist Party of Great Britain 32
Communist Party of the United States of America (CPUSA) 12–13, 31–3, 46
Conde, Raymond 25, 94
Conference on Security and Cooperation in Europe (CSCE) 145, 147
Congress 9, 48, 51–2, 67, 152–3
Congress for Cultural Freedom (CCF) 84, 93; Masterpieces of the Twentieth Century festival 84
Conover, Willis: and Americanism 47; and VOA 1, 2, 47; and Duke Ellington's birthday party 1, 71; and Presidential Medal of Freedom 153; and rock music 74, 134; in the subcommittee of jazz 72–4; visit to Poland 131–4, 139; visit to the Soviet Union 72, 120
Consular Treaty 113
Conyers, John Jr. 152, 154
cool jazz 55, 92, 131
Copeland, Ray 77
Coriden, Guy E. 117
Côte d'Ivoire 97
Cousens, Charles 25
Creative Jazz Ensemble Japan 160
Croce, Benedetto 84
Crosby, Israel 53
cross-cultural dialogue 5, 9, 165
Crossman, Richard 90
Crow, Bill 108, 112
Cuba 70; missile crisis 106
Cultural Association of the Democratic Reconstruction of Germany 11
Cultural Presentations Program 47–8, 69, 74, 76, 79
Czech crisis 120–1, 144
Czechoslovakia 8, 131; jazz festivals in 143; Jazz Section in 144–7, 167; and Madeleine Albright 156–7; "pasek" in 38; Willis Conover 139; Zhdanov doctrine in 37
Czechoslovak Musicians' Union 144–5

Dahomey 97
Daily Worker 12
Dália 134
Davenport, Lisa 5–6, 44n42, 61n4
Davis, Benjamin J. 31
Davis, Miles 37, 73, 87–8, 95
Davis, Mel 54
Davis, Richard 113
Davis, Richard H. 135
Dawson, Alan 137
Dean, John G. 68
De Beauvoir, Simone 4, 88, 90–1, 96
decolonization 68, 126, 165; in Africa 52, 97; era of 8; process of 60, 68, 95; wave of 46, 65, 68
De Gaulle, Charles 19, 88
DeJohnette, Jack 119
Delaunay, Charles 15–16, 102n11
Deming, Olcott 76
Democratic Republic of the Congo 76
Denmark 130, 142
Dennis, Sandy 117
Dennis, Willie 111–12
De Paris, Wilbur 7, 52
Derrida, Jacques 95
Der Spiegel 92
Desmond, Paul 1, 55
de-Stalinization 106, 130
détente 8, 152, 165; dawn of 120; little 113; momentum of 143; politics of 145
Deutsches Tanz- und Unterhaltungs-sorchester (DTU) 18, 166
Dixieland jazz 49, 113; and Earl Hines 113; in East Germany 40–1; and Jack Teagarden 57, 59
Djanger Bali 93
Dmytryk, Edward 32
Doldinger, Klaus 99
Donkey's Tail 106
Donovan, Bob 116
"Double V" campaign 23
Down Beat: Benny Goodman's Soviet tour 112–12; Charles Delaunay 16; Charles Lloyd quartet 119; the editor-in-chief of 68; Iola Brubeck 132; Leonard Feather 96; Marshall Stearns 13
Downbeat Jazz Festival 100
Drunken Angel 95, 104n36
Dubček, Alexander 144
DuBois, W. E. B. 4
Dudziak, Urszula 134
Duke Ellington Big Band 139
Dulles, Allen 38

188 Index

Dulles, John Foster: at the Advisory Committee on the Arts 165–6; and Dave Brubeck 131; and Dizzy Gillespie's tour 49; and Jack Teagarden's tour 59; and Little Rock crisis 67; and Van Cliburn 85; and Wilbur De Paris's tour 52; and Willis Conover 133

East Berlin uprising 38, 40
Eastern Europe (*see also* Europe) 8, 37–40, 93, 126, 130–1, 136–7, 139, 142; of the 1970s 136; free jazz in 136; jazz festivals in 131, 167; Lionel Hampton in 140; and Lyndon B. Johnson 135; Ornette Coleman in 74; and NATO 157; and RFE 38; Willis Conover in 133, 139; Woody Herman in 75; youth in 38–9, 143
East Germany 36, 40, 93
Easy Rider 144
Ehrenburg, Ilya 36
Eisenhower, Dwight D.: administration 3, 41, 45–7; and Dizzy Gillespie 48, 51, 72; and Little Rock crisis 66, 85; and Van Cliburn 87
Eldridge, Roy 86, 94
Ellender, Allen J. 51
Ellington, Edward Kennedy "Duke" 7–8, 36, 126; 100th anniversary of the birth of 158; and Americanism 125–6; and American National Exhibition 107; birthday party at the White House 1–3, 47, 71–2, 140; in Congress resolution 153; and FBI 31, 42n6; in the interwar period 12, 15; in the jazz ambassador selection process 48, 68–70; *Jazz* (film) 155; Nixon's condolences 126; and Pulitzer Prize 71, 154; Soviet audience's reaction 122–3; Soviet authorities' reaction 124; Soviet media's reaction 124–5; as a suitable choice for the Soviet tour 120; unusual events in the Soviet Union 123–4; tour in Poland 142; visit to Senegal 70–1, 75; in the war period 21, 23, 27n27
Ellington, Mercer 123, 139
Elliott, Don 73
Ellis, Herb 86
Ellison, Ralph 68
El Moudjahid 79
El Sistema 167
English, Robert D. 36

"Entartete Musik" exhibition 17
Erenberg, Lewis A. 11, 23
Estado Novo 143
Ethiopia 12, 52
Europe (*see also* Eastern Europe and Western Europe) 3, 5–6, 13, 18–9, 84, 161; audience 75–6; Central 146; civilization 14; classical music in 66; Count Basie in 73; détente in 145; fascism in 11; First World War 13, 15; intellectuals 4, 13; musical forms in 159; Southern 49, 158
European Jazz All Stars 101
European Nuclear Disarmament (END) 146
Europe, James Reese 13
Evans, Bill 73, 138,
Evans, Gil 73, 146
Evening News 99
Existentialist 4, 8, 88

Faisal II of Iraq 49
Fanon, Frantz 95, 104n41
Farmer, Art 73
Faubus, Orval 65
Feather, Leonard 23, 96, 112
Federal Bureau of Investigation (FBI) 30–2, 42n6, 70
Federation of Malaya 58
Federation of Mali 68
Feigin, Leo 167
Feldman, Victor 108
Festival International de Jazz 87–8
First World Festival of Black Arts 70
First World War 10, 13–15
Fitzgerald, Ella 94, 136, 153, 157
Fitzgerald, F. Scott 10
Flanagan, Tommy 146
Forces françaises libres 19
Ford, Gerald 142
Ford, Henry 33
Ford Motor Company 33
Foucault, Michel 95
Founding Fathers 3–4, 7, 11, 52
Four Freedoms 22–3
France 13–16, 76, 80, 95, 104n41; Americanism in 4, 8, 11, 87–9, 167; in First World War 13; Geneva Summit (1955) 45; jazz criticism in the 1950s 87–8; jazz diplomacy of 97; jazz musicians' visit to Poland 142; *La Revue Nègre* in 14, 70; occupied 16–17, 21, 34;Van Cliburn in 85; Vichy 7, 16, 19; youth in 19, 36,

Frankfurt All Stars 131
Frankfurt School 17
Freeman, Bud 73, 117
Freie Deutsche Jugend (FDJ) 41
Freund, Joki 98, 131
Furtwängler, Wilhelm 99

Gabler, Milt 13
Gabon 78
Ganelin Trio 166
Garment, Leonard 71–2
Garner, Erroll 73
General Electric 33
General Headquarters, the Supreme Commander for the Allied Powers (GHQ/SCAP) 94
Geneva Summit (1955) 45, 61n4
Geneva Summit (1985) 155
George V, King (Britain) 14
German All Stars 99
German/Soviet Nonaggression Pact 34
German Wehrmacht Hour 23
Germany *see* East Germany, Nazi, Weimar Germany and West Germany
Gershwin, George 10, 156
Getz/Gilberto 93
Getz, Stan 73, 86, 93
Ghana 52, 67, 78
Ghana Arts Festival 78
Ghetto Swingers 24, 91
Giants of Jazz 142
Gierek, Edward 137
Gilberto, Astrud 93
Gilberto, João 93
Gillespie, Dizzy 7, 53–4, 79; arrest of 32; as bebopper 29, 41; in Congress resolution 153; Congress's perception of 51–2; as the first jazz ambassador 49–51, 97–8, 117, 136, 158; JATP tour 86; in the jazz ambassador selection process 48
Gilroy, Paul 165
Giuffre, Jimmy 73
Globe and Mail 99
Gnawa musicians 75
Goebbels, Joseph 18, 91
Goethe Institut 8, 98, 100
Goethe, Johann Wolfgang von 40
Gojković, Duško 136
Goldberg, Richie 138
Goldwater, Barry 51
Gomułka, Władysław 130, 137
Gonsalves, Paul 122–3

Goodman, Benny 7, 13, 59, 87, 153; as an advocate of racial integration 11–12, 53, 107; arrival to Moscow 107–8; in Congress resolution 153; early proposal of the Soviet tour 10; friction with band members 111–12; Orchestra 10, 153; personality of 108–9; Soviet audience's reaction 110; Soviet authorities' reaction 110; and Soviet jazz scene 112; as a suitable choice for the Soviet tour 110–1; and swing 10–11; tour in Asia 53–5, 58; tour in the Soviet Union 8, 97, 112–5, 120, 124, 134; in the war period 22, 27n27
Gorbachev, Mikhail 156
Gordon, Joe 50
Gorky, Maxim 33, 112
Goskonsert 108, 118, 124
gospel 158
"Goulash Communism" 134
grandeur 88
Granz, Norman: arrest of 32, 87; and FBI 30, 32; and HUAC 32; and JATP 7, 30–3, 40; and JATP tour in Europe 86, 88; and Presidential Medal of Freedom 153; as a social entrepreneur 30–1
Grappelli, Stéphane 15, 17, 97
Great Depression 10
Great East Asia Co-Prosperity Sphere 21
Greece 49–50, 90
Greeks 90, 167
Green, Urbie 1
Greenwich Village 13
Gregor and His Gregorians 15

Haile Selassie I, Emperor (Ethiopia) 52
Halbstarke 92
Haley, Bill 92
Hall, Jim 1
Hamilton, Chico 70, 73
Hammond, John 13, 23, 31
Hampton, Lionel 11, 24, 140–1, 153; and His All Star Jazz Inner Circle 140
Hampton, Slide 73
Hancock, Herbie 158–60; Institute of Jazz 159
Handy, John 73
Hara, Nobuo 94; and His Sharps & Flats 96, 100–1
Harlem 12, 15, 31, 48; Hellfighters 13; in Montmartre 14; Renaissance 12, 14
Hatano, Fukutaro 20

Hatschek, Keith 133
Hattori, Ryoichi 20, 22
Havel, Václav 146–7, 157
Hawes, Hampton 73
Hawkins, Coleman 24, 27n27, 68, 73, 86
Hayashi, Eitetsu 161
Helsinki: Final Act 145–7, 167; process 145; Watch 146
Henderson, Fletcher 12, 21
Henry, Haywood 138
Hentoff, Nat 71, 146
Herman, Woody 39–40; in the jazz ambassador selection process 70; Orchestra 71; tour in Africa 75–8; tour in Romania 135; tour in South America 63n39; tour in Yugoslavia 136
Hershorn, Tad 31
Herter, Christian 51
Himmler, Heinrich 19
Hindemith, Paul 17, 99; Case 99
Hines, Earl 1, 112; early life of 113; personality 113–4; Soviet audience's reaction 115; Soviet authorities' reaction 115–6; tour in Romania 138–9, 141; tour in the Soviet Union 8, 116–17; visit to Portugal 143
Hino, Terumasa 100–1
Hinton, Milt 1
hip hop 158
Hiraoka, Masaaki 96
Hitler, Adolf 17, 23
Hitlerism 11, 23
Hitlerjugend 18–9
Hobsbawm, Eric 32, 89, 96
Hoggart, Richard 89
Holiday, Billie 12–13, 160
Hollywood 31; Independent Citizens Committee of the Sciences, Arts, and Professions (HICCASP) 31; Screen Actors Guild in 152; Ten 32
Hong Kong 58
Hoover, John Edgar 31
Horn, Shirley 154
Hot Club de France 13, 15–17
hot jazz 10, 15, 33
House I Live In, The 31
House Un-American Activities Committee (HUAC) 31–2, 48, 72
Houston city police 32, 87
Hrabal, Bohumil 145
Hucko, Peanuts 59
Hungarian Uprising 36, 41, 136

Hungarian Young Communist League 134
Hungary 38–9, 61n4, 133–4, 139, 142, 145; "jampecek" in 38; jazz festival in 100; Lionel Hampton's tour in 140
Hussein, King (Jordan) 71, 156

Ida, Ichiro 20
Ikezaki, Tadataka 20
Il Tempo 86
"imperialism" 20, 35, 96
Imperial Rule Assistance Association 22
India: Dave Brubeck's tour in 55–7, 168; Dizzy Gillespie's tour in 49; Jack Teagarden's tour in 57–8; West German musicians' tour in 99
Indian Express 58, 99
Indonesia 93, 162
Indonesian All Stars 93, 101
Informatia Bucurestiului 138
International Jazz Day 9, 159–60
International Jazz Federation 145
International Jazz Festival (Tallinn) 119
International Red Cross Committee 24
Iran 49
Iraq 49, 99; War 155
I Served the King of England 145
Ishihara, Yujiro 104n36
Isono, Teruo 54
I Spit on Your Graves 88

Jackson, Oliver 114–15
Jacquet, Illinois 140–1
"jampecek" 38
Janis, Byron 85
Japan 5–8, 11, 17, 71, 80, 91, 166–7; African Americans in 14; Benny Goodman's tour in 54–5; Giants of Jazz's tour in 142; International Jazz Day in 160; in the interwar period 17, 20–1; Jack Teagarden's tour in 59–60; JATP tour in 32, 94; jazz criticism in the 1960s of 95–6; jazz in films of 95; musicians in the Berliner Jazztage 93; musicians' search for national style of jazz 100–1; in the occupation period 94, 103n33, 104n34; "unprecedented jazz boom" 94; Van Cliburn in 85; in the war period 21–2; wartime propaganda in 24–5; West German musicians in 99; jazz diplomacy of 160–2
Japan Foundation 160–1
Japan-US Security Treaty 100

Jarrett, Keith 119
Jaspers, Karl 84
"jass" 11
Jazz (film) 154–5
Jazz (journal) 130
Jazz Age 10, 14
Jazz Appreciation Month 154
Jazz at Lincoln Center (JALC) 153–4, 158, 167
Jazz at the Philharmonic (JATP) 7, 30–3, 153; and Americanism 30–1; tour in Japan 94; tour in Western Europe 51, 86, 88
Jazz Book, The 92
Jazz Hot 15–16, 87, 97
Jazz Jamboree 131, 137, 139, 142, 167
Jazz Mission to Moscow 112
Jazzpetit 144
Jazz Scene, The 89, 96
Jazz Section 144–7, 167; creation of 144; and European Nuclear Disarmament 146; and Madeleine Albright 156–7
Jim Crow 4, 14, 87–8
jitterbugs 11
John, Elton 146
Johnson, Budd 53–4, 114
Johnson, Harold 114, 116, 122, 128n46
Johnson, J. J. 1, 95,
Johnson, Lyndon B. 71, 135, 156
Johnson, Pete 86
Jones, Hank 1, 53
Jones, G. Lewis 52
Jones, LeRoi *see* Baraka, Amiri
Jones, Quincy 49, 73, 97
Jones, Rufus 122
Jones, Thad 73
Joplin, Janis 74
Jordan, Clifford 77
Jornal do Brasil 100
Josephson, Barney 13, 31
Josephson, Leon 31
Josie, Marva 138
Judt, Tony 86
Juilliard School of Music 48, 69, 116–17
Juilliard String Quartet 111

Kádár, János 134
Kamayatsu, Tib 25
Kamerton 123–4
Kami, Kyosuke 103n33
Kater, Michael H. 18, 91
Katowice Academy of Music 137
Kawaguchi, George 54, 94
Kelly, Wynton 95

Kennan, George F. 29
Kennedy Center 157
Kennedy, John F. 156
Kenton, Stan 38, 40, 48, 73
Kenya 52, 161
Khachaturian, Aram 35, 37, 109
Khrennikov, Tikhon 109
Khrushchev, Nikita: and Benny Goodman's Soviet tour 109, 112–13; and cultural "thaw" 106; and "Kitchen Debate" 106; secret speech 36, 41, 131
Kikuchi, Masabumi 100
Kikuchi, Shigeya 103n33
Kind of Blue 154
King, Martin Luther 125, 168
"Kitchen Debate" 106
Klosson, Boris H. 121, 123, 125
KM Quartet 118
Knepper, Jimmy 108, 111
Kohler, Foy D. 114–16
Komeda, Krzysztof 37, 131, 134, 166
Komitet Gosudarstvennoy Bezopasnosti (KGB) 124
Kommunisticheskiy Soyuz Molodyozhi (Komsomol): and Byeliye Nochi 123; and Duke Ellington's Soviet tour 124; and jazz cafes 107; and Molodezhnoe 117, 119–20; and stilyagi 36
Komsomolskaya Pravda 124
Konitz, Lee 50
Kosygin, Alexei 109
Kozlov, Alexey 37, 120, 123
Krupa, Gene 59, 73, 94–5, 117; Trio 94
Kubota, Jiro 54
Kulisy 134
Kuriya, Makoto 160

Land of Folk 130
La Revue Nègre 14, 70
Larkin, Philip 89
Laski, Harold 30
Lateef, Yusef 73
Laughing Stars 20
Lebanon 49
Legrand, Michel 37, 97, 113
Le Journal d'Égypt 78
Le Monde 87
Leningrad Ballet 110
Leningrad Philharmonic Orchestra 45, 85
Lenin, Vladimir 112
Leo Records 166
Les Temps modernes 8, 88
Levitt, Rod 73

Levy, Lou 86
Lewis, Mel 108, 111–12
Lewis, Ramsey 73
Life 84
Lifetime Achievement Award 153
Light Music Hour 22
Lincoln, Abbey 65, 73, 160
Lincoln Center 79
Liston, Melba 49–50
Little Rock crisis 65–7, 87, 106, 108, 132
Live at Birdland 65
Living Theater 144
Lloyd, Charles 73, 117, 119–20, 135–6
London air raids 23
Look Back in Anger 89
Los Angeles Philharmonic 136
Love Supreme, A 154
Luceafărul 141
Luce, Henry 84
Luftwaffe 18, 24
Lumumba, Patrice 76
Lunacharsky, Anatoly 33

MacArthur, Douglas II 85
Machito 73
Macmillan, Harold 90–1, 96
Mainichi Shimbun 24
Makowicz, Adam 134, 139, 166
Malaysia 162
Malle, Louis 95
Mangelsdorff, Albert 98–9, 101, 131
Mangelsdorff, Emil 98
Mann, Herbie 71
Man Who Causes a Storm 95, 104n36
Maoism 95
Maria Fisher Founder's Award 157
Marsalis, Wynton 146, 154–5, 159, 167
Marshall Plan 84, 86–7
Masekela, Hugh 74, 82n31
Mathis der Maler 99
Matsumoto, Hidehiko 96, 100
Matsumoto, Shin 24–5, 94, 103n33
Mayo, Mary 1
McCartney, Paul 146
McClure, Ron 119
McKibbon, Al 142
McKinley, Ray 148n8
McRae, Carmen 96
Meeker, Leonard C. 138–9
Meeropol, Abel 13, 31
Melodie 144
Melodiya 119
Melody Maker 91
Mennin, Peter 117

Metronome 50
MI5 32, 42n11
Middle East 48, 158; Dave Brubeck's tour in 55, 63n39; Dizzy Gillespie's tour in 49; Duke Ellington's tour in 71; Japanese musicians' tour in 161; in the jazz ambassador selection process 70, 73; West German musicians' tour in 98–9
Mifune, Toshiro 104n36
Mikoyan, Anastas 109
Milhaud, Darius 14, 55, 138
Military Relief Department 24
Miller, Arthur 146
Miller, Glenn 39; and Americanism 22–3; in the war period 18, 25, 34; Orchestra 63n39, 148n8
Miller, Marcus 160
Mine, Koichi (Dick Mine) 103n33
Mingus, Charles 42n6, 65, 73, 114; "Fables of Faubus" 65, 143; "Remember Rockefeller at Attica" 143; tour in Romania 142–3; visit to Portugal 143
Mitchell, Billy 50
Mitchell-Ruff Trio 73
Mitsuaki Kanno quintet 100
Mitterrand, François 147
mobo 20
Modern Jazz Quartet 73, 117
moga 20
Moiseyev, Igor 110; Dance Company 110
Molasky, Mike 95, 104n36
Mölders, Werner 18
"moldy figs" 102n11
Molodezhnoe 117–19
Monk, Thelonious 73, 117, 142, 158
Monk, T. S. 158
Monnet Plan 86
Monson, Ingrid 66
Monterey Jazz Festival 100
Montreux Jazz Festival 101
Morello, Joe 55–6
Morgenstern, Dan 146
Moriyama, Hisashi 25
Morocco 75–6, 97
Moscow Conservatory 108
Moscow International Film Festival 72, 117
Moscow Philharmonic Orchestra 116
Moscow State Symphony Orchestra 110, 115
Moscow summit (1972) 35

Moscow summit (1988) 156
Moskonsert 118
Mozart, Wolfgang Amadeus 21, 69
Mulligan, Gerry 124, 146; and Duke Ellington's birthday party 1, 71; in the jazz ambassador selection process 73; tour in Poland 137–8, 141; visit to the Soviet Union 117–20
Mulligan, Robert 118
Munongo, Godefroid 76
Music Advisory Panel 72, 117; and Africa 68–70, 74, 77; and Dizzy Gillespie 48; establishment of 48; and Louis Armstrong's African tour 81n11
Music for Zen Meditation 100
Music USA 1, 36, 40, 47, 111, 121

Nabokov, Nicolas 84, 93
Nagy, Earnest A. 39–40
Nanri, Fumio 20, 24, 54, 59, 94
Nation 54
National Association for the Advancement of Colored People (NAACP) 23
National Endowment for the Arts 168
National Medal of Arts 153, 156
National Mobilization Act 21
National Security Council (NSC) 38
Nazi: Germany 7, 16, 18, 21–2, 24, 34, 36, 166; history 91; ideology 19; occupation 84; party 34; past 41; period 92, 94, 144; regime 23, 33, 40, 98–9, 144
Nazis 132, 144
Nazism 15
NBC 108–9
Nedelya 125
Négritude 70–1, 125
négrophilie 14–15
neoclassicists 154–5
Nepal 162
New Cold War 152
New Deal 12; era 7, 11–12, 46; Liberalism 7, 29, 42
New Economic Policy 33
Ne Win 54
new jazz 166–7
Newman, Joe 110
New Orleans jazz 2, 88, 102n11, 131
New Orleans Jazz National Historical Park 155
New Pacific Hour 94
New Pacific Orchestra 94

Newport Jazz Festival: 60th anniversary of the first opening of 154; European tour of 137, 142; Japanese musicians in 100; start of 87; Wreckers in 134
Newsweek 25, 74
Newton, Francis 32, 42n11
Newton, Frankie 32
New York City Ballet 110
New York city police
New York Jazz Festival
New York Philharmonic 111
New York Times 11, 46, 48, 87, 153
New York Times Magazine 47
Nichols, Red 95–6
Niger 78
Nigeria 77, 161
Niki, Takio 24, 103n33
Nippon Hoso Kyokai (NHK) 22, 25, 94
Nishiyo, Muneyoshi 59
Nixon, Richard: and Ceaușescu 138; and Charles Mingus 143; and Duke Ellington 126; and Duke Ellington's birthday party 1–3, 71–2; and era of negotiation 120; in HUAC 31; and "Kitchen Debate" 106; and Lionel Hampton 140, 162; visit to Moscow 35, 121
Nkrumah, Kwame 52, 67
Nogawa, Kobun 103n33
"normalization" 146
North Atlantic Treaty 84, 157
Novy Mir 106

Oborin, Lev 54, 85
Occupation Forces 25, 103n33
O'Day, Anita 157
Oder–Neisse line 136
Odwira festival 67
Oe, Kenzaburo 96
Office of War Information (OWI) 23
Oistrakh, David 54, 85
One Day in the Life of Ivan Denisovich 106
Ongaku Bunka Shimbun 22
Ongaku Chishiki 22
Original Dixieland Jazz Band (ODJB) 14
Ormandy, Eugene 124
Orwell, George 89, 137, 144
Osaka World Expo 101, 167
Osborne, John 89
Ostpolitik 93
Overton, Hall 72

194   Index

Pakistan 49
Panassié, Hugues 15–16, 102n11
Parker, Charlie 45–6, 50, 79, 161; in Congress resolution 153; in Czechoslovakia 144; in East Germany 41; and Festival International de Jazz 87–8; in Poland 133; and social issues 29
Parks, Rosa 152
Parnakh, Valentin 33
Partial Test Ban Treaty 113
Partisan Review 89
Partnership for Peace 157
"pasek" 38
Pather Panchali 99
PBS 154
peace movements 5
Pedersen, Niels 101
Pemberton, Bill 116
Pershing, John 14
Peterson, Oscar 94, 153
Peukert, Detlev 19
Peyton, Benny 33
Philippines 99, 162
Pillai, Palani Subramania 56
Pittsburgh Courier 23, 31
Pleshakov, Constantine 35
Poe, Edgar Allan 13
Poiger, Uta G. 40
Poland 37, 130, 134, 137, 166; "bikiniarze" in 38; bilateral treaty with West Germany 136–7; Dave Brubeck's tour in 55, 63n39, 132–3, 137–9, 158; de-Stalinization in 130; Eddie Rosner in 34; Edward Gierek in 137; Glenn Miller Orchestra's tour in 63n39, 148n8; Japanese musicians in 100; jazz festival in Sopot 98, 131; Lionel Hampton's tour in 140–1; martial law in 152; Willis Conover's visit to 133–4, 139; youth in 38
Polish Jazz Clubs Federation 133
Ponty, Jean-Luc 101
Ponomarenko, Panteleimon 34
Porter, Eric 66
Portugal 143
Powell Jr., Adam Clayton 48, 70
Prague Jazz Days festival 144–5
Prague Spring 136, 144
Pravda 109, 124
Presel, Joseph A. 122–2, 125
Preservation Hall Jazz Band 142
Presidential Medal of Freedom 1–2, 125, 153

Preston, Eddie 123
Priestley, J. B. 89
Przekroy 132
Puente, Tito 73
Pulitzer Prize 71, 154

Quintette du Hot Club de France 15, 166

Rachmaninov, Sergei 85
Radio Free Europe (RFE) 38, 40–1, 130, 145–7
ragtime 10, 20
Ramadan 51
Ravel, Maurice 14
Ray Ventura and His Collegians 15
RCA Victor 112
Reagan, Ronald 152, 155–6, 162
Recreation and Amusement Association (RAA) 94
Reinhardt, Django 15–7, 24
Republic of Mali 68, 78
Republic of the Congo 97
Republika 50
Reyes, Francisco "Kiko" 25, 94
Reyes, Norman 25
Rhee, Syngman 59
rhythm and blues 140
Rhythm Road 158
Rice, Condoleezza 158
Rice, Susan 159
Richardson, Larry 138
Rimsky-Korsakov, Nikolai 122
Ritter, Rüdiger 120
Roach, Max 65–6, 73, 79, 87
Roaring Twenties 14
Robert Shaw Chorale 110
Robeson, Paul 13, 29
Rock Around the Clock 92
Rockefeller, Nelson 143
rock music: in Africa 78; in Burma 58; in Communist countries 166; in Czechoslovakia; in Eastern Europe 8; in East Germany 41; growing popularity of 65; in Hungary 135; in India 57; and Lionel Hampton 140; in Poland 132, 134, 140; in Romania 138; in the Soviet Union 107, 116, 121; in West Germany 92; and Willis Conover 74, 134; in Yugoslavia 136
Rolling Stone 157
Rollins, Sonny 146
Romania: Charles Lloyd's tour in 135–6; Charles Mingus's tour in 142–3; Dave Brubeck's tour in 137–9; Earl Hines's

tour in 138–9; Lionel Hampton's tour in 140–1; Woody Herman's tour in 135
Romania Libera 138–9
Romania Literara 138
Romanian Writers' Union 141
Roman, Martin 24
Romans 90, 167
Roosevelt, Eleanor 13
Roosevelt, Franklin D. 22–4
Rosenberg, Ethel 13
Rosenberg, Julius 13
Rosner, Eddie 34–5
Rudorf, Reginald 41, 130
Russell, Bertrand 84
Russell, Pee Wee 73

Sakura Sakura 93
Sales, Grover 152
San Francisco Peace Treaty 94
Santamaria, Mongo 73
Sartre, Jean-Paul 4, 88
Sato, Eisaku 71
Sato, Masahiko 100; & NoModismo 162
Saury, Maxim 97
Schiller, Friedrich 40
Schnitzer, Robert C. 48
Schoenberg, Arnold 55, 138
Schubart, Mark 69
Schuller, Gunther 72, 74
Schulz-Köhn, Dietrich 17, 91
Schumann, Coco 24, 91
Schuman, William 48
Schutzstaffel (SS) 19
Schwedler, Karl 23
Scott, Hazel 48
Scottsboro case 12
Scott, Tony 93, 100
Second Sino–Japanese war 21
Second World War 2, 29, 84, 91, 132, 166; French jazz scene during 16; German jazz scene during 18; jazz and propaganda in 22–3; Oder–Neisse line since the end of 136
Seifert, Jaroslav 145
Semaine du Jazz festival 97
Senegal 68–71, 75, 97, 161
Senghor, Léopold 70–1
September 11, 2001 terrorist attacks 155
September 30 incident of 1965 93
Shankar, Ravi 99
Sharpeville massacre 82n31
Shaw, Artie 25, 31
Shimura, Takashi 104n36

Shiraki, Hideo 93, 100; Quintet and Three Koto Girls 93
Shochiku 24
Shorter, Wayne 158, 160
Shostakovich, Dmitri 35, 85; "Lady Macbeth of the Mtsensk District" 84
Sibelius, Jean 84
Sihanouk, Norodom, Prince (Cambodia) 53
Silver, Horace 73
Simon Bolivar Youth Orchestra 167
Simone, Nina 160
Sims, Zoot 108, 112
Sinatra, Frank 23, 31
Singapore 24, 162
Siniaia Ptitsa 120
Sino–Soviet conflict 113, 120
Situace 144
Six, Jack 137
Sixty Eight Publishers 144
Škvorecký, Josef 144
Sleepy Lagoon case 30
Smith, Carleton Sprague 69
Smithsonian National Museum of American History 154
socialist realism 37, 84, 106, 125, 145, 156
Solzhenitsyn, Aleksandr 106
Sontag, Susan 146
South America 63n39, 67, 98–9, 152
Southern Europe 49, 158
Southern Syncopated Orchestra 14
South Korea 59
Sovetskaya Kultura 124–5, 127n21
Sovetskaya Rossiya 124–5
Soviet cultural offensive 3, 45, 54, 61n4, 166
Sovietization 8, 130
Soviet Union 2, 8, 36, 38, 101, 139; Benny Goodman's tour in 55, 107–12; categorization of jazz in 33, 41; Charles Lloyd's tour in 119–20; Chick Corea and Gary Burton's visit to 163n16; and CSCE 145; Dave Brubeck's visit to 155–6; Duke Ellington's tour in 120–6; Earl Hines's tour in 112–17; Eddie Rosner in 34; Geneva Summit (1955) 45; Gerry Mulligan's visit to 117–19; of the interwar period 33; Khrushchev's criticisms of Stalin 36, 41, 134; Louis Armstrong's tour plan in 67; "new jazz" in 167; relations with East European countries 130, 136; relations

with Romania 135; and the Rosenbergs 13; thaw in 36–7, 106–7; of the war period 34; Willis Conover's visit to 72, 120; and Woody Herman 75
Sozialistische Einheitspartei Deutschlands (SED) 41
Spalding, Esperanza 160
Spanish Civil War 12–13
spiritual 49
Spree City Stompers 98
Sputnik I 106
Sri Lanka 162
Srp, Karel 145–7
Stalinism 131
Stalin, Joseph 3, 37, 45, 130, 166; and Eddie Rosner 34; jazz during the rule of 33; Khrushchev's secret speech denouncing 36, 41, 134; "little" 130–1; and Zhdanov doctrine 35
Starr, S. Frederick 33–4
Stasi 41
State Jazz Orchestra 34
Stearns, Marshall 13; and American National Exhibition 107; and Dizzy Gillespie's tour 49, 98; and Music Advisory Panel 48, 69–70, 72
Stern, Isaac 85, 136
stilyagi 36–8, 107, 143
Stitt, Sonny 86, 96, 142
Stoessel, Walter J. 138, 141–2
Stokowski, Leopold 124
Stowe, David W. 11
Strategic Arms Limitation Talks (SALT) 120
Strayhorn, Billy 2, 156
Studio 136
Suez crisis 88, 90
Suharto 93
Sukarno 93
Sunday Promenade Concert 25
Sun Valley Serenade 34
Suramarit, Norodom, King (Cambodia) 53
Suzuki, Shoji 54–5
swing 2, 10–13, 33, 49, 92, 98, 140, 144, 147, 161; and Americanism 12, 29; and Benny Goodman 10–12, 55, 111; and Earl Hines 113; in East Germany 41; in France 15; in Germany 18–19; and Glenn Miller Orchestra 148n8; in Japan 20–1, 25, 94; in *Jazz* (film) 154; and Karel Vlach orchestra 37–9; and Lionel Hampton 144; and rise of bebop 29–30; as a social phenomenon of the mid-1930s 10–13; stilyagi 36; and wartime propaganda 22–3; and Woody Herman 75
swing ideology 11, 15, 23, 31, 42, 46–7
Swing Journal 54, 59
Swingjugend 18–20, 36, 38, 143
Switzerland 32, 101
symphonic jazz 10, 15, 21, 33
Symphony of the Air 54
Syria 49
Sztandar Młodych 141

Tanzania 75–6, 161
Taylor, A. J. P. 89
Taylor, Billy 1, 73, 146, 152
Taylor, Cecil 117
Taylor, Malcolm 123
Taylor, Paul B. 52
Tchaikovsky, Pyotr Ilyich 85; Competition 85
Teagarden, Charlie 59
Teagarden, Jack 7, 55, 63n39; tour in Burma 58; tour in India 57–8; tour in Japan 59–60; tour in Korea 58–9
Templin, Lutz 23
Terry, Clark 1, 73, 95, 117
Thailand 53, 71, 98–9, 158, 162
"thaw" 41, 106, 126
Thaw, The 36
Thelonious Monk Institute of Jazz 157–9
Theresienstadt camp (Terezín ghetto) 24, 91, 144
Third Reich 17–8
Thompson, Llewellyn 112, 118
Threepenny Opera, The 17
Tienken, Arthur T. 76
Time 84
Times of India 56–7
Tjader, Cal 73
Togashi, Masahiko 100
Togo 97
Toguri D'Aquino, Iva 25
Tokyo Music School 20
Tokyo Rose 25
Toscanini, Arturo 124
Truman Doctrine 29, 35, 90
Truman, Harry 33, 153
Tsfasman, Alexander 112, 119
Tsuneishi, Shigetsugu 25
Tsunoda, Takashi 103n33
Tunisia 52, 97
Turkey 49–50, 55
Turner, Joe 86

Uganda 75–6
Uhuru Afrika 77
Ukrainian Composer Union 125
Ukrainian Dance Ensemble 110
Ulbricht, Walter 106
un-American values 7, 29, 32
Union of Moscow Composers 123
Union of Polish Composers 37
Union of Soviet Composers 112, 119, 156
Unit Asia 161
United Hot Clubs of America 13, 16
United Nations (UN) 53, 157, 159
United Nations Educational, Scientific and Cultural Organization (UNESCO) 9, 145–6, 159–60
United Nations Jazz Society 77
United Service Organizations (USO) 23
United States Information Agency (USIA) 72, 113, 142, 156–7
United States Information Service (USIS) 52, 54, 72, 143
University of North Texas jazz band 71
U Nu 53
Updike, John 146
Up the Down Staircase 117
Urbaniak, Michal 134
USA Patriot Act 155
Uses of Literacy, The 89
US-Soviet confrontation 6
US-Soviet Cultural Exchange Agreement 108
US-Soviet relations 3, 5, 112–13, 120, 152
Utesov, Leonid 36, 112, 127
U Thant 53

Van Lake, Turk 108
Vaughan, Sarah 3, 71, 86
"V Discs" 22
Večernje Novosti 136
Velvet Revolution 147, 157
Venezuela 167
Vian, Boris 88, 144
Vietnam 155, 158; War 95, 113; and Randy Weston 79; and Ronald Reagan 152; and US-Soviet relations 135
Viets, Richard N. 142
Vlach, Karel 37–9
Vogel, Eric 24
Voice of America (VOA) 1–2, 47, 72; in Eastern Europe 40, 133–4, 139, 145

Von Eschen, Penny M. 5–6, 61n6, 83n57
Vonnegut, Kurt 146
Vostok II 106

Wallace, Henry 33
Waller, Fats 12–13, 31
Warsaw Pact 130, 135–6
Warsaw Philharmonic Orchestra 139
Waschko, Roman 133–4
Washington, Dinah 153
Watanabe, Hiroshi 94, 103n33
Watanabe, Ryo 25
Watanabe, Sadao 94, 100–1
Watergate scandal 126, 143
Weill, Kurt 17
Weimar Germany 14, 17, 33–4
Wein, George 137–8, 140, 142
We Insist! 65–6
Weintraub Syncopators 34
Weiße Rose 18
Western Europe (*see also* Europe) 86, 89, 97, 100–1, 137, 140, 142; Coca-Cola in 87; JATP tour in 51; jazz ambassadors in 46, 61n6, 85, 97; relationship with America 84, 88, 90, 167; Van Cliburn in 85
West Germany: Americanism in 11, 167; bilateral treaty with Poland 136; break with the past 8, 80, 91–4, 98; jazz diplomacy of 98–9; jazz musicians' visit to Poland 131, 142
Weston, Randy: and African music 77; criticism of America 79–80, 83n57; in the jazz ambassador selection process 73; tour in Africa 7, 75, 78–9; visit to Nigeria 77
White House 1–2, 47, 71–2, 156
Whiteman, Paul 10, 15, 22
Wild One, The 92
Williams, Joe 1
Williams, William L. S. 49, 57
Wilson, John 72, 74
Wilson, Teddy 11, 73, 108, 117
Wilson, Woodrow 14
Winding, Kai 73, 142
Wolfe, Glenn G. 81n11
Wood, Bill 77
Wooding, Sam 17, 33
Woods, Phil 49–50, 108, 110–12
World Festival of Youth and Students: fifth 130; sixth 37, 97, 113
World Jazz Festival 95
Wreckers 134

Wretched of the Earth, The 95
Wright, Eugene 55, 87, 132

Yamamoto, Hozan 100
Yamashita, Yosuke 100, 161
YMCA 37
Young, Lester 23
Yugoslavia 49–50, 63n39, 100, 136, 140
Yui, Shoichi 54, 94, 100
Yuize, Shinichi 93, 100

Zaire 161
Zambia 161
Zappa, Frank 146
zazou 19–20, 36, 38, 143
Zero Hour 25
Zhdanov, Andrei 35; doctrine 35, 37
Zoller, Attila 73
Zubok, Vladislav 35
Zwerin, Mike 19
Życie Warszawy 132, 141